PHYSICAL RELIGION

D1880420

PHYSICAL RELIGION

The Gifford Lectures

DELIVERED

BEFORE THE UNIVERSITY OF GLASGOW

IN 1890

BY

F. MAX MÜLLER, K.M.

GYAN

Published by

Gyan Publishing House
5, Ansari Road
Daryaganj, New Delhi-110002
Phone: 011-47034999, 9811692060
E-mail: books@gyanbooks.com

Distribution Network
gyanbooks.com
India, USA, Canada, UK, Australia

© Publisher
All rights reserved. No part of this work may be reproduced, stored, adapted, or transmitted in any form or by any means, electronic, mechanical, photocopying, micro-filming, recording or otherwise, or translated in any language, without the prior written permission of the copyright owner and the publisher.

ISBN: 978-81-212-5697-1 (PB)
First Published, 1891

2nd Impression 2024

Printed at: Gyan Press, Delhi.

The book is sold subject to the condition that it shall not, by way of trade or otherwise, be lent, resold, hired out, or otherwise circulated without the prior publisher's written consent.

PHYSICAL RELIGION
Author: F. MAX MÜLLER

PHYSICAL RELIGION

MAX MÜLLER

PHYSICAL RELIGION

The Gifford Lectures

DELIVERED

BEFORE THE UNIVERSITY OF GLASGOW
IN 1890

BY

F. MAX MULLER, K.M.
FOREIGN MEMBER OF THE FRENCH INSTITUTE

NEW EDITION

LONGMANS, GREEN, AND CO.
39 PATERNOSTER ROW, LONDON
NEW YORK AND BOMBAY
1898

PREFACE.

THIS volume contains my second course of Gifford Lectures, as I delivered them before the University of Glasgow in the beginning of this year, with a few additions, mostly printed at the end of the volume.

In lecturing before an academic audience, I felt in duty bound to make my meaning as clear as possible, even at the risk of becoming tedious in driving the nail home more than once.

Nor could I avoid repeating here and there what I had written elsewhere, if I wished to place the subject before my hearers in a complete and systematic form.

Attentive readers will find, however, that in re-stating what I had said before, I often had to modify or correct my former statements, and I hope the time may never come, when I can no longer say, We live and learn.

F. MAX MÜLLER.

OXFORD, *Dec.* 6, 1890.

TABLE OF CONTENTS.

PAGE

PREFACE V

LECTURE I.

HOW TO STUDY PHYSICAL RELIGION.

The three divisions of natural religion.—The three phases of religion often contemporaneous.—Physical religion.—The historical method.—Historical continuity.—Varieties of physical religion.—Physical religion best studied in India.—The Vedic period.—Natural phenomena as viewed by nomad and agricultural people.—Physical religion outside of India.—The meaning of primitive.—Discoveries of ancient life.—Discovery of the Veda.—Unique character of the Veda 1–21

LECTURE II.

THE VEDA AND THE TESTIMONIES TO ITS EARLY EXISTENCE.

How did the Veda become known?—No foreign nations mentioned in the Veda.—The Veda not mentioned by foreign nations.—Early contact between India and Egypt, Babylon, and Persia.—Greek accounts of India.—Skylax.—Alexander's expedition to India.—Contact with China.—Buddhist Pilgrims.—Later contact with Persia.—Al-Birûnî, 1000 A.D.—The Emperor Akbar, 1556–1605.—Prince Dârâ, translator of the Upanishads.—Schopenhauer 22–36

LECTURE III.

THE VEDA AS STUDIED BY EUROPEAN SCHOLARS.

Thread of our argument.—European missionaries in India.—European scholars acquainted with the Vedas.—Asiatic Society of Bengal.—Interest aroused in Germany.—Bunsen's projected journey to India.—MSS. of the Veda brought to Europe.—Eugène Burnouf in France.—First edition of the Rig-veda 37–54

LECTURE IV.

SURVEY OF VEDIC LITERATURE.

PAGE

Peculiar character of Indian antiquity.—Meaning of Veda.—The Rig-veda, the only true Veda.—Brahmanic view of the Vedas.—The Rig-veda.—The ten Ma*n*dalas.—Method in the collection of the ten Ma*n*dalas.—Number of hymns.—The Prâti*s*âkhyas.—Date of the Prâti*s*âkhya.—Minutiae of the Prâti*s*âkhya.—The Anukrama*n*is of *S*aunaka.—Number of verses in the Rig-veda.—The Sâma-veda.—Ya*g*ur-veda.—The *Kh*andas or Mantra period.—The prose Brâhma*n*as.—The Brâhma*n*as of the Ya*g*ur-veda.—The Brâhma*n*as of the Sâma-veda.—The Brâhma*n*as of the Rig-veda.—The true Veda.—The Brâhma*n*as of the Brâhmans.—Life during the Vedic period.—Poem on trades and professions.—Poem of the gambler.—Independent speculation.—Âra*n*yakas and Upanishads.—Duration of Brâhma*n*a period.—The Atharva-veda 55–83

LECTURE V.

AGE OF THE VEDA.

An accurate knowledge of the Veda necessary for a study of physical religion.—How to fix the date of the Veda.—Aryan immigration into India.—Sindhu, cotton, mentioned 3000 B. C.—The Sûtras.—The three literary periods of the Vedic age.—Chronological *terminus ad quem.*—Sandrocottus, died 291 B. C.—Buddhism, a reaction against the Vedic religion.—The word Upanishad.—The word Sûtra.—Relation of Buddhism to Brâhmanism.—Constructive chronology.—Character of the Veda.—Simplicity of Vedic hymns.—Moral elements.—Early sacrifices.—Childish thoughts in the Veda.—More exalted ideas.—The sacrificial character of the Vedic hymns.—Ya*g*, to sacrifice.—Hu, to pour out.—Sacrificial terms.—Other sacrificial terms.—Prayer better than sacrifice.—The primitive sacrifice.—Morning and evening meal.—Lighting and keeping of the fire.—New and full moon.—The three seasons.—The meaning of solemn 84–114

LECTURE VI.

PHYSICAL RELIGION.

Definition of physical religion.—God as a predicate.—Deification.—The natural and the supernatural.—Agni, fire, as one of the

PAGE

Devas.—Early conceptions of fire.—The etymological meaning of Agni.—Names of fire.—Fire, named as active.—Agni as a human or animal agent.—New explanation of animism, personification, and anthropomorphism.—Mr. Herbert Spencer, against animism.—Professor Tiele's theory of the gods as *facteurs*.—The agents in nature.—The categories of the understanding.—The categories of language.—Fire, as a Deva.—Greek and Roman gods.—Ruskin on the ancient gods.—Evolution of the word deva.—Natural revelation of God.—The biography of Agni 115–143

LECTURE VII.

THE BIOGRAPHY OF AGNI.

Facts against theories.—Premature generalisation.—Agni in his physical character.—Agni, as the sun.—Agni, the sun, or the fire on the hearth.—Sun and fire in America.—Sun and fire among the Fins.—Agni, as lightning.—Mâtarisvan.—Fire from flint.—Fire from wood.—Mythological ideas connected with fire.—Agni, as deva, bright, amartya, undying, &c.—Agni, the immortal among mortals.—Agni, the friend, helper, father.—Agni, helper in battle.—Fireless races.—Agricultural Âryas.—Agni, destroying forests.—Agni's horses.—Agni, as sacrificial fire.—Agni, the messenger between gods and men.—Agni, as priest.—Hymn to Agni 144–176

LECTURE VIII.

AGNI, AS DIVESTED OF HIS MATERIAL CHARACTER.

Later development of Agni.—Agni identical with other gods.—Henotheism.—Henotheism in Finland.—Early scepticism.—Exchange of gods.—Dual deities.—Reconciliation of the solar and meteoric theories.—Supremacy of Agni.—The general name of deity.—Evolution of concepts.—The highest concept of deity.—Agni, as creator, ruler, judge.—The dark side of Indian religion. —Anthropomorphism.—The sage Nârada.—Influence of children on religion 177–203

LECTURE IX.

THE USEFULNESS OF THE VEDIC RELIGION FOR A COMPARATIVE STUDY OF OTHER RELIGIONS.

Agni, fire, in other religions.—No religious literature in Greece and Italy.—Religion in Egypt.—Brugsch on Egyptian religion.—Le Page Renouf on the gods of Egypt.—Religion in

PAGE

Babylon and Assyria.—Where to study the historical growth of religious ideas.—The Old Testament.—Invention of alphabetic writing.—The sixth century B. C.—The Old Testament as an historical book.—Monotheistic instinct of the Semitic race.—Abraham.—Elijah.—The god of fire in the Old Testament . 204–224

LECTURE X.

Fire as conceived in Other Religions.

Fire widely worshipped.—Fire in the Avesta.—Ormazd, not fire.—Âtar, fire.—Âtar fights with Azi Dahâka.—Plurality of Âtar.—Âtar, son of Ormazd.—Difference between Âtar and Agni.—Is the Avestic religion dualistic?—Fire in Egypt.—Modern character of the Egyptian religion.—Ra.—Osiris.—Ptah.—Tvash*tri* in the Veda.—Fire in Greece, Hephaestos.—Fire in Italy, Vulcanus.—Philosophical concepts of fire in Greece.—The fire of Herakleitos.—Zoroaster.—Fire and water in the Brâhma*n*as.—Fire as worshipped in Babylon.—The true antiquity of the Veda 225–251

LECTURE XI.

The Mythological Development of Agni.

Tales about Agni.—Euhemeristic explanations of mythology.—Ancient riddles.—Brahmodya.—The disappearance of Agni.—Dialogue between Agni and Varu*n*a.—Later accounts of the hiding of Agni.—The meaning or hyponoia of mythology.—Lessons of comparative mythology 252–275

LECTURE XII.

Religion, Myth, and Custom.

Difference between religion and mythology.—Secular ideas become religious.—Lighting and keeping of fire.—Religious sanction for customs.—Baptism by water and fire.—Purification by fire.—Lustration of animals.—Need-fire.—Tinegin in Ireland.—Purpose of customs often forgotten.—Essential difference between religion, mythology, and ceremonial.—Theogonic development of Agni.—Mythological development of Agni.—Ceremonial development of Agni.—Definition of religion re-exami ed.—The meaning of the Infinite.—The religious element 276–302

LECTURE XIII.

Other Gods of Nature.

PAGE

The development of fire.—The agents behind the other phenomena of nature.—The theogonic process.—Wordsworth.—The storm-wind.—The storm-wind in America.—The storm-wind in Babylon.—The storm-wind in India.—The Marus of the Buddhists.—Rudra, the father of the Maruts.—The storm-wind in Germany.—Odin, Wuotan.—The mixed character of ancient gods.—The theogonic development 303–328

LECTURE XIV.

What does it lead to?

Value of historical studies.—Lessons of natural religion.—The agents in nature.—One agent in nature.—Craving for the supernatural.—Miracles condemned by Mohammed.—Miracles condemned by Buddha.—Miracles condemned by Christ.—The supernatural as natural.—Common elements of all religions; the Ten Commandments.—Similarities between Christianity and Buddhism.—Divine character ascribed to the founders of religions.—Buddha's birth.—Birth of Mahâvîra.—Mohammed's birth.—Other prophets.—The birth of Christ.—Signs changed to miracles.—Dr. Robert Lee.—The highest commandments.—Conclusion 329–367

APPENDICES.

Appendix I.

Are Parthians, Persians, and Bactrians mentioned in the Veda? 369

Appendix II.

Skylax and the Paktyes, the Pashtu or Afghans 371

Appendix III.

Buddhist Pilgrims acquainted with the Veda 373

PAGE

APPENDIX IV.

Sanskrit MSS. bought by Guizot 376

APPENDIX V.

Date of the Prâtisâkhya 376

APPENDIX VI.

Minutiae of the Prâtisâkhya 377

APPENDIX VII.

Number of verses in the Rig-veda 378

APPENDIX VIII.

Brâhmanas of the Sâma-veda 381

APPENDIX IX.

Sanskrit words in Sumerian 381

APPENDIX X.

Technical terms borrowed by the Buddhists 382

APPENDIX XI.

Pischel and Geldner's 'Vedische Studien' 384

APPENDIX XII.

Egyptian Zoolatry 387

APPENDIX XIII.

Writing mentioned in the Old Testament 388

APPENDIX XIV.

Need-fire 389

APPENDIX XV.

Similarities between Christianity and Buddhism 390

INDEX 397

LECTURE I.

HOW TO STUDY PHYSICAL RELIGION.

The Three Divisions of Natural Religion.

THE first course of lectures on Natural Religion which I had the honour to deliver in this University was chiefly of an introductory character. It was then my object to discuss, and to answer, as far as was in my power, three principal questions:

(1) What are the limits of Natural Religion?

(2) What is the proper method of studying it? and

(3) What are the materials accessible for such study?

In the present course of lectures I mean to treat of Natural Religion in one of its three great manifestations, namely, as *Physical Religion*. Natural Religion, as I tried to show last year, manifests itself under three different aspects, according as its object, what I called the Infinite or the Divine, is discovered either in *nature*, or in *man*, or in the *self*. I shall repeat from the last lecture of my first course a short description of these three forms of religious thought.

'In treating of Physical Religion,' I said, 'we shall have to examine the numerous names, derived from the phenomena of nature, by which the early inhabitants of this small planet of ours—some of them our direct ancestors—endeavoured to apprehend what lies behind the veil of nature, beyond the horizon of our sensuous perception. We shall meet there with the so-called gods of the sky, the earth, the air, the fire, the storm and lightning, the rivers and mountains, and we shall see how the god of the sky, or, in some countries, the god of the fire and of the storm-wind, assumes gradually a supreme character, and then is slowly divested again, in the minds of his more enlightened worshippers, of what we may call his original, purely physical, or mythological attributes. When the idea had once sprung up in the human mind that nothing unworthy should ever be believed of the gods, or, at least, of the father of gods and men, this process of divestment proceeded very rapidly, and there remained in the end the concept of a Supreme Being, still called, it may be, by its ancient and often no longer intelligible names, but representing in reality the highest ideal of the Infinite, as a father, as a creator, and as a wise and loving ruler of the universe. What we ourselves call our belief in God, the Father, is the last result of this irresistible development of human thought.

'But the Infinite has been discovered, not only behind the phenomena of nature, but likewise behind man, taking man as an objective reality, and as the representative of all that we comprehend under the name of mankind. Something not merely human, or very soon, something superhuman was discovered at a very early time in parents and ancestors, particularly after they had departed this life. Their names were preserved, their memory was honoured, their sayings were recorded, and assumed very soon the authority of law, of sacred law, of revealed truth. As the recollection of fathers, grandfathers, great-grandfathers, and still more distant ancestors became vaguer and vaguer, their names were surrounded by a dim religious light. The ancestors, no longer merely human, approached more and more to the superhuman, and this is never very far removed from the divine.

'Offerings, similar to those that had been presented to the gods of nature, were tendered likewise to the ancestral spirits, and when the very natural question arose, who was the ancestor of all ancestors, the father of all fathers, the answer was equally natural,—it could only be the same father, the same creator, the same wise and loving ruler of the universe who had been discovered behind the veil of nature.

'This second sphere of thought may be comprehended under the name of *Anthropological Religion*. Under the form of worship of ancestral spirits it seems among some people to constitute almost the whole of their religion, but more generally we find it mixed with what we call Physical Religion, not only in ancient, but also in modern times. Christianity itself has been obliged to admit some remnants of that ancestral worship, and in Roman Catholic countries the immense popularity of the Festival of All Souls seems to show that a loving homage paid to the spirits of the departed satisfies one of the deepest and oldest yearnings of the human heart.

'The third sphere of religious thought, the *Psychological*, is filled with endeavours to discover what lies hidden in man, considered not merely as a creature, or as a part of nature, but as a self-conscious subject.

That self of which man became conscious, as different from his merely phenomenal, or even his personal being, has been called by many names in the different languages of the world. It was called breath, spirit, ghost, soul, mind, genius, and many more names, which constitute a kind of psychological mythology, full of interest to the student of religion as well as to the student of language and thought. It was afterwards called the *Ego*, or the *person*, but even these names did not satisfy man, as he became more and more conscious of his higher self. The person was discovered to be a *persona* only, that is a mask; and even the *Ego* was but a pronoun, not yet the true noun, the true word which self-conscious man was in search of. At last, the consciousness of self arose from out the clouds of psychological mythology, and became the consciousness of the Infinite or the Divine within us. The individual self found itself again in the Divine Self, not absorbed in it, but hidden in it, and united with it by a half-human and half-divine relationship. We find the earliest name for the Infinite, as discovered by man within himself, in the ancient Upanishads. There it is called Âtman, the Self, or Pratyag-âtman, the Self that lies behind, looking and longing for the Paramâtman, the Highest Self—and yet it is not far from every one of us. Sokrates knew the same Self, but he called it *Daimonion*, the indwelling God. The early Christian philosophers called it the *Holy Ghost*, a name which has received many interpretations and misinterpretations in different schools of theology, but which ought to become again, what it was meant for in the beginning, the spirit which unites all that is holy within man with the Holy of Holies or the Infinite behind the veil of the Ego, or of the merely personal and phenomenal self.'

The Three Phases of Religion, often contemporaneous.

It must not be supposed that these three phases of natural religion, the *Physical*, the *Anthropological*, and the *Psychological*, exist each by itself, that one race worships the powers of nature only, while another venerates the spirits of human ancestors, and a third meditates on the Divine, as discovered in the deepest depth of the human heart. As a general rule, physical religion everywhere comes first, and is succeeded by anthropological, and lastly by psychological religion. Among most nations whose historical antecedents are known to us, we can see that the idea of something divine is elaborated first from elements supplied by nature, and that afterwards the spirits of the departed are raised to a fellowship with the gods of nature, while the recognition of a universal Self, underlying the gods of nature, and the spirits of the departed, and recognised as the immortal element within ourselves, comes last, nay belongs even now to the future rather than to the past. The germs of these three developments may be discovered in most religions. Sometimes the one, sometimes the other, becomes more prominent. But I doubt whether any nation, whose earlier history is known to us, has been found devoted exclusively to the worship of physical deities, still less, devoted exclusively to the worship of ancestral spirits. What I call psychological religion is a phase of thought which we generally comprehend under the name of philosophy rather than under that of religion, and though it may have been anticipated here and there by prophets and poets, it presupposes in its developed form the existence of religion, both physical and anthropological.

The ancient Vedic religion, for instance, is pre-eminently a physical religion, but to maintain, as some philosophers have done, that it contained no traces of ancestor-worship, shows simply an ignorance of facts. The worship of the Fathers, the Pitaras, is presupposed by a number of Vedic hymns, and to the present day, the most truly religious ceremony of the Hindus, that which still touches their hearts, and not their eyes only, is the so-called *S*râddha, the sacrifice in memory of their ancestors.

Even the third phase, the *Psychological*, though in its fully elaborated form it belongs to a later age, and assumes the character of a philosophy rather than of a religion, is never entirely absent in any religion. The very recognition of superior beings implies some kind of perception of man's own being, some recognition of what really constitutes his own self. If he calls the gods immortals, that would seem to imply that he considered himself as mortal; but when he begins to implore the favour of the immortal gods, not only for this life, but for a life to come, when he prays to be united again with those whom he loved and lost on earth, a new conception of his own self must have sprung up in his heart, and though mortal and liable to death, he must have felt himself or something within himself as eternal, and as beyond the reach of annihilation.

Ancestor-worship also implies always the recognition of something immortal in man, however dim that primitive belief in immortality may have been.

Physical Religion.

But though we find these three roads on which a belief in the Infinite was reached by different nations, running closely parallel or even crossing each other, it is possible, and, for the sake of systematic study, almost indispensable, that we should explore each of them by itself. This present course of lectures will therefore be devoted to a study of *Physical Religion*, though from time to time we shall hardly be able to avoid a consideration of such influences as *Anthropological* and *Psychological* ideas exercise on *Physical Religion* in its historical progress to higher ideas.

The Historical Method.

How that exploration is to be carried out I need not tell you, after what I have said in my first course of lectures. There is but one method that leads to really trustworthy and solid results, and that is the *Historical Method.* We must try to discover the historical vestiges of that long pilgrimage which the human race has performed, not once, but many times, in search of what lies beyond the horizon of our senses,—in search of the Infinite, in search of a true religion; and this we can only achieve by a careful study of all truly historical documents in which that pilgrimage has been recorded.

Historical Continuity.

There is an unbroken continuity in the religious and philosophical concepts, as there is in the languages of the world. We know that the language spoken by Hume and Kant is substantially the same as that which was spoken by the poets of the Veda in India, four thousand years ago. And we shall see that the problem of causality which occupied the powerful minds of Hume and Kant is substantially the same as that which occupied the earliest framers of Aryan language and Aryan thought, when, driven by the very necessities of pure reason, or, as we may now call it by a better name, by the very necessities of Logos or language, they conceived and named for the first time the sky, the sun, the fire, and all the other great phenomena of nature by means of roots, expressive of agency, of force, or, in the end, of causality. Physical Religion owes its origin to the category of causality, or, in other words, to the predicating of roots, expressive of agency and causality, as applied to the phenomena of nature. And this intellectual work, performed thousands of years ago by millions of human beings, deserves, it would seem, at least as much attention as the speculations of two individuals, even though they be Hume and Kant, as to the legitimacy of the concept of causality, when applied to the data of the senses. 'Without the doctrine, the true doctrine, of substance and of cause,' I am quoting the words of the founder of these lectures, Lord Gifford, 'philosophy would be a delusion, and religion a dream' (Lord Gifford's Lectures, pp. 139–140). 'Just let me say,' he adds, 'and I say it with the deep seriousness of profoundest conviction, that true philosophy and true religion must stand or fall together. If philosophy be a delusion, religion can hardly escape being shown to be a dream.'

Varieties of Physical Religion.

But here, again, we must not try to attempt too much. Though we find traces of physical religion everywhere among ancient and modern, among civilised and uncivilised races, it would lead to confusion only were we to attempt to treat them all as one. Physical Religion is the same, and yet not the same at different times and in different places. The lessons which nature teaches in a small and fertile island, surrounded by a horizon, half sky and half sea, are very different from the lessons which man reads when living in narrow valleys, overawed by snow-decked mountains, and hemmed in by rivers which, though they are looked upon as beneficent, may at any moment bring destruction and death on what man calls his own, his home on earth. The Nile in Egypt assumes a very different aspect in the religious imagery of its worshippers from that which the river Sarasvatî bears in the hymns of the Rig-veda; and the cupola of the sky, resting all around on the monotonous desert as its sole foundation, forms a very different temple from that in which the most gigantic snowy mountains support on all sides, like lofty pillars, the blue roof of heaven.

For practical purposes, therefore, it will be best to study, first of all, the origin and growth of Physical Religion in one country only, and then to turn our eyes to other countries where the same ideas, though under varying outward conditions, have found expression in mythology or religion.

Physical Religion best studied in India.

And here there can be little doubt as to which

country is the typical country for the study of Physical Religion. In no country do we find Physical Religion in its simplest form so completely developed as in India. Not in India, as it is popularly known, not in modern India, not in mediaeval India, not even in the ancient India, as represented to us in the Epic Poems of the Mahâbhârata and Râmâya*n*a, least of all in the India of the Buddhists, whose religion, old as it is—for Buddha died 477 B.C.—was built up on the very ruins of that religion which interests us at present.

No, the original, simple, and intelligible religion of India is to be found in the Vedic period only, which preceded the rise of Buddhism, just as the religion of the Old Testament preceded that of the New. Here and here only can we see Physical Religion in all its fulness, in all its simplicity, nay, I should say, in all its necessity. Suppose we had known Christianity only as it appears after the Council of Nicaea, after it had become a state-religion, and had once for all settled its dogmas and ceremonial, and then had suddenly discovered a manuscript of the Gospels—the new insight into the true nature of Christianity could not have been more startling and surprising than was the new light which the discovery of the Veda has thrown on the origin and growth of religion, not only in India, but in every part of the world. That the gods of the Greeks and the Romans, the Teutonic, Slavonic, and Celtic nations, that the gods of the Babylonians and Assyrians and other Semitic nations, not excepting the Jews, that the gods of Egypt and the whole of Africa, that the gods of Finland and Lapland, of Mongolia and China, of the Polynesian islands, and of the North as well as the South of America, that all these gods had in the beginning something to do with the most prominent sights of nature, could hardly have escaped even the least thoughtful student of antiquity. But it was only like guessing at the former existence of a geological stratum which does not come to the surface except in scattered fragments. That *Helios* was originally the sun and *Mênê* the moon, no one could have doubted, except he who is proud of his ignorance of Greek; but that *Apollo* too had a solar, and *Lucina* a lunar, origin was contested by many a classical scholar with the same eagerness with which many a theologian would fight even now against the admission of physical elements in the original character of Jehovah.

The Vedic Period.

With the discovery of the Veda all this has been changed. Here was the very stratum, the very period of language and thought before our eyes, the existence, nay, the very possibility of which had been so keenly contested. That *Zeus* was originally a name of the sky, could hardly have been denied by any Greek scholar; but it was not till the corresponding deity, *Dyaus*, was discovered in the Veda that all opposition was silenced, and silenced for ever.

How can we imagine, it used to be said again and again, that the whole of the ancient Greek religion and mythology should have consisted in talk about the sun and the moon, the sky and the dawn, day and night, summer and winter. Surely the Greeks would have been mere idiots if they had found nothing better to engage their thoughts or to supply their religious cravings.

Natural Phenomena as viewed by Nomad and Agricultural People.

No doubt, even without the evidence supplied by the Veda, one might have asked in return what better subjects there could have been in an early state of society, to engage the thoughts and to satisfy even the higher aspirations of mankind, than the wonders of nature—the daily return of the sun, which meant the return of light and warmth, that is, the possibility of life and the joy of life,—or the yearly return of the sun, which meant again the return of spring and summer after the horrors of winter, that is, the possibility of life and the joy of life. In days when a violent storm might turn a happy homestead to wrack and ruin, when a sudden rain might sweep away a whole harvest, and bring famine and death on a prosperous village, when the hot rays of the sun might parch the fields, kill the cattle, and spread pestilence among children and servants, what subjects could there have been nearer to the heart of man than the strange and startling movements of the heavenly bodies, the apparent cause of all their happiness, the apparent cause of all their misery on earth?

What does a farmer talk about even now, before and during and after the harvest, but the weather? We have now calendars to tell us when the spring returns, when the summer heat may be expected, how long the autumn may last, and when the winter will set in with its snow and frost. But with the ancient tillers of the soil, the most highly-prized wisdom consisted in sayings and rules, handed down from father to son, which told when it was safe to sow, when it was time to mow, and how much provision was wanted for a long winter, to prevent children and parents from dying of hunger. In our days, with all the experience gathered in our books, with all the precautions taken against the violent freaks of nature, with the forecasts of the weather published in all the newspapers, we can afford to neglect the signs and warnings of nature, or leave their observation to those whom they more specially concern. But ancient superstitions connected with Physical Religion are not quite extinct even now. We may be sceptical as to the Halcyon birds having the power of quieting the sea, and unwilling to postpone our voyage until the return of the Pleiades. We should hardly believe that if Zeus has visited the earth with rain on a certain day, he will repeat his visits for many days to follow. But sailors still object to embark on a Friday, and farmers still believe that if St. Swithin sends rain, rain will continue for forty days. If, then, even in our own enlightened century, a simple-minded peasant may still be found here or there uttering a prayer or presenting an offering to St. Swithin, is it so very strange that in early days, when the very possibility of life depended on the success of the harvest, the thoughts of people should have been almost entirely absorbed in watching those powers of nature on whom they felt themselves dependent for life, and breath, and all things?

If these powers had to be named, they could be named, as I tried to explain in my first course of lectures, as active only, as doing deeds, as working works; as raining, not as rain; as storming, not as storm; as feeding and protecting, like a loving father, or as punishing and chastising, like an angry father.

Given these few germs of thought which are found in every human heart, what is there strange or unintelligible in the luxuriant growth of physical mythology and physical religion?

But we need not argue this point any more. What was a mere postulate before the discovery of the Veda, has now become a fact. We have that whole primitive stratum of thought laid open before our eyes, in one, and that a very important part of the world. To those who will not see, who will put what they think ought to be in the place of what is, we can only say with all the frankness of the Hindu logician, 'It is not the fault of the post, if the blind man does not see it.'

Physical Religion outside of India.

On the other hand, we must guard against exaggerating the importance of the Veda. If we wished to study Dutch art, we should feel it our duty, first of all, to go to Holland, and to examine there on the spot, not only the master-works, but the whole school of Dutch painters. But we should not imagine that we had thus done our whole duty, and that the vast galleries in the other capitals of Europe had nothing to teach us. In the same way Physical Religion has to be studied, not only in the Veda and in India, but almost everywhere where historical documents enable us to study the gradual growth of religion. A study of the Veda is the best preparation for the study of Physical Religion; but it does not claim to teach us all that can be known about the gods of nature.

The meaning of Primitive.

Secondly, if we call the Veda primitive, it must not

be supposed that we imagine we can find in the Veda the earliest thoughts that ever passed through a human brain. If we call the Veda primitive, we mean two things; first, that it is more primitive than any other literary work we are acquainted with; secondly, that it contains many thoughts which require no antecedents, which are perfectly intelligible in themselves, thoughts, in fact, which we should call primitive, even if we met with them in the works of modern poets.

But it would be the greatest mistake to imagine that everything in the Veda is primitive, everything is intelligible, everything without antecedents. The student of the Veda knows but too well how much there still remains in the Veda that is hard, petrified, unintelligible, artificial, secondary, nay tertiary, and altogether modern in one sense of the word. The collection of hymns which we chiefly mean when we speak of the Veda in general, is a collection of various collections, and in each of these there are relics of different ages, mixed up together. We have to search carefully for what is really primary in thought, for the later rubbish is much more abundant than the original gold. The Vedic poets themselves make no secret of this. They speak of old and of living poets, they know of ancient and recent deeds of the gods. Their very language bewrays the date of many of the Vedic hymns. The distances between the intellectual layers forming the collection of the Rig-veda are so enormous that most scholars would hesitate to translate them into any chronological language. And yet, for all that and for all that, we possess in the whole world no literary relics intellectually older than the oldest hymns of the Rig-veda, and I doubt whether we possess any literary relics chronologically older, at all events in our own, the Aryan world.

Discoveries of Ancient Life.

We have lived to see many discoveries, revealing to us the buried life of ancient nations. I still remember the amazement produced by the resurrection of Pompeii and Herculanum. If you want to realise the feelings with which the highest intellects regarded that discovery, read Schiller's poems, or read a novel which I can still read with undiminished admiration, particularly when I remember that it was written in 1832 by a young man, not more than twenty-seven years of age—I mean Bulwer's 'Last Days of Pompeii.' I have seen and known the most learned and the most brilliant young men whom our Universities now send out into the world—I must confess I have never met with one who, at the age of twenty-seven, could have produced a work so full of genius and so full of learning also.

Then followed the wonderful discoveries in Egypt, the Rosetta stone supplying to Champollion the key to the decipherment of the hieroglyphic inscriptions, and every year adding new treasures to our museums, new materials to our Egyptian grammars and dictionaries, till now it would seem as if all Egyptian mysteries had been revealed, and the ancient language, spoken and written there thousands of years B. C., could be read with the same ease as Greek and Latin.

About the same time the kingdoms of Persia, of Babylon and Nineveh shook off the shroud of sand under which they had so long been buried. And here too the genius of Grotefend, of Burnouf, Lassen and Rawlinson broke the spell of those long rows of wedges or arrows, which seemed more meaningless even than hieroglyphics, and restored to us first the contemporaneous edicts of Darius and Xerxes, and afterwards the very archives of the ancient kings of Babylon and Nineveh. With the help of cuneiform grammars and dictionaries the Persian, Babylonian, and Assyrian texts can now be read by all who possess the patience of real students. We were told at the International Congress of Orientalists at Stockholm in 1889 that there are at present in the United States of America thirty chairs filled by professors who lecture to good audiences on Cuneiform Inscriptions, on the language, religion, and history of Persia, Babylon, Nineveh, and Accadia. This shows how rapidly a discovery can progress, and how widely-spread an interest still exists, even in our utilitarian age, in the earliest history of the human race.

Discovery of the Veda.

Less remarked, though certainly not less remarkable than these unexpected finds in Egypt and Babylon, was the discovery of the Veda, which took place about the same time. It was in one sense even more important, for it revealed to us, not only inscriptions, but a real full-grown literature, and a literature containing the annals of our own, the Aryan, race. The French have a saying that it is always the unexpected that happens. And certainly, if anything was unexpected, it was the discovery of a literature in India, in distant India, among dark-skinned people, of a literature more ancient than Homer, of a language less changed than Latin, of a religion more primitive than that of the Germans as described by Tacitus, and yet intimately connected with all of them. It is true the literature of ancient India had not been buried in the earth, it was never altogether lost in its own country. But so far as Europe and European science were concerned, the Veda was as good as buried, nay as non-existent, and what is more extraordinary still, it remained as if non-existent for European scholars long after the discovery of India, long after the discovery of the ordinary Sanskrit literature.

The Veda has now become the foundation of all linguistic, mythological, and religious studies. Even the minutest changes of vowels in Greek and in English find their final explanation nowhere but in the accents of Vedic words. Many of the most important names of Greek and Roman gods and goddesses remain dumb, till they are made to speak once more, when brought face to face with the gods and goddesses of the Veda. Nay, religion itself, which seemed to some scholars so irrational and unnatural a creation 'that it could have been invented by one man only, and he probably a madman,' assumes, when watched in the Veda, a character so perfectly natural and rational, that we may boldly call it now an inevitable phase in the growth of the human mind.

Unique Character of the Veda.

In saying this I am not afraid that I shall be charged with exaggerating the importance of the Veda. There was a time when it was thought necessary to protest against the assumption that the Veda reflected the image of the earliest phase of Aryan life, nay of all human life on earth. I am not aware that so preposterous a claim in favour of the Veda had really ever been made by any scholar. It seems only another instance of a very common practice in the republic of letters. A purely imaginary danger is conjured up, in order to claim the merit of having stemmed it. I do not mean to say that there may not have been an unguarded expression here and there which could be construed as claiming for the Veda a primordial antiquity. After all, scholars write for scholars, and they take it for granted that even their somewhat enthusiastic expressions will not be misinterpreted so as to become unmeaning and absurd. Now for a scholar it would be nothing short of absurd to claim for the Vedic poetry a primordial character. Whoever the first inhabitants of our earthly Paradise may have been, they certainly did not speak the language of the Veda, which shows as many rings within rings as the oldest trunks in the Yosemité valley. Nor would it be less absurd to represent the Veda as a literary monument dating from the undivided Aryan period. The division of the Aryan race into its two chief branches, the North-Western and South-Eastern, belongs to a time beyond the reach of historical chronology, whereas the date claimed for the Veda does not exceed the second millennium B. C.

There are misunderstandings against which one does not guard, because they seem impossible, at least 'within the profession.'

But, on the other hand, who can deny that the Veda is the oldest monument of Aryan speech and Aryan thought which we possess? Who can wonder at the enthusiasm with which its discovery was greeted, at the eagerness with which the Vedic MSS. were seized, copied, collated, and published, and at the zeal with which its treasures have been ransacked and brought to light? What Aryan nation could produce anything to match the Veda? Beautiful as the Homeric poems are—for power of description infinitely superior to anything in the Veda—yet they exhibit a far more advanced state of society, so modern in many of its aspects that we ourselves could almost feel at home in it. Besides, they represent chiefly the outward life, and allow us but few glimpses into those inward thoughts about gods and men, about this life and the next, which find expression in the hymns of the Veda. And if no one would blame the historian who drew the picture of early chivalry from the Iliad, or the idyl of early domestic life from the Odyssey, why should we wonder at the student of religion drawing his most valuable lessons from the Veda? We shall certainly not find in the Veda the archives either of the first man or of the undivided Aryan race, but we do find there, and there alone, the oldest record of what one branch of that race thought about this life and its many problems, and what it believed about the gods and another life. And if among the gods worshipped in the Veda we find some that have the same names as the gods of other Aryan nations, such as, for instance, Dyaus and Zeus, is it so wild an assumption to maintain that some of the antecedents of the Greek and Roman gods may be discovered in the Veda? May we not say with the Preacher, 'Be not righteous over much, neither make thyself over wise: why shouldest thou destroy thyself?'

Neither the hieroglyphic inscriptions of Egypt nor the cylinders of Babylon can lend us such assistance for our studies, more particularly for the study of the historical growth of that Aryan race, to which we and the greatest historical nations of the world belong, as the Veda. The first thing, therefore, which I shall have to do is to give you an account of how the Veda was discovered, and what the Veda really is.

LECTURE II.

THE VEDA AND THE TESTIMONIES TO ITS EARLY EXISTENCE.

How did the Veda become known?

THERE seems to be a general agreement among Sanskrit scholars that the Vedic hymns, as we now possess them, collected in the Rig-veda-sa*m*hitâ, were composed between 1500 and 1000 B.C. Why that date has been fixed upon we shall have to consider hereafter; but it is well to say at once, that we must not expect the same kind of historical evidence for a date reaching back to 1500 B.C. which we have a right to demand for a date 1500 A.D. There are different degrees of certainty, and it is the neglect of this inevitable fact which causes so much needless controversy between specialists and outsiders. The date assigned to the poetry of the Veda is and will always remain hypothetical. To critical scholars it would, I believe, be a real relief if a later date could be assigned to some portions of that sacred collection. But we can hardly hope for new evidence to enable us to fix Vedic dates. Historical dates require the evidence of contemporary witnesses, and it is difficult to say where we should look for witnesses, outside of India, and contemporary with the Vedic Rishis.

No Foreign Nations mentioned in the Veda.

We find no traces in the ancient Vedic literature of India of any contact with foreign nations. It has been supposed by some scholars that the names of the Parthians and Persians, or even of the Bactrians, were known to the poets of the Veda, but the evidence on which they rely is very uncertain[1].

The Veda not mentioned by Foreign Nations.

Nor do we find in the annals of other nations any traces of their acquaintance with India before the sixth century B.C.

Early Contact between India and Egypt, Babylon, Persia.

Whether there had been any intercourse, direct or indirect, between India and Greece before the sixth century B.C. we cannot tell. Some scholars imagine that Homer's Ethiopians, who dwelt towards the rising of the sun, were meant for the people of India, but this belongs to a class of conjectures to which we can say neither yes nor no. If India was known to the Greeks at that early time, it could only have been through the Phenicians. It is well known that among the articles of merchandise brought home by the fleets of Hiram and Solomon, there were some which by their origin and name point to India. If we look at a map on which the stations are marked which were established by Phenician merchants before

[1] See Appendix I.

500 B.C., we see that the whole coast of the Mediterranean, from Tyre and Sidon to Gibraltar, from Carthage to Marseilles, had been explored by them. The Mediterranean was then, as it is still, the mart of the world. The Greeks in Asia Minor and in Europe, the Phenicians and the Egyptians occupied its borders, and we know now from Babylonian and Egyptian inscriptions that there was a very early diplomatic and commercial intercourse between Egypt and Babylon. We must remember also that the people on the Egyptian or Ethiopian side of the Red Sea could hardly have been ignorant of the people on the Arabian side, or the people on the Arabian side of the Persian gulf unacquainted with the existence of people on the Persian side. Commerce was even then a magnetic force that attracted nation to nation, and merchants, less bold even than the Phenicians, would not have been frightened by a voyage from the sea that received the Tigris and Euphrates to the sea that received the Indus and the rivers of the Penjâb.

Yet the name of India, to say nothing of the name of the Veda, is never mentioned in the more ancient inscriptions of Egypt and Babylon. The only evidence of a possible contact between India and Egypt at that early time is the occurrence of the word *kafu*, ape, which is said by Professor Dümichen to be found in a text of the seventeenth century [1]. This *kafu* is supposed to be the same word as the Hebrew *koph*, ape, which occurs in the first book of Kings, x. 22. Here we read that 'Solomon had at sea a navy of Tharshish with the navy of Hiram, and that once in three years

[1] Die Flotte einer aegyptischen Königin in dem 17. Jahrhundert, 1868; table II, p. 17.

came the navy of Tharshish, bringing gold, silver, ivory, and *apes*, and peacocks.' All these articles were the products of the soil and climate of India, and the Sanskrit name for ape is *kapi*. Here then the single word *kapi* may possibly indicate the route of commerce from India to Judaea and Phenicia, and from thence to Egypt, in the seventeenth century B. C.

The same animal, the ape, is supposed to attest an early intercourse between India and Babylon also. It occurs with other animals on the black obelisc from Nineveh, now in the British Museum.

Though the armies of the great conquerors of Mesopotamia must have approached very near to the frontiers of India, they have left no traces of their presence there, nor have they brought any intelligence of India back to Babylon or Nineveh. The idea that the Indian division of the heavens into twenty-seven or twenty-eight Nakshatras was of Babylonian origin, and the assertion that the name of the Babylonian weight, *mna* or *mina*, occurred in the Veda as manâ, rest both on no valid authority. In the half-legendary account given by Diodorus Siculus (ii. 16–19) of the expedition of Semiramis against India, possibly derived from Ctesias, the name of the Indian king who in the end repels the foreign invaders, has been supposed to bear evidence of the Sanskrit language being known to the people of Babylon. It is *Stabrobates*, which may represent the Sk. sthavira-patī, the strong lord; but this also is doubtful[1].

[1] Lassen explains Stabrobates as sthauri-pati, lord of bulls; Bohlen as sthavara-pati, lord of the continent, both impossible.

Greek Accounts of India.—Skylax.

The first Greek who is supposed to have actually visited India and to have written an account of it, was *Skylax*. He lived before Herodotus, who tells us (iv. 44) that Darius Hystargus (512–486), wishing to know where the river Indus fell into the sea, sent a naval expedition, and with it Skylax of Karyanda in Karia[1].

As soon, however, as Greek historiography begins, we find that the name of India was known. Hekataeos knows it, Herodotus knows it, both living in Asia Minor. But why did they call the country India?

Persia has formed at all times a connecting link between India and the Greeks of Asia Minor. In the ancient sacred literature of Media and Persia, in the Avesta of Zoroaster, India is mentioned under the same peculiar name which it has in the Veda. In the Veda the home of the Âryas in India is called Sapta Sindhava*h*, the Seven Rivers, that is, the five rivers of the Penjâb with the Sarasvatî, a river which afterwards disappeared, and the Indus. The very same peculiar name, which is used during the Vedic age only, appears in the Avesta as Hapta He*n*du. This cannot be a mere accident, but proves, like many other coincidences between Vedic Sanskrit and Zend, that, long after the Aryan separation, there was a continued historical contact between the Vedic poets and the people among whom at one time the Zoroastrian religion flourished.

Hapta He*n*du is exactly the same name as Sapta Sindhu, by a change of s into h. The name

[1] See Appendix II.

of India must have reached the Greeks through a language in which, as in Persian, every initial s was represented by h, for it is thus only that we can account for the Greek form *India*, instead of what we should expect, if the Sanskrit word Sindhu had reached the Greeks directly, namely Sindia.

Persia continued to serve as a bridge between India and Greece in later times also, for in the Persian cuneiform inscription at Nakshi Rustam we find among the provinces paying tribute to Darius, *Hindu* mentioned by the side of *Ionians*, *Spartans*, *Bactrians*, *Parthians*, and *Medes*. Long before Alexander's discovery of India, Greek writers, such as Hekataeos (B.C. 549–486) and Herodotus, possessed some information about that distant country beyond its mere name. Hekataeos mentions the river *Indus*, Herodotus speaks of the *Gandarioi*, a race evidently identical with the Gandhâras, mentioned in the Rig-veda, whose town Kaspapyros was known to Hekataeos. Herodotus (i. 131) knows even the name of one of the deities, worshipped in common by the Vedic Indians and the Persian Zoroastrians, namely *Mitra*; but how superficial his knowledge was is best shown by the fact that he takes Mitra for a female deity, corresponding to the Assyrian Mylitta, the Arabian Alitta.

Alexander's Expedition to India.

There seems to have been from very early times a vague impression that India, like Egypt, was the home of an ancient wisdom. Alexander himself shared that idea, and was most anxious therefore to get a glimpse of the wisdom of the Brâhmans, by conversing with them through the aid of various interpreters. It is quite possible that those of his companions who were entrusted with a description of Alexander's campaigns may have written down a full account of the Brâhmans, particularly of the so-called Hylóbioi, the dwellers in the forest, called in Sanskrit vânaprastha, and of the ancient literature which they possessed. But whether by accident or through the indifference of the later Greeks, scanty fragments only have been preserved of these writings. Nor do we possess more than fragments of the description of India, composed by Megasthenes, who stayed at Patna (Pâ*t*aliputra = Palibothra) as ambassador of Seleucos to the King of the Prasii, the famous *K*andragupta, about 295 B.C.; still less of Ktesias, who, though he did not actually live in India, gathered much information about that wonderful country, when staying at the court of Darius II and Artaxerxes Mnemon, about 400 B.C.

Certain it is that the name of the *Veda* is never mentioned in Greek literature, and that nothing but vague ideas about the wisdom of the Brâhmans were current among the philosophers of Greece and Rome. Early Christian writers also, who speak of the religions of India, and are able to distinguish between the religion of Brâhmans and Buddhists, never refer to the sacred literature of the Brâhmans under the name of Veda.

Contact with China.

The first people who give us authentic information about the Veda, you will be surprised to hear, are the Chinese. There exists a curious prejudice against all that is Chinese. We seem to look upon the Chinese very much as they look upon us, as Outer Barbarians.

We find it very difficult to take them, as the French say, *au grand sérieux*. They seem to us queer, funny, not quite like other people—certainly not like Greeks and Romans, not even like Indians and Persians. And yet when we examine their literature, whether ancient or modern, it is by no means so very different from that of other nations. Their interests are much the same as ours, and there is certainly no lack of seriousness in their treatment of the highest problems of religion, morality, and philosophy.

There are in China three religions, that of Confucius, that of Lao-tze, and that of Buddha. Confucius and Lao-tze lived both in the sixth century B.C. They were, however, restorers rather than founders of religion. The religion of Buddha reached China from India about the beginning of our era.

The name of *K*îna occurs in the epic literature of India as the name of a people on the North-Eastern frontiers of the country. But whether it was intended as a name of China is doubtful[1].

The three religions of China have had their controversies and their hostile conflicts. But all three are now regarded as recognised systems of faith in China, and the Emperor of China is expected to profess all three, and to attend their special services on great occasions. Here we are at once inclined to smile, and to doubt the seriousness of a religious faith that could thus conform to three systems, so different from each other as Confucianism, Taoism, and Buddhism. We pride ourselves on attending the services of none but our own sect or subdivision of the great divisions of

[1] See Lassen, *Indische Alterthumskunde*, I². p. 1029.

Christendom. We are apt to suspect indifference, latitudinarianism, or scepticism in any member of the Church of England who should attend the communion of any other Christian sect. But the official attendance of the Emperor of China in the temples of Confucianists, Taoists, and Buddhists admits of a different interpretation also. May it not show that the wisest of their statesmen had recognised that there was some truth, some eternal truth, in every one of these three religions; that the amount of truth on which they all agreed was much greater and much more important than the points of doctrine on which they differed, and that the presence of the Emperor at the services of the three religions of his subjects was the most efficient way of preaching tolerance, humility, or, if you like, Christian charity. We are but too ready to judge heathen nations, without considering how much of charitable interpretation we have to claim for ourselves.

Buddhist Pilgrims.

How serious a Chinaman can be about his religion, you will be able to gather from the lives of those Buddhist Pilgrims to whom we owe the first authentic account of the Veda. Why did these pilgrims go from China to India—a journey which even now is considered by geographical explorers as one of the most perilous, and as requiring no less of human endurance and bravery than Stanley's exploration of Africa?

They went there for the sake of their religion. India was to them their Holy Land. Buddhism had reached China at the beginning of our era from Northern India, and to visit the holy places where Buddha had been born, had lived, taught, and died, was as much the dream of a devout Buddhist in China as to visit the Holy Sepulchre at Jerusalem was the dream of many a poor palmer and many a valiant Crusader in Christendom.

We possess the descriptions of these Buddhist pilgrimages, extending from about 400 A.D. to 1000 A.D. The most important are those of Fâ-hian, 399–414, Hiouen-thsang, 629–645, and I-tsing, 673–695. Their works have been translated into French and into English too by Stanislas Julien, Professor Legge, Dr. Beal, and others. While the companions of Alexander had no eyes to see the existence of Sacred Books, such as the Veda, in India, the Chinese pilgrims not only give us the name of the Veda, but they actually learnt Sanskrit, and they were able to point out the differences between the ordinary Sanskrit and the more ancient language used in the Veda. You know how highly Christian apologists value any mention of, or quotations from the New Testament, occurring in ancient authors, in order to prove the existence of the Gospels at a certain date, or to confirm the authenticity of certain Epistles as read in the first, second, and third centuries A.D. The critical student of the Veda has the same interest in collecting independent testimonies as to the existence and authenticity of the Veda from century to century, and here the testimony of the Chinese pilgrims stands first among those coming from people outside India, from what the Brâhmans also would call 'Outer Barbarians,' or Mle*kkh*as[1].

[1] See note in Appendix III.

Later Contact with Persia.

The next people from whom we might have expected direct information about the ancient Vedic literature of India are the Persians. I do not mean the ancient Persians, the subjects of Darius or Xerxes, for they have left us no information about their own sacred literature, much less about that of their neighbours. I mean the Persians of the sixth century A. D. The kings of Persia at that time, such as Khosru Nushirvan, were men of literary tastes, patrons of poets and philosophers. We know that they entertained the greatest admiration for the literature of India, and patronised the translation of several Sanskrit works into Pehlevi, the literary language of Persia at that time. But we look in vain for any mention of the sacred books of the Brâhman, and it is doubtful whether the translators of the other Sanskrit texts were aware of their existence [1].

Al-Birûnî, 1000 A. D.

Some of the books which during the Sassanian

[1] It is stated in the Dînkard, as translated by Mr. West, that the Sassanians collected information from *Arûm* (the Byzantine Empire) and from *Hindûkân* (the Hindus). The names even of MSS. are given, but there is nothing in them that points to India. One curious coincidence, however, has been pointed out by Mr. West. The human body is apportioned between the four professions, priesthood being on the head, warriorship on the hand, husbandry on the belly, and artizanship on the foot. The names of the four castes are derived from the Avesta, but the idea itself seems to have been borrowed from the Veda. Here we read, X. 90, 12,

Brâhma*n*á*h* asya múkham âsît, bâhû râ*g*anyâ*h* k*r*itá*h*
Ûrû tát asya yát vaí*s*ya*h* padbhyâm *s*ûdrá*h* a*g*âyata.

'The Brâhma*n*a was his mouth, the Râ*g*anya was made his two arms, his two legs were the Vaisya, from his two feet the *S*ûdra was born.'

period had been translated from Sanskrit into Pehlevi or ancient Persian were afterwards, in the eighth century, translated into Arabic, and some of them, such as the fables of Bidpai, have served to carry the fame of the wisdom of the Brâhmans all over Europe. But the Vedas remained unknown to other Oriental nations till about 1000 A. D. At that time the north of India was conquered by Sultân Mahmud of Ghazna, who from time to time made predatory expeditions to plunder and destroy the richest temples of India at Taneshar, Mathurâ, Kanoj, and Somnâth[1]. After taking Khîva in 1017, he carried off among other prisoners and hostages a learned astronomer and astrologer, best known by the name of Al-Birûnî. During thirteen years which he spent in India, 1017–1030, Al-Birûnî devoted himself sedulously to the study of Sanskrit and Sanskrit literature. It was formerly supposed that he translated not only from Sanskrit into Arabic and Persian, but likewise, what would have been a much more arduous task, from Arabic and Persian into Sanskrit. Dr. Sachau, the learned editor and translator of Al-Birûnî's great work on India, has shown that this was not the case, and that all we can say with safety is that he was able to read Sanskrit texts with the help of native Pandits. But for all that, Al-Birûnî was a most remarkable and exceptional man for his time, a man of wide sympathies, a true philosopher, and an acute observer. The very idea of learning a foreign language, except perhaps Persian or Turkish, had never entered at that time the head of any Mohammedan. As to studying the religion

[1] Al-Birûnî, translated by Sachau, vol. i. p. xvii.

of the infidels, it would have been considered damnable. Al-Birûnî showed himself free from all such prejudices, and the world owes to him the first accurate and comprehensive account of Indian literature and religion [1]. If his writings had been more widely known, and if, more particularly, European scholars had been acquainted with them at the time when Sanskrit literature began to attract the interest of Sir William Jones, Colebrooke, and others, many discoveries which taxed the ingenuity of European scholars need not have been made at all, for Al-Birûnî would have told us all we wanted to know. He knew the four Vedas, the Rig-veda, Ya*g*ur-veda, Sâma-veda, and Atharva-veda. He knew that the Vedas, even in his time, in the eleventh century, were not allowed to be written, but were handed down by oral tradition, which was considered far safer than the pen of a ready writer (vol. i. p. 126). He tells us, what we can hardly accept as true for the whole of India, that it was not long before his time when Vasukra, a native of Kashmir, a famous Brâhman, undertook the task of explaining the Veda and committing it to writing (vol. i. p. 126), because he was afraid that it might be forgotten and entirely vanish from the memories of men. He asserts that the Hindu consider as canonical only that which is known by heart, not that which is written, and he remarks that even their scientific works were composed in metre, in order to facilitate their being learnt by heart (vol. i. p. 19). All this and a great deal more he tells us as an eye-

[1] Al-Birûnî's India, *An Account of the Religion, Philosophy, Literature, Chronology, Astronomy, Customs, Law, and Astrology of India, about* 1030, edited and translated by Dr. Sachau.

witness, and as one who could command the services of the best native scholars.

Emperor Akbar, 1556–1605.

It is strange, however, that the account he gave of the Vedas should have attracted so little attention either in the East or in the West. Five centuries passed before the Vedas were really placed in the bright light of history, and even then only a small portion of the Vedas was rendered accessible by means of translation. This took place during the reign of the great Emperor Akbar, 1556–1605. He knew of the Vedas, and in his eagerness to become acquainted with all the religions of the world before founding his own religion, he made great efforts to obtain a translation of them. But his efforts were in vain. We hear indeed of a translation of the Atharva-veda, made for Akbar. But the Atharva-veda, as we shall see, is very different from the other Vedas, and the portions of that Veda, translated for Akbar, were most likely the Upanishads only. These Upanishads are the philosophical appendices of the Veda, more particularly of the Atharva-veda. They are deeply interesting, though as philosophy rather than as religion.

Prince Dârâ, translator of the Upanishads.

One hundred years after Akbar they fascinated Dârâ, the unfortunate son of Shâh Jehan, as they have fascinated others in later times. Prince Dârâ is said to have learnt Sanskrit in order to translate the Upanishads from Sanskrit into Persian, and a year after he had accomplished his task, he was murdered by his brother Aurungzebe. It was this Persian translation of the Upanishads which Anquetil Duperron translated again into Latin in 1795, and it was Duperron's Latin translation which inspired Schopenhauer, and furnished to him, as he himself declares, the fundamental principles of his own philosophy.

Schopenhauer.

Nothing shows more clearly the indefatigable industry and at the same time the wonderful perspicacity of that great philosopher, than his being able to find his way through the labyrinth of an uncouth Latin translation, and to discover behind the strangest disguises the sublime truths hidden in the Upanishads. Honest as he was, Schopenhauer declared openly that his own philosophy was founded on that of the Upanishads. 'From every sentence of these Upanishads,' he writes, 'deep, original, and sublime thoughts arise, and the whole is pervaded by a high and holy and earnest spirit. Indian air surrounds us, and original thoughts of kindred spirits. And oh, how thoroughly is the mind here washed clean of all early engrafted Jewish superstitions, and of all philosophy that cringes before those superstitions! In the whole world there is no study, except that of the originals, so beneficial and so elevating as that of the Oupnekhat. It has been the solace of my life, it will be the solace of my death[1].'

[1] The Upanishads, translated by F. M. M., in *Sacred Books of the East*, vol. i. p. lxi.

LECTURE III.

THE VEDA AS STUDIED BY EUROPEAN SCHOLARS.

Thread of our Argument.

IN a course of lectures we must try never to lose our way.

Where are we?

We are studying Physical Religion—the roads that led from Nature to Nature's gods—to Nature's God. I stated that this phase of religious growth can best be studied in the Veda. And the next question was, What is the Veda—and, How did we come to know it?

Now, if you had asked the most learned Professor, not more than a hundred years ago, What is the Veda?—he would most likely have had to say, what no Professor likes to say, *I don't know.* Not quite so many years ago, when Professor Wilson offered a translation of the Veda to one of our greatest publishers, he was met by the question, 'And pray, Sir, what is the Veda?'

I therefore feel in duty bound to explain, first of all, how the world came to know the Veda, and who are the first people outside of India that bear witness to its existence.

The Greeks did not mention the Veda, though no doubt it existed long before Alexander, nor the Persians, nor the Jews. The first people outside India who knew the Veda were the Chinese. Then followed Al-Birûnî, at the court of Mahmud of Ghazna (about 1000 A.D.), and lastly the Emperor Akbar and his literary friends, in the second half of the sixteenth century. All these bear witness to the existence of the Veda. But they are witnesses who lived in the East. We have now to see how the Veda became known in the West, how a knowledge of that ancient literature reached the scholars of Europe.

European Missionaries in India.

At the court of Akbar, and again at the court of Aurungzebe (1658–1707), there were several European missionaries who took part in the religious and philosophical discussions of the time, and who ought to have been acquainted with the Vedas, if only by name. But it would seem as if the Brâhmans, though anxious to have their literature known and appreciated by their conquerors, were more anxious still to keep their sacred literature, the Vedas, out of sight of any strangers. Their law-books are full of threatenings against any one who should divulge the Veda, and it seems certainly a fact that the Emperor Akbar, omnipotent as he was, did not succeed in persuading any Brâhman to translate the real Veda for him [1].

It was only when Christian missionaries began themselves to learn the classical language of the Brâhmans, the so-called Sanskrit, that they became

[1] See a story about an attempted translation of the Veda in *Science of Language*, vol. i. p. 206.

aware of the existence of the old sacred books, called the Veda.

Francis Xavier, who went as a missionary to India in the first half of the sixteenth century, was honest enough to confess that he could not learn the language. 'I do not understand that people,' he writes, 'nor do they understand me.' Yet this is the same Xavier who is always mentioned as one of the first successful missionaries in India, nay to whom, under the name of St. Francis Xavier, his admirers ascribed the gift of tongues.

In the second half of that century, however, a successful attempt was made by some Roman Catholic missionaries at Goa to learn Sanskrit with the help of a converted Brâhman, and early in the seventeenth century the famous missionary, Roberto de' Nobili, had made himself thoroughly acquainted, not only with the Sanskrit language, but with Sanskrit literature also. That he knew the Veda, and that he had learnt to appreciate its enormous authority among the higher classes in India, is best shown by the fact that he announced himself as come to preach a new Veda. Whether he actually composed such a work we do not know, but it seems quite certain that the notorious Ezour-veda was not his work. This Ezour-veda was a poor compilation of Hindu and Christian doctrines mixed up together in the most childish way, and was probably the work of a half-educated native convert at Pondicherry. A French translation of this work was sent to Voltaire, who presented it to the Royal Library at Paris in 1761. It was published by Sainte-Croix in 1778, under the title of *L'Ezour Védam, ou ancien commentaire du*

Védam, contenant l'exposition des opinions religieuses et philosophiques des Indous, traduit du Samscretam par un Brame. How a man of Voltaire's taste could have been taken in by such a work is difficult to understand to any one who takes the trouble to read the two volumes. Yet Voltaire spoke of it as 'the most precious gift for which the West has ever been indebted to the East,' and he placed its date four centuries before Alexander. In plain English, the whole book is childish drivel.

To us the book is chiefly interesting as showing when the name of Veda began first to be more generally known among the literary men of Europe. The Roman Catholic missionaries in India had begun to grapple with the real Veda early in the eighteenth century, but their communications in the *Lettres édifiantes* attracted much less attention than the eulogies of a spurious Veda, trumpeted forth by so powerful a trumpeter as Voltaire. Father Calmette, for instance, in a letter from Carnata in the south of India, dated January, 1733, assures us that his friends were not only well grounded in Sanskrit, but were able to read the Veda. This shows decided progress, and a recognition of the fact of which Sanskrit students are painfully aware, that a man may be well grounded in Sanskrit, and yet unable to read the Veda. He also knows that there are four Vedas which, as he states, 'contain the law of the Brâhmans, and which the Indians from time immemorial regarded as their sacred books, as books of an irrefragable authority and as coming from God Himself.' Father Calmette was evidently quite aware of the importance of a knowledge of the Vedas for missionary purposes, and of the immense influence which the Vedas continued to exercise on the religious convictions of the people. 'From the time,' he writes, 'that missionaries first went to India, it has always been thought to be impossible to find this book which is so much respected by the Indians. And, indeed, we should never have succeeded, if we had not had Brâhmans, who are Christians, hidden among them. For how would they have communicated this book to Europeans, and particularly to the enemies of their religion, as they do not communicate it even to the Indians, except to those of their own caste.' He then adds what shows that his informants had been *bona fide* students of the Veda. 'The most extraordinary part is that those who are the depositaries of the Veda do not understand its meaning; for the Veda is written in a very ancient language, and the Samouscroutam (that is, the Sanskrit), which is as familiar to their learned men as Latin is to us, is not sufficient, without the help of a commentary, to explain the thoughts as well as the words of the Veda.'

This statement is important in several respects. You will have remarked the expression, 'those who are the depositaries of the Veda.' He does not say that he has as yet seen or handled the books containing the text of the Veda; he speaks only of depositaries of the Veda. This shows, what we now know to have been the case always, that the Brâhmans at his time, and in the south of India, did not depend on books or manuscripts for the preservation of the Veda, but that they knew it by heart, and learnt it by heart from the mouth of a teacher. It does not follow that they did not possess manuscripts also of the Veda. It is true that in their law-books the copying of the Veda and the selling of manuscripts is strictly forbidden, but the fact that it was necessary to forbid this shows, of course, that the law was broken. Manuscripts of the Veda did exist in the last century, for we possess them, and Father Calmette also succeeded after a time in procuring some of them. They may have existed as soon as the art of writing for literary purposes began to be practised in India, say a century or two before the beginning of the Christian era. But they never assumed the authority which the *litera scripta* assumed in Europe. The Brâhmans themselves were the true depositaries of the Veda; they were the books, and more than the books, inasmuch as an unbroken oral tradition was supposed to connect each successive generation with the original composers, or, speaking more accurately, with the original recipients of these sacred hymns.

Another remark too of Father Calmette is very significant. He says, 'They who are the depositaries of the Veda, do not understand its meaning.' Now this is again perfectly true. The Veda is learnt by heart at first, without any attempt at understanding it. It is only after the text has thus been mechanically engraved on the tablets of the memory, that the more learned among the Brâhmans endeavour to understand it under the guidance of their teachers and with the help of ancient commentaries. All this is in accordance with their ancient law-books, and exists still as the recognised system of education in several parts of India, particularly in the south. Some schools go even so far as to maintain that a text of the Veda, if *not* understood, is more efficient at a sacrifice than if it is understood by the person who recites it. I doubt whether any other priesthood has gone so far in their admiration of ignorance.

However, it is quite clear that Father Calmette was one of the first who succeeded in getting hold of actual manuscripts of the Veda.

Father Calmette tells us that for a long time he thought that the Vedas could not be found in manuscript. Other missionaries also tell the same story. Marco della Tomba, for instance, who was in India between 1757 and 1774, and who declares that he knew Sanskrit well enough to carry on disputations in it with the Brâhmans, confesses that he was never allowed to see a manuscript of the Vedas. He doubts the very existence of the Vedas, but he speaks with the greatest admiration of the Brâhmans who knew whole books by heart. At last, however, Father Calmette was successful. 'It is only five or six years ago,' he writes, 'that I was allowed to form an Oriental library for the King, and charged to seek for Indian books for that purpose. I then made discoveries of great importance for religion, among which I count that of the four Vedas or sacred books.'

And here, after Father Calmette had got actual possession of the Veda, and had succeeded with the help of some Brâhmans to decipher some of its chapters, it is most instructive to watch the bent of his thoughts, and of the thoughts of many of the early missionaries in India. He is not bent on extracting from the Veda passages showing the depravity and absurdity of the ancient Indian religion, an occupation which some of our present missionaries seem to consider their principal duty. No, the very contrary.

'Since the Veda is in our hands,' he writes, 'we have extracted from it texts which serve to convince them of those fundamental truths that must destroy idolatry; for the unity of God, the qualities of the true God, and a state of blessedness and condemnation, are all in the Veda. But the truths which are to be found in this book are only scattered there like grains of gold in a heap of sand.'

What would some of the present Bishops in India say to this truly Pauline sentiment, to this attempt to discover in the sacred books of other nations some grains of gold, some common ground, on which a mutual understanding and a real brotherhood might be established between Christians and non-Christians? The Brâhmans themselves are quite aware of the existence of these grains of gold, and when accused of polytheism and idolatry, they themselves quote certain verses from the Veda to show that even in ancient times their prophets knew perfectly well that the different gods invoked for different blessings were only different names of the one Supreme Being. Thus they quote from Rig-veda I. 164, 46:

> Índram Mitrám Várunam Agním âhuh,
> Átho divyáh sáh suparnáh Garútmân.
> Ékam sát víprâh bahudhấ vadanti,
> Agním, Yamám, Mâtarísvânam âhuh.

'They call Indra, Mitra, Varuna, Agni, then there is that heavenly Garutmat with beautiful wings: the One that is they speak of in different ways, they call it Agni, Yama, Mâtarisvan.'

This is a clear confession, if not of Monotheism, at least of Monism, for it should be remarked that the Vedic poet, when he speaks of the one that truly exists, the bearer of many divine names, does not even venture to put it in the masculine gender, but calls it the Ekam Sat, the only Being that exists.

Another well-known verse of a similar character, in which, however, the masculine gender and a certain amount of human metaphor are still preserved, occurs in Rig-veda X. 82, 3:

> Yáh nah pitấ ganitấ yáh vidhâtấ,
> dhấmâni véda, bhúvanâni visvâ,
> Yáh devấnâm nâmadhấh ékah evá,
> tám samprasnám bhúvanâ yanti anyấ.

> 'He who is our father that begot us, he who is the creator,
> He who knows all places and all creatures,
> He who gave names to the gods, being one only,
> To him all other creatures go, to ask him.'

I could add other passages, particularly from the Brâhma*n*as and Upanishads, all confirming Father Calmette's idea that the Veda is the best key to the religion of India, and that a thorough knowledge of it, of its strong as well as of its weak points, is indispensable to the student of religion, and more particularly to the missionary who is anxious to make sincere converts. What is extraordinary is that the announcement of Father Calmette's discovery of the Veda passed off almost unheeded in Europe.

Another French missionary, Father Pons, in 1740, sent a still more complete account of the literary treasures discovered in India. In it he describes the four Vedas, the grammatical treatises, the six systems of philosophy, and the astronomy of the Hindus. But his communications also excited no curiosity except among a few members of the French Institute. The world at large, which would have greeted the discovery of a single ancient Greek statue with shouts of applause, had nothing to say to the unearthing of a whole literature, of a whole world of ancient thought.

European Scholars acquainted with the Vedas.

The Abbé Barthélemy was one of the few European scholars who perceived the true import of the communications sent home from India by French missionaries, and he asked Father Cœurdoux in 1763 to send home a Sanskrit grammar. This shows that he was in real earnest, and felt impressed with the duty which these extraordinary Indian discoveries imposed on the learned men of Europe. After a time, grammars of the Sanskrit language reached Europe, and it will always remain an honour to Rome that the first grammar of the Sanskrit language was published at Rome in 1790, by a Carmelite friar, Paolino da S. Bartolomeo. He was a German, by name of Johann Philip Werdin, not Wesdin, as he is often called, and had been actively employed as a missionary in the south of India from 1776 to 1789.

But after giving full credit to the labours of Paolino da S. Bartolomeo and other Roman missionaries, the fact remains that there was as yet a smouldering curiosity only for all that concerned India. The flames of a true scientific enthusiasm for the ancient literature of that country did not burst forth till they were lighted by a spark of genius. That spark came from Sir William Jones. Sir William Jones was a man of classical culture and of wide interests. He was at home in the best literary society of the age. He could speak with authority, as a scholar to scholars, as a philosopher to philosophers, and as a man of the world to men of the world. When in

1789[1] he published his translation of *S*akuntalâ, he forced the attention of the world, not only by the unexpected character of his discovery of a perfect dramatic work composed by a dark-skinned poet, but by the pure and classical style of his translation. His subsequent translation of the Laws of Manu did infinite credit to his patience and his ingenuity, and coming from the hand of a professed lawyer and a judge, it could not but attract the serious attention of all who were interested in ancient history, and more particularly, in ancient law. Of course, Sanskrit scholarship has made progress since the days of Sir William Jones, and it is easy now to point out a few mistakes in his renderings. But true scholars who, like Professor Bühler, have given us better translations of Manu, have been the first to acknowledge Sir William Jones' great merits: whereas others who have never done a stitch of independent work, have dared to call his translations 'meretricious.'

Asiatic Society of Bengal.

With the foundation of the Asiatic Society of Bengal in 1784, the history of Sanskrit philology begins, and after a hundred years that society still holds the foremost place as the Royal Exchange between Asia and Europe. I cannot here attempt to give an account of all the brilliant work done by Sanskrit scholars during the first century of Indo-European scholarship. We are concerned with the Vedas only. And here it

[1] A translation of the Bhagavadgîtâ, by Charles Wilkins, had appeared before, in 1785. Wilkins' translation of the Hitopadesa appeared in 1787. The first original Sanskrit text published was, I believe, the *Ri*tusa*m*hâra, in 1792, under the auspices of Sir William Jones.

is certainly surprising that the Vedas, the supreme importance of which was so clearly perceived by men like Father Calmette, Pons, Paolino da S. Bartolomeo, and others, should have remained so long neglected. Sir W. Jones was fully impressed with their importance. He knew that the Laws of Manu, to which he assigned the extravagant antiquity of 1500 B.C. (they are now referred to about 400 A. D.), were modern in comparison with the Vedas, and derived their chief authority from them.

A much greater scholar than even Sir William Jones, Henry Thomas Colebrooke, who with indefatigable industry had worked his way through the text and the enormous commentaries of the Veda, and whose essay on the Vedas, published in 1805, is still a work of the highest authority, so far from exciting an active interest in these works, rather damped the enthusiasm of scholars who might have wished to devote themselves to Vedic studies, by saying, as he does at the end of his essay: 'The Vedas are too voluminous for a complete translation of the whole, and what they contain would hardly reward the labour of the reader, much less that of the translator.'

Interest aroused in Germany.

Still the curiosity of the learned world had been roused, not only in England, but in Germany also. While Goethe admired the graceful simplicity of *S*akuntalâ, his friend Herder, with the true instinct of the historian, was thirsting for the Veda. While others ascribed an extreme antiquity to the Laws of Manu and even to plays like *S*akuntalâ, he saw clearly that whatever had been hitherto published of Sanskrit literature, was comparatively modern and secondary in its character. 'For the real Veda of the Indians,' he sighed, 'as well as for the real Sanskrit language, we shall probably have to wait a long time.'

Bunsen's projected Journey to India.

How strong a desire had been awakened in Germany at that time for a real and authentic knowledge of the Veda, I learnt from my dear old friend Bunsen, when I first made his acquaintance in London in 1846. He was then Prussian Minister in London. He told me that when he was quite a young man, he had made up his mind to go himself to India, to see whether there really was such a book as the Veda, and what it was like. But Bunsen was then a poor student at Göttingen, poorer even, I believe, than the poorest student in England or Scotland. What did he do to realize his dream? He became tutor to a young and very rich American gentleman, well known in later life as one of the American millionaires, Mr. Astor. Instead of accepting payment for his lessons, he stipulated with the young American, who had to return to the United States, that they should meet in Italy, and from thence proceed together to India on a voyage of literary discovery. Bunsen went to Italy, and waited and waited for his friend, but in vain. Mr. Astor was detained at home, and Bunsen, in despair, had to become private secretary to Niebuhr, who was then Prussian Minister at Rome. Brilliant as Bunsen's career became afterwards, he always regretted the failure of his youthful scheme. 'I have been stranded,' he used to say, 'on the sands of diplomacy; I should have been happier had I remained a scholar.' This was the origin of my own friendship with Bunsen.

When I called on him as Prussian Minister to have my passport *visé* in order to return to Germany, and when I explained to him how I had worked to bring out an edition of the text and commentary of the Rig-veda from MSS. scattered about in different libraries in Europe, and was now obliged to return to Germany, unable to complete my copies and collations of manuscripts, he took my hand, and said, 'I look upon you as myself, young again. Stay in London, and as to ways and means, let me see to that.' Mind, I was then a young, unknown man. Bunsen had never seen me before. Let that be a lesson to young men, never to despair. If you have found a work to which you are ready to sacrifice the whole of your life, and if you have faith in yourselves, others will have faith in you, and, sooner or later, a work that must be done will be done.

MSS. of the Veda brought to Europe.

But I have not yet finished the account of the final discovery of the Veda.

After Colebrooke's return from India, manuscripts of the Veda and its commentaries had become accessible in London. The first who made an attempt to study these manuscripts, to copy and collate them, and prepare them for publication, was Rosen. As the result of his labours he published in 1830 his *Rigvedae Specimen*. It contained a few hymns only, but it produced a great impression, because, after all, it was the first authentic specimen of the ancient Vedic language submitted to the scholars of Europe. Rosen undertook to bring out the whole of the Rig-veda, but he found the preliminary work, the study of Sâyana's commentary and of all the literature pertaining to it, far more difficult than he expected. When after seven years of hard and patient labour Rosen died in 1837, all that there was to be published after his death in 1838, was the first book of the Rig-veda in Sanskrit, with a Latin translation and notes.

With Rosen's death the thread of the history of Vedic scholarship seems broken again. Many learned papers were written on the Veda, all based on Rosen's posthumous volume. Bopp constantly availed himself of the Veda for his *Comparative Grammar*. Lassen, Benfey, Kuhn, and others, all drew as much information as possible out of the 121 hymns which Rosen had placed within their reach. But the only scholar in Europe who went beyond Rosen, and who really forms the connecting link between the first and the second periods of Vedic scholarship, was Eugène Burnouf at Paris.

Eugène Burnouf in France.

Historical justice requires that Burnouf's merits should be fully recognised, because, owing to his being called away to Buddhistic studies, and owing to his early death, very little of his work on the Veda has come to the knowledge of the world, except through his disciples. First of all, Burnouf worked hard in collecting MSS. of the principal Vedas, of their commentaries, and of other works necessary for their elucidation. He had persuaded Guizot[1], who was then

[1] See Appendix IV.

Prime Minister in France, to provide the funds necessary for the acquisition of these MSS.; others he had acquired at his own expense. With the help of these MSS. he gained a wider acquaintance with Vedic literature than was possessed at that time by any other scholar. Scholars came from all parts of Europe to attend his lectures. These lectures were given at the *Collège de France*. They were attended by Nève, Gorresio, Roth, Goldstücker, Barthélemy St. Hilaire, Bardelli, and others, who have all done good work, though some of them have gone to rest from their labours. In these lectures Burnouf laid before us in the most generous spirit his own views on the interpretation of the Veda, his own results, and his own plans for the future. The true principles of the interpretation of the Veda, the necessity of beginning with the native commentaries, and the equal necessity of going beyond them and discovering the true meaning of the Vedic language by the same method of decipherment which Burnouf himself had so triumphantly applied to the Avesta and to the cuneiform inscriptions, were then for the first time clearly enunciated. And not only was all his knowledge freely communicated to his pupils, but his own MSS. were readily placed at their disposal, if only they would work and help in the advancement of Vedic scholarship.

We were allowed to handle for the first time, not only the texts of the Vedas and their commentaries, but such books as the Nirukta, the Prâtisâkhyas, the Kalpa-sûtras were freely placed at our disposal. There can be no question whatever that the founder of the critical school of Vedic scholarship was Burnouf, though he himself was the very last man to claim any credit for what he had done. The seed which he had sown bore ample fruit, and that was all he cared for. In Roth's *Essays on the Veda* (1846) we see the first results of Burnouf's teaching, and in his later works, his edition of the Nirukta (1852) and his valuable contributions to the *Petersburg Dictionary*, the same scholar has proved himself a worthy disciple of that great French savant.

My edition of the Rig-veda.

I had come to Paris to attend Burnouf's lectures, and with very vague notions as to an edition of the text and the commentary of the Rig-veda. You must remember that the Vedas had never been published in India, though for more than three thousand years they had held there the same place which the Bible holds with us. They existed both in oral tradition, as they still exist, and in MSS., more or less perfect, more or less correct. These MSS. therefore had to be copied, and then to be collated. This was comparatively an easy task. The real difficulty began with the commentary. First of all, that commentary was enormous, and filled about four volumes quarto of a thousand pages each. While the MSS. of the text were generally correct, those of the commentary were mostly very carelessly written, full of omissions, and often perfectly unintelligible. But the greatest difficulty of all was that Sâya*n*a, the compiler of the great commentary, who lived in the fourteenth century A.D.[1], quoted largely from a literature which was at that time entirely unknown to us, which existed in

[1] He became president of the College of *S*ri*n*gerî in 1331, and died in 1386.

MSS. only, and often not even in MSS. accessible in Europe. My idea was to give extracts only from this commentary, but on this point Burnouf resisted with all his might. We must have the whole or nothing, he used to say, and often when I despaired of my task, he encouraged and helped me with his advice. Before I could begin the first volume of my edition of Sayâ*n*a's commentary, I had to read, to copy, and to index the principal works which were constantly referred to by Sâya*n*a—a little library by itself. However, in 1849 the first volume appeared, and twenty-five years later, in 1875, the whole work was finished.

I have thus tried to give you a short sketch of the discovery of the Veda. My own task was not that of a discoverer, but that of a patient excavator only. With every new platform that was laid bare, with every new volume that was published, scholars rushed in to examine what had been found, to sift the ashes, to clear the genuine antiquities from the rubbish. Critical scholarship did not wait till the whole of Sâya*n*a's commentary was finished. A number of excellent young scholars have been at work on the Veda in every country of Europe. In India also a new interest has sprung up in Vedic literature, and with every year new light is thrown on the enigmatic utterances of the Vedic Rishis. What these utterances are, what the Rig-veda really is, what the whole of Vedic literature contains, I shall have to explain to you in my next lecture.

LECTURE IV.

SURVEY OF VEDIC LITERATURE.

Peculiar Character of Indian Antiquity.

WE saw how the Veda was discovered, how the ancient city of Vedic thought was excavated, and how a world which had lain buried for thousands of years was called back to life in our own time. No doubt the ruins of Carnac in Egypt look grander, the palaces of Nineveh are more magnificent, the streets and houses and temples at Pompeii are more imposing than a hundred volumes of Vedic literature. But what is it that gives life to the colossal ruins of Carnac, what allows us a real insight into the palaces of Nineveh, what imparts to the streets and houses and temples of Pompeii a meaning and a real human interest, if not the inscriptions on their walls and the rolls of papyrus and parchment which tell us of the thoughts of the ancient Egyptians, or Assyrians, or Romans? Mere monuments, mere lists of kings, mere names of battles, what do they teach us? But give us *one* thought, *one* truly human sentiment, and we feel at home among those ancient ruins, the Babylonian statues begin to live, the Egyptian mummies begin to speak, and the streets of ancient Pompeii swarm once more with senators, with philosophers, and the gay society of ancient Italy.

Here it is where the discoveries in India assert their superiority over all other discoveries in ancient history. It is true we have no really ancient temples or palaces in that country. Massive stone buildings were probably unknown in India before the rise of Buddhism and the conquests of Alexander, and even if they had existed, they would have perished long ago in the peculiar climate of India. The Indian mind had no faith in that small immortality which the kings of Egypt and Babylon valued so much, and strove to secure for themselves by their stupendous edifices. The Hindu always felt himself a mere stranger on earth, a sojourner in a foreign land, and the idea of perpetuating his name and fame for a few thousand years by brick and mortar never entered his mind, till he had learnt it from outsiders.

But if the Âryas in India have left us no stones, they have left us bread—thoughts to feed on, riddles to solve, lessons to learn, such as we find nowhere else.

Meaning of Veda.

We call what they have left us Veda. Now what does Veda mean? It means knowledge, and it is letter by letter the same word as the Greek *οἶδα*, i.e. *ϝοῖδα*, only that Veda is a noun, while *οἶδα* is a verb. But the verb also exists in Sanskrit, and as we have to learn in Greek that *οἶδα* is a perfect with the meaning of the present, we have to learn in Sanskrit that veda is a perfect, but means 'I know.'

Is this a mere accident, a mere coincidence? Certainly not. It is one of those small facts of the

Science of Language which can teach us volumes. This similarity between, or rather this identity of, Sanskrit veda and Greek *οἶδα*, clenches with the force of an hydraulic hammer the original unity of the speakers of Greek and Sanskrit. If perfect Sanskrit was spoken 1500 B.C., and if perfect Greek was spoken about the same time, then these two streams of language which had diverged even at that time so much that not one word in them was exactly the same, that Homer and Vasish*th*a would have been perfectly unintelligible to each other, these two streams of language, I say, must once have formed one stream, and in that one stream this so-called irregular perfect must have been formed once for all. No other explanation is possible for that simple equation veda=*οἶδα*.

But this perfect veda and *οἶδα*, with the meaning of the present, may teach us another lesson also, namely, that these early framers of language held the same, whether right or wrong, view on the nature of human knowledge which Locke held. If he said, *Nihil in intellectu quod non ante fuerit in sensu*, they expressed 'I know' by 'I have seen,'—the only saving clause being in the implied *I*, which may represent what Leibnitz added, *nihil, nisi intellectus.*

But it is time now to ask what this Veda really is. The Veda has become such a power, not only in linguistic research, but in all antiquarian, religious, and philosophical studies, that no honest student can be satisfied with a vague idea of what the Veda is. I am afraid a more detailed survey of Vedic literature will prove somewhat tedious, but to a real student of religion such knowledge is absolutely indispensable.

The Rig-veda, the only true Veda.

It has been usual to speak of three or even of four Vedas, namely, the Rig-veda, Ya*g*ur-veda, Sâma-veda, to which the Atharva-veda has been added as the fourth. Now although from an Indian point of view this is perfectly correct, nothing can be more misleading from an historical point of view. From an historical point of view there is but *one* real Veda, the Rig-veda, and when we say the Rig-veda, what we mean is the Rig-veda-sa*m*hitâ only, the collection of hymns, and nothing else. When we speak of the Veda as representing the earliest phase of thought and language accessible to the historian on Aryan ground, that phase of thought must not be looked for in what are called the Ya*g*ur-veda and Sâma-veda, but in the hymns of the Rig-veda only, to which possibly some popular verses collected in the Atharva-veda may have to be added. Whenever therefore I speak of the Veda in general, whenever I appeal to the Veda as the foundation of the science of language, mythology, and religion, what I mean is the Rig-veda, the Veda of the sacred hymns which belonged to the ancient inhabitants of the country of the Seven Rivers.

Brahmanic View of the Vedas.

In order to explain how the confusion between the Rig-veda and the other so-called Vedas arose, I must explain to you the view which the Brâhmans themselves take of their ancient sacred literature.

According to them there are three Vedas (trayî vidyâ), or, according to later authorities, four, the Rig-veda, Ya*g*ur-veda, Sâma-veda, and, as the fourth, the Atharva-veda.

Each of these Vedas, as we now possess it, consists of two parts, called Sa*m*hitâ and Brâhma*n*a. The Sa*m*hitâs, literally collections, consist of Mantras, or metrical compositions, the Brâhma*n*as are in prose.

The Rig-veda.

Let us begin with the Rig-veda. *Rig*, which is a modification of *rik*, means a verse, originally a verse of praise, for the root ark in one of its ramifications has taken the sense of praising and celebrating. Hence arka also, a hymn of praise.

The Sa*m*hitâ of the Rig-veda, as we find it in our MSS., is a large collection of hymns, chiefly but not exclusively of a religious character. It is really a collection of collections, for it consists of ten so-called Ma*nd*alas, lit. rounds or spheres, and each of these Ma*nd*alas forms by itself an independent collection, and belonged originally to one or other of the great Vedic families.

The Ten Ma*nd*alas.

We can distinguish between Ma*nd*alas II to VII, which are distinctly Ma*nd*alas belonging to certain families, and the remaining four Ma*nd*alas, which are less distinctly the property of Vedic families.

Thus the second Ma*nd*ala belongs to the family of G*ri*tsamada (Bhârgava).
The third to that of Visvâmitra.
The fourth „ „ Vâmadeva (Gautama).
The fifth „ „ Atri.
The sixth „ „ Bharadvâ*g*a.
The seventh „ „ Vasish*th*a.

The first Ma*nd*ala is not ascribed to any family in particular, but is called by native authorities the Ma*nd*ala of the *S*atar*k*ins, that is of the poets who each contributed about a hundred verses to this book. The eighth Ma*nd*ala contains a large number of hymns composed in a peculiar metre, called Pragâthas.

While the eighth Ma*nd*ala seems to have been collected chiefly on the strength of the similarity of metre, the ninth was evidently intended to comprehend hymns addressed to one and the same deity, namely, Soma.

The families who principally contributed to these three books, the first, the eighth, and the ninth, are the Kâ*n*vas and Ângirasas, though other families are not excluded.

Lastly, the tenth book seems to contain whatever was left over of Vedic poetry. It is called the Ma*nd*ala of the long and short, or miscellaneous hymns. The poets also seem to belong promiscuously to every one of the ancient Vedic families.

It was very natural on the strength of these facts to suppose that the six Family Ma*nd*alas, II to VII, were the oldest collections; that they were followed by the eighth and ninth Ma*nd*alas, each having its own distinctive character and purpose, and that in the end the first and tenth Ma*nd*alas were added, containing the last gleanings of the ancient collectors.

Method in the Collection of the Ten Ma*nd*alas.

But if we examine the character of the ten Ma*n*-*d*alas more closely, we shall find that such a theory can hardly be justified. There is clearly one and the same system, according to which every one of these ten books has been collected. It is not by accident, as I pointed out long ago[1], that in every one of these Ma*n*d*a*las, except the eighth[2] and ninth, the first hymns are those addressed to Agni, and that these are followed by hymns addressed to Indra. Native students of the Veda were fully aware of this fact, and we can only account for it by admitting that the collection of all, or at least of eight of the Ma*n*d*a*las, was carried out under the same presiding spirit.

Another feature common to several of the Ma*n*d*a*las[3] is a certain arithmetical order of the hymns. Here I should mention first of all that each Ma*n*d*a*la is divided into a number of Anuvâkas, i.e. recitations or chapters. In many of these Anuvâkas the hymns follow each other according to the diminishing number of verses. This fact no one could help perceiving who looked at the tabular index printed at the end of my edition of the Rig-veda[4]. But the frequency with which this law was broken prevented most scholars from drawing the important lesson which, I believe, Professor Grassmann was the first to draw, namely, that whenever that rule is broken, there must have been a reason for it. The chief reason is supposed to have been that the hymns which break the rule were later additions, and that in some cases shorter hymns at the end of an Anuvâka had been

[1] Rig-veda-Sanhita, translation, vol. i. p. xxv.

[2] The eighth Ma*n*d*a*la begins with hymns to Indra, not, as Prof. Weber asserts, with hymns to Agni. The tenth Ma*n*d*a*la begins with hymns to Agni.

[3] Cf. Delbrück in *Jenaer Literaturzeitung*, 1875, p. 867.

[4] Bergaigne, *Journal Asiatique*, 1886, p. 197.

wrongly united into one large hymn. This has been a most useful lesson for critical purposes, though in some cases the knife of the operating critics may have been handled with too great boldness[1].

There are many characteristics, however, which all the Ma*nd*alas share in common, and which show the working of a common system on the part of the collectors. The collectors were evidently impressed with the idea that every hymn must have a poet, and that every poet must belong to a certain family. In many cases it is quite evident that these names were fanciful; still in none of the Ma*nd*alas do we find a hymn without the names of poet or deity. That hymns addressed to the same deity were generally kept together, we have seen already. There is the same tendency also to keep hymns of the same poets together. Nor can there be any doubt that the same general theory of metre had been accepted by the compilers of all the ten Ma*nd*alas.

It seems to me quite clear from these facts that we must admit a period, it may be of one or of two generations only, during which a few individuals agreed to collect the sacred poetry that had been preserved in six of the most prominent Brahmanic

[1] This, as has been shown by Delbrück, Grassmann, and others, is very clear in the seventh Ma*nd*ala. There the hymns addressed to each deity diminish regularly in succession, except at the end of each group.

(1)	Hymns addressed to		Agni, regular 1–14, irregular 15–17.
(2)	,,	,,	Indra, ,, 18–30, ,, 31–33.
(3)	,,	,,	the Visve, regular 34–54, irregular 55.
(4)	,,	,,	the Marutas, regular 56–58, irregular 59.
(5)	,,	,,	Sûrya, the Marutas, and Varu*n*a, regular 60–65, irregular 66.
(6)	,,	,,	the Asvinau, regular 67–73, irregular 74.
(7)	,,	,,	Ushas, regular 75–80, irregular 81.

families, that the same individuals, or their immediate successors, superintended the other four collections also, which are contained in the eighth, the ninth, the first, and the tenth Ma*n*d*alas, and that in this way one great collection, the Rig-veda-sa*m*hitâ, was finished. The whole collection of hymns is sometimes called Dâsatayî, i.e. consisting of ten parts, as it were, the Decamerone. Dâ*s*ataya is an adjective, meaning what belongs to the ten Ma*n*d*alas.

Number of Hymns.

This collection, as we now possess it, handed down in the school of the *S*âkalas, consists of 1017 hymns (Mantras or Sûktas), while in the school of the Bâshkalas their number amounted to 1025. There are besides eleven hymns, called the Vâlakhilya hymns [1], which were added at the end of the sixth Anuvâka of the eighth Ma*n*d*ala. If we count them together with the 1017 hymns of the *S*âkalas, we get a sum total of 1028 Vedic hymns. There are other spurious hymns called Khilas, but they are not counted with the hymns of the Sa*m*hitâ.

The Prâtisâkhyas.

These 1028 hymns became soon the subject of a most minute study, a kind of Masoretic exegesis. They had to be learnt by heart, and their exact pronunciation was laid down with the greatest care in works called Prâtisâkhyas [2]. The date of these Prâtisâ-

[1] There can be no doubt that these eleven hymns were added at a later time, and that they had existed before as a separate collection. This is best shown by the fact that they admit Galitas from themselves only, except in one doubtful case, tam tvâ vayam.

[2] The Prâtisâkhyas form one of the six Vedângas, viz. the *S*ikshâ. Goldstücker denied it, but he is refuted by the *Ri*k-prâtisâkhya itself, which says, S. 827, that it is k*ri*tsna*m* vedângam anindyam

khyas has been fixed with as much probability as is attainable in such matters, in about the fifth or sixth century B.C. They are certainly prior to the great grammarian Pâ*n*ini who quotes *verbatim* from the Prâti*s*âkhya belonging to the *S*âkala school of the Rig-veda [1].

Date of the Prâti*s*âkhya.

In this Prâti*s*âkhya we have clear proof that the author of it, commonly called *S*aunaka, knew our collection of hymns, consisting of ten Ma*nd*alas. He speaks of dâ*s*atayî [2] verses, i.e. verses found in the ten Ma*nd*alas. He actually quotes a passage as coming from the tenth Ma*nd*ala [3] (Sûtra 313). In fact, his various rules presuppose not only the collection of the ten Ma*nd*alas, but the exact collocation also of the hymns in each Ma*nd*ala, such as we now possess them. It is thus and thus only that he is able to say, as he does, that a certain verse (I. 133, 6) is the longest, and another the shortest (VI. 45, 29), among all the verses of the ten Ma*nd*alas.

He goes even further, and he shows himself so certain of every consonant and vowel of the whole text of the ten Ma*nd*alas being in its right place, that he can say (S. 309) with perfect assurance and with

ârsham, 'a complete Vedânga, faultless, and canonical.' The first Prâti*s*âkhya published was that of the Rig-veda (1856–69). There are, besides the two Prâti*s*âkhyas of the Ya*g*ur-veda, one for the Vâ*g*asaneyi-sa*m*hitâ, the other for the Taittirîya, and the Atharva-prâti*s*âkhya. A Sâma-prâti*s*âkhya has been published by Satyavrata Sâma*s*rami in the Ushâ, vol. i. No. 3 seq.

[1] See Appendix V.

[2] Rig-veda-prâti*s*âkhya, 997, *g*yesh*th*â dâ*s*atayîshu *rik*âm, the longest of the verses among the Dâ*s*atayîs. I thought that Dâ*s*atayî might here be meant as a name of Ma*nd*ala, because the text has *rik*âm, not *rik*shu. See, however, Sûtras 946 and 993.

[3] The technical term Ma*nd*ala occurs first in the Aitareya-âra*n*yaka and in the G*ri*hya-sûtras.

perfect correctness, that, for instance, compounds ending with the words varu*n*a and vrata shorten their last vowel, provided a consonant or semi-vowel follows, and this through the whole of the Rig-veda, except in thirteen hymns which are ascribed to Medhâtithi[1] (I. 12; I. 24).

Minutiae of the Prâtisâkhya.

Such statements occur again and again, and leave us in no doubt that not a single hymn could have been added to our collection, nor a single line be changed, after the date of the Prâtisâkhyas.

This is a most important point, for unless our arguments can be upset, we now possess the certainty that the Masoretic studies of the sixth and fifth centuries B.C. presuppose, nay postulate the existence, not only of Vedic hymns in general, but of our collection of these hymns in ten Ma*nd*alas; and not only of our collection in ten Ma*nd*alas, but of every hymn exactly in that place in which we now find it, with every word in its right place, nay with every vowel, either lengthened or shortened, exactly as they are lengthened or shortened in our MSS. This means that the text, exactly as we possess it in MSS. not more than about 500 years old, had become the subject of most minute scholastic studies about 500 B.C.

The Anukrama*n*îs of *S*aunaka.

And now we may advance another step. The same author, *S*aunaka, to whom the authorship of one Prâtisâkhya is ascribed, is also mentioned as the author of certain *indices* to the Rig-veda, called Anukrama*n*îs, literally, 'after-steppings.' These indices

[1] See Appendix VI.

contain the number of Ma*nd*alas, of Anuvâkas, and of hymns, the names of the authors and the deities, and the metres.

Most of these single indices have been preserved to us, or they existed at least as late as the time of Sâya*n*a, fourteenth century. They were superseded, however, by the more comprehensive index of Kâtyâyana, the Sarvânukrama*n*î. These indices again presuppose the text of the ten Ma*nd*alas in all its important features exactly such as we now possess it, and thus enable us to say that the bridge of our argument spans a distance of more than two thousand years, and lands us about 500 B. C. in the schools of the Brâhmans, the so-called Parishads, where we see teacher and pupils learning by heart exactly the same Veda which we are studying at present.

Number of Verses of the Rig-veda.

We saw that, according to the calculation of those ancient scholars, the Rig-veda-sa*m*hitâ consisted then, as it does now, of ten Ma*nd*alas, eighty-five Anuvâkas, and 1028 Sûktas or hymns. But they went further in their calculations, and counted 10,402 verses[1], 153,826 words, 432,000 syllables. These calculations, I am obliged to confess, have not yet been checked, except that of the verses, and here there is a discrepancy, but only a slight one. On an average, however, a hymn may be said to consist of ten verses, so that the number of 10,402 verses for 1028 hymns cannot be far wrong.

This will give you an idea of the extent of the real Veda, or the Rig-veda-sa*m*hitâ. If we take into

[1] See Appendix VII.

account the length of the Vedic verses, as compared with the Greek hexameter, the Rig-veda may be said to contain nearly as much as the Iliad and Odyssey together.

This is all we have and ever shall have for studying that ancient period in the history of the Aryan race which precedes in language, mythology, and religion the Homeric period, hitherto the most ancient known period in the history of our race.

The Sâma-veda.

If all the rest of what is called Vedic literature had been lost, we should not have been much the poorer for it. To the student of the history of Sanskrit literature the other so-called Vedas are no doubt of very high interest, as they form the connecting link between the ancient Vedic period and the later Sanskrit literature. But in the eyes of the general historian they cannot compare with what is really unique in the literature of the whole world, the hymns of the Rig-veda.

What then are the other so-called Vedas?

What is called the Sâma-veda-sa*m*hitâ is no more than a compilation of verses contained in the Rig-veda, which had to be sung at certain sacrifices, and not simply to be recited, as were the hymns of the Rig-veda. Sâman means melody. Very often single verses are taken out of the hymn to which they originally belonged, in order to be sung together at certain sacrifices. There are only seventy-eight out of the 1549 verses of the Sâma-veda[1] which have not

[1] See Ludwig, Rig-veda, iii. pp. 419–426. Aufrecht, Rig-veda, second edition, vol. ii. p. xlv.

been found in our text of the Rig-veda. All the rest are simply the same as we find them in the Rig-veda, with slight variations, representing the various readings of different recensions (*s*âkhâ), but by no means, as was once supposed[1], a more ancient text.

Ya*g*ur-veda.

What we call the Ya*g*ur-veda-sa*m*hitâ is a collection of verses and sacrificial formulas, intended for the use of the priests who, while performing the sacrifice, had to mutter these verses and formulas. Ya*g*us[2] is the name for these sacrificial formulas, as ya*gñ*a is the name of sacrifice.

What then is the difference between the collection of hymns of the Rig-veda and the two collections of hymns of the Ya*g*ur-veda and Sâma-veda?

The collection of hymns of the Rig-veda represents an historical event, like the final collection of the books of the Old Testament. It arose from a desire to preserve from destruction the sacred poetry that was the property of certain families, in order to hand it down as a whole from generation to generation.

The *Kh*andas or Mantra Period.

I have formerly called the period during which the hymns collected in the Rig-veda were originally composed, the *Kh*andas period, *kh*andas being one of

[1] This idea of Prof. Weber's has been sufficiently refuted by Burnell, Ârsheya-brâhma*n*a, p. xvi, and by Aufrecht, Rig-veda, second edition, p. xxxvii.

[2] The distinction of *rik*, sâman, and ya*g*us is clearly laid down in the Aitareya-âra*n*yaka, II. 3, 6, 8: 'A *rik* verse, a gâthâ, a kumbyâ (a moral saw) are measured (metrical). A Ya*g*us line, an invocation (nigada), and general remarks, these are not measured. A Sâman, or any portion of it (gesh*n*a, i.e. parvan) is musical.'

the oldest names for these sacred verses, and I have tried to distinguish it from the period in which these verses were collected and studied as a whole, which I called the Mantra period, mantra being the technical name for these hymns. But later researches have convinced me that with regard to the Rig-veda the Mantra period simply represents the closing of the *Kh*andas period, while with regard to the Ya*g*ur-veda and Sâma-veda it has now become clear that there never was a Mantra period at all, but that even the first collection of these hymns and formulas belongs to a later period, that of the prose Brâhma*n*as, and certainly did not precede that period.

The Prose Brâhma*n*as.

I mentioned before that, according to Hindu authorities, every Veda consists of a collection of hymns, Sa*m*hitâs, and Brâhma*n*as. These Brâhma*n*as are the earliest specimens of prose literature in India which we possess, and their object was to describe the elaborate system of sacrifices which had grown up among the Brâhmans, and to show how the hymns or portions of the hymns should be used at each sacrifice.

For the performance of these sacrifices, particularly of the great sacrifices, three distinct classes of priests were required. One class had to perform the manual labour, which was very considerable, the clearing of the sacrificial ground, the erection of altars, the lighting of the fire, the preparation of the offerings, &c. They were called Adhvaryus, the labouring priests, and their duties, mixed up with endless speculations, were described in the Brâhma*n*as of the

Adhvaryus. They formed the Brâhma*n*as of the Ya*g*ur-veda.

Another class of priests had to sing. They were called Udgât*ri*s, the singing priests, and their respective duties were in the same way described in the Brâhma*n*as of the Udgât*ri*s, or, as they are also called, the *Kh*andogas, i.e. the singers of the *kh*andas. These formed the Brâhma*n*as of the Sâma-veda.

A third class of priests had to recite certain hymns with the utmost correctness of articulation. They were called Hot*ri*s, the reciting priests, and their duties were described in the Brâhma*n*as of the Hot*ri* priests. They formed the Brâhma*n*as of the Rig-veda.

The Brâhma*n*as of the Ya*g*ur-veda.

We can best study the historical growth of the Brâhma*n*as in the case of the Adhvaryu priests, the actual performers of the sacrifices.

We possess for the Adhvaryus four ancient works containing explanations of the sacrifice,—

(1) The Kâ*th*aka, belonging to the school of the Ka*th*as,

(2) The Kapish*th*ala-ka*th*a Sa*m*hitâ, belonging to the school of the Kapish*th*ala-ka*th*as,

(3) The Maitrâya*n*î Sa*m*hitâ, belonging to the school of the Maitrâya*n*as, and

(4) The Taittirîyaka.

In these four works the verses to be used by the Adhvaryu priest are given in proper order for each sacrifice, and they are accompanied by prose portions, containing instructions and general observations.

It will be observed that two of them are called Sa*m*hitâs, though they would more correctly have been called Brâhma*n*as. There is, in fact, no other Brâhma*n*a for the Kapish*th*ala-ka*th*as and the Maitrâya*n*îyas, besides what is here called their Sa*m*hitâ. The Taittirîyaka, however, exists in two portions, one called Sa*m*hitâ, the other Brâhma*n*a. But here again there is really no distinction between the two, the Brâhma*n*a being simply a continuation and appendix of the Sa*m*hitâ. Sa*m*hitâ, in fact, is a misnomer, as applied to the Maitrâya*n*îya and the Kapish*th*ala-ka*th*a Sa*m*hitâs, and, in spite of native tradition, it would be far better to call these collections of the Taittirîyas, Maitrâya*n*as, and Kapish*th*ala-ka*th*as, Brâhma*n*as.

After a time, however, it was felt to be useful for the priests, when performing the sacrifice, to have a separate collection of the hymns and sacrificial formulas, and another containing the rules of the sacrifice and the explanatory notes. And thus we find in the school of the Vâ*g*asaneyins a Sa*m*hitâ, containing nothing but the hymns, and a Brâhma*n*a, containing nothing but the explanations. In this form the Ya*g*ur-veda is called the Bright Ya*g*ur-veda, in contradistinction from the Dark Ya*g*ur-veda, in which hymns and explanations are mixed. The Brâhma*n*a of the Bright Ya*g*ur-veda is called the *S*atapatha-brâhma*n*a, and it exists in two texts, as handed down by the two schools of the Mâdhyandinas and Kâ*n*vas.

We are thus enabled to see how the so-called Sa*m*hitâ of the Ya*g*ur-veda, the collection of verses and formulas to be used by the Adhvaryu priest, arose. It existed first as part and parcel of a Brâhma*n*a, and was afterwards extracted and separated from it for the benefit of the officiating priest. It is therefore really subsequent, not antecedent to the Brâhma*n*a. It is no more than a manual for the use of the Adhvaryus, the labouring priests, extracted from a previous work in prose, which gave a full account of that portion of the sacrifice which this one class of priests, the Adhvaryus, had to perform, together with the necessary verses.

The Brâhma*n*as of the Sâma-veda.

Exactly the same seems to have taken place with the Sâma-veda. Here too we have Brâhma*n*as, such as the Tâ*nd*ya-brâhma*n*a in twenty-five books, discoursing on that portion of the sacrifice which fell to the share of the singing priests. After a time a hymn-book was felt to be useful, and a Sâma-veda-sa*m*hitâ was put together which we still possess in two forms, either as simple texts (Sâma-veda-âr*k*ika), or as adapted to the melodies (Grâmageyagâna, Ara*n*yagâna)[1].

We shall now be better able to see the difference between the collection of the hymns of the Rig-veda, the Rig-veda-sa*m*hitâ, and the other collections of hymns, the Ya*g*ur-veda-sa*m*hitâ, and the Sâma-veda-sa*m*hitâ. The latter were collected for the special benefit of certain classes of priests, and were, so far as we can judge, put together subsequently to the composition of the prose Brâhma*n*as. They were mere extracts from more ancient Brâhma*n*as. The Rig-veda-sa*m*hitâ, on the contrary, has nothing to do with the sacrifice. It is true that a third class of priests, the Hot*ri*s, have likewise to recite many

[1] See Appendix VIII.

of the hymns of the Rig-veda during the performance of the sacrifice. But there is no collection giving these hymns in the order in which they have to be recited by the Hot*ri* priests. Such a collection would have been analogous to the hymn-books of the labouring and the singing priests, while the collection of the Rig-veda hymns, as we possess it, is really an historical collection, carried out in common, as we saw, by a number of Brahmanic families, and by itself utterly useless for sacrificial purposes.

The Brâhma*n*a of the Rig-veda.

It seems that the Hot*ri* priests, the reciters, were the most highly educated Brâhmans. It was their duty not only to know the whole of the hymns of the Rig-veda by heart, and to learn to pronounce them with the greatest accuracy, but likewise to learn from their Brâhma*n*as at what part of the sacrifice certain hymns and portions of hymns had to be recited. We still possess two of these Brâhma*n*as, intended for the use of the reciting priests,

(1) The Aitareya-brâhma*n*a, belonging, according to Satyavrata, to the *S*âkhâ of the *S*âkalas,

(2) The Kaushîtaki-brâhma*n*a, also called the *S*ânkhâyana-brâhma*n*a.

If, according to the indications contained in these Brâhma*n*as, the hymns and verses to be recited by the Hot*ri* priests had been collected and arranged according to the order of the different sacrifices, we should then have had a Rig-veda-sa*m*hitâ on a level with the Sa*m*hitâs of the other Vedas. As it is, the Rig-veda-sa*m*hitâ stands by itself. It had a different, not a purely priestly origin, and, so far as we can judge at present, it was anterior, not posterior, to the Brâhma*n*a period.

The true Veda.

What is the result of all this? It is this, that we really possess one collection only of ancient hymns which by itself represents the earliest period of Indian language, mythology, and religion. This is called the Rig-veda-sa*m*hitâ, and can alone be spoken of as the true Veda.

Between the period represented by these hymns, the duration of which may have been many centuries, and the period which gave rise to the prose works called Brâhma*n*as, there is a complete break. How it came about we cannot tell, but it is a fact that the authors of the Brâhma*n*as had completely lost the true meaning of the Vedic hymns. Their interpretations, or rather misinterpretations, of these ancient hymns are perfectly astounding. Their one idea is the sacrifice, which had assumed such proportions, and had been elaborated with such hair-splitting minuteness that we may well understand how the Brâhmans had no thoughts left for anything else. The hymns had become in time a merely subordinate portion of the sacrifice. The proper position of a log of wood or of a blade of grass round the sacrificial fire, seemed of more consequence than the expressions of gratitude, the prayers for forgiveness of sin, or the praises of the mighty deeds of the gods, contained in the hymns of their ancestors.

The Brâhma*n*as of the Brâhmans.

I think, therefore, that we may speak of a period of Brâhma*n*as following on the period of the hymns, and the very name of Brâhma*n*a period would fully characterise it. The name Brâhma*n*a has nothing to do with brahman, in the special sense of prayer, or sacrificial formula and ceremony. These are not the principal or exclusive objects of the Brâhma*n*as. The name Brâhma*n*a was derived either from brahman, neuter, meaning the clergy or priesthood, just as kshatram means the nobility, or directly from brahman, nom., brahmâ, masc., the priest, and more especially the superintending priest. For it should be remembered that, in addition to the three classes of priests whom I mentioned before, the labouring, the singing, and the reciting priests, there was a fourth class who had to watch the progress of the sacrifice and see that all was done and spoken and sung correctly and in proper order. For that purpose the priests who performed the office of the Brahman had to be acquainted with the other Vedas also, and especially with the rules laid down in the works which were called Brâhma*n*as. These Brâhma*n*as could hardly have been so called except because they were the books of the Brahman, neut., the clergy in general, or of the Brahman, masc., the superintending priest. Brâhma*n*a, the Brâhman, is a derivative of brahman, masc.

We possess at present a limited number of these Brâhma*n*as only, but the number of Brâhma*n*as quoted is very large. We also know of numerous schools who followed the same Brâhma*n*a, though with slight variations—variations which may seem small to us, but which seemed very important in the eyes of the Vedic priesthood. That there were ancient and modern Brâhma*n*as we know from unimpeachable authorities of the fourth century B.C., for instance, the great grammarian, Pâ*n*ini. We saw before how the separation of the hymns from the Brâhma*n*as, a work ascribed to Yâ*gñ*avalkya, led to the introduction of a new Brâhma*n*a for the Ya*g*ur-veda, viz. the *S*atapatha-brâhma*n*a, and this very Brâhma*n*a, ascribed to Yâ*gñ*avalkya, is reckoned among those which were not old[1].

Life during the Vedic Period.

It ought not to be supposed, however, that what we call the Brâhma*n*a period represents to us the whole of the intellectual, or even of the religious life of India. It would be fearful to think that millions of people should for generations have fed on such stuff as we find in the Brâhma*n*as, and on nothing else. All we can say is that these Brâhma*n*as represent to us the only pillars left standing in a vast field of ruins, but that they need not have been the pillars of the only temples which once stood there. Besides, every temple presupposes a vast surrounding of busy life, without which a priesthood would find itself stranded high and dry.

Even in the hymns of the Rig-veda we find a great deal more than merely religious sentiments. We find in them traces of a busy life in all its phases, peace and war, study and trade. Thus we read in hymn IX. 112:

Poem on Trades and Professions.

'Different indeed are our desires, different the works of men. The carpenter looks for something that is

[1] Pâ*n*. IV. 3, 105, vârtt., IV. 2, 66, vârtt. *History of Ancient Sanskrit Literature*, p. 329.

broken, the leach for something that is sprained, the priest for one who offers oblations. . . . The smith with his dry sticks, with his wings of birds (in place of bellows), and his stones (anvil), looks day after day for a man who possesses gold. . . . I am a poet, my father is a leach, my mother works the mill; with different desires, all striving for wealth, we are as if running after cows[1].'

Poem of the Gambler.

The next hymn, if hymn it can be called, contains the lamentations of a gambler. That gambling is not a modern invention, but one of the oldest, one of the most universal vices of the human race, has been clearly proved, not only from ancient literature, but likewise from the study of the customs of uncivilised races. Still it is startling when we meet in this poem, not only with dice and public gambling places, but with all the miseries entailed on wife and mother and brothers by the recklessness of a gambler. Some people who know all about primitive society declare without hesitation that such verses cannot be genuine. If they would prove it, we should feel most grateful. As it is, we must simply take note of them; we must live and learn.

[1] 'Nânânám vaí u na*h* dhíya*h* ví vratā̃ni *g*ánânâm;
tákshâ rish*t*ám rutám bhishák brahmā̃ sunvántam i*kkh*ati . . .
*G*áratîbhi*h* óshadhîbhi*h* par*n*ébhi*h* *s*akunā̃nâm
kârmârá*h* ásmabhi*h* dyúbhi*h* híra*n*yavantam i*kkh*ati . . .
Kârú*h* ahám tatá*h* bhishák upalaprakshí*n*î nanā̃;
nā̃nâdhiya*h* vasuyáva*h* ánu gā̃*h* iva tasthima' . . .
Rig-veda IX. 112, 1–3.

X. 34.

1. These dice that have grown in the air on the great (Vibhîdaka) tree, drive me wild when they roll about on the board. This Vibhîdaka seems to me intoxicating like a draught of Soma, that has grown on mount Mu*g*âvat.

2. She (my wife) never troubled or chid me, she was kind to me and to my friends. But I, for the sake of these only-beloved dice, have spurned my devoted wife.

3. My mother-in-law hates me, my wife avoids me, the miserable finds no one to pity him; nor do I see what is the use of a gambler, as little as of an old horse, offered for sale.

4. Others pet his wife, while his war-horse, the dice, thirsts for booty. Father, mother, and brothers say of him, 'We do not know him, lead him away bound.'

5. And when I think that I shall not play with them again, then I am left by my friends who run away. But when the brown dice are thrown down and utter speech, then I rush to their rendezvous, like a love-sick maiden.

6. The gambler goes to the assembly, his body glowing, asking, Shall I win? Alas, the dice cross his desire, handing over to his opponent all that he has made.

7. These dice hook, prick, undo, burn, and inflame. After giving childish playthings they ruin the winner; yet to the gambler they are all covered with honey.

8. Their company of fifty-three plays about, like the bright Savit*ri*, whose laws are never broken.

They do not bend before the anger of the mighty, even the king bends down before them.

9. They roll down, they jump up; though having no hands themselves, they resist him who has hands. These playing[1] coals, though cold, when thrown on the board, burn the heart through and through.

10. The wife of the gambler mourns forlorn, so does the mother of the son who is gone away, she knows not whither. In debt, trembling, longing for money, the gambler goes to the house of others by night.

11. It grieves the gambler when he sees his wife, and the wives of others and their well-ordered house. In the fore-noon he has harnessed his brown horses (the dice); and when the fire is out, the wretch sinks down.

12. He who is the general of your large company, the king of the troop, the first, to him I stretch forth my ten fingers to swear,—I do not refuse my stake,—I now speak the truth:

13. 'Do not play with dice, plough thy field, enjoy what thou hast, consider it much. There are thy cows, O gambler, there thy wife—this is what the noble Savit*ri* has told me.

14. 'Make (other) friends, O dice, have mercy on us, do not bewitch us with powerful enchantment. May your wrath abate, and your enmity; let some one else be held in the snare of the brown dice.'

Independent Speculation.

In the Brâhma*n*as, particularly in the legends scattered about in them, we get many a glimpse of active life, and we see at all events that the Brâhmans did not constitute the whole of India. On the contrary,

[1] Read dîvyâ*h* for dívyâ*h*.

the nobility, though willing to work together with the priests, had evidently opened for themselves new avenues of thought, and begun to assert great independence in religious speculation, while among some of the Brâhmans also a desire seems to have arisen to be freed from the tedious routine of their life, and to retire into the forest for silent contemplation. It is curious that in both directions the Brahmanic system should have yielded so readily. People who had done their duty as students and as married men, were allowed to retire into the forest, free from nearly all religious restrictions, and to meditate there with perfect freedom on the highest problems of life. In these philosophical meditations princes and noblemen took an active part, and we hear of kings instructing the wisest among the Brâhmans in the knowledge of the Highest Self.

Âra*n*yakas and Upanishads.

All these later phases of life are reflected in the Brâhma*n*as, and particularly in the latest portions of them, the so-called Âra*n*yakas and Upanishads. Âra*n*yaka means a forest-book, Upanishad[1] a sitting down at the feet of a teacher to listen to his instruction[2].

[1] See Upanishads, translated by M. M., in *S. B. E.*, vol. i. p. lxxx.

[2] We have for the Rig-veda,
the Aitareya-âra*n*yaka, with an Upanishad,
and the Kaushîtaki-âra*n*yaka, with an Upanishad;
for the Taittirîya,
the Taittirîya-âra*n*yaka, with an Upanishad;
for the Vâ*g*asaneyins,
the B*ri*had-âra*n*yaka, with an Upanishad;
for the *Kh*andogas,
the *Kh*ândogya-upanishad, following the Mantra-brâhma*n*a.
The number of independent Upanishads is very large. See M. M., *Sacred Books of the East*, vol. i. p. lxviii.

Duration of Brâhma*n*a Period.

How long that Brâhma*n*a period lasted, how long it took to elaborate the stupendous system of sacrificial rules, and afterwards the lofty speculations of the Âra*n*yakas and Upanishads, which in their turn may be said to have neutralised and superseded all sacrifices, we can only guess. If we allowed ourselves to be guided by the large number of ancient and modern authorities quoted in the Brâhma*n*as, and by the long lists of successive teachers preserved in different schools, we should say that three or four centuries would hardly suffice for the whole of the Brâhma*n*a period. But ancient Indian chronology is built up on ever so many ifs, and against an uncompromising scepticism our arguments would prove of little avail.

The Atharva-veda.

Before we proceed, however, to a consideration of these chronological questions, I have still a few words to say about the fourth so-called Veda, the Atharva-veda.

The Atharva-veda possesses a Sa*m*hitâ or collection of verses, a Brâhma*n*a, and Sûtras, like the other Vedas. But it is difficult as yét to say what special purpose this Veda was intended to serve. Some native authorities maintain that the Atharva-veda was meant specially for the superintending priest, the Brahman, and was therefore called Brahma-veda ; but there is nothing to confirm this view. It seems a mere guess that, because there are four classes of priests and four Vedas, therefore the fourth Veda must have belonged to the fourth class of priests. So far as we know at present, hymns from the Atharva-veda were used for domestic ceremonies, at the celebration of the birth of children, at weddings, funerals, and likewise at the coronation of kings. Many of its verses are simply taken from the Rig-veda; the rest, and those the most interesting, contain all kinds of imprecations, blessings, charms, formulas to drive away diseases, prayers for success on journeys or in gambling, and lines for conjuring, often quite unintelligible. Supposing that these verses had been in use among the people, they would allow us an insight into their more homely thoughts, and deserve therefore to be studied more carefully than they have hitherto been. Some native authorities stoutly refuse to recognise the Atharva as a real Veda, others defend its authority with equal zeal. The old name of the Atharva-veda is Atharvângirasas, which would seem to indicate that the families of the Atharvans and the Angiras, or the Atharvângiras, were the original collectors or possessors of this Veda.

We possess the text of the Atharva-veda as handed down in two schools, the *S*aunakas and the Paippalâdas; but there is as yet no really critical edition of the text. A commentary lately discovered in India has not yet been published.

In our next lecture I shall try to explain to you how it is possible to assign certain dates to this large mass of Vedic literature which has come down to us, partly by oral tradition, partly in MSS. If you consider that most of these MSS. do not go back beyond the fifteenth century, you will understand that it is no easy undertaking to throw a bridge from the fifteenth century A.D. to the fifteenth century B.C.

Still the attempt must be made, for unless an historical date can be assigned to these relics of an ancient world, they would dwindle down in the eyes of the historian to mere curiosities. They would lose what alone makes them worthy of serious study, their historical character.

LECTURE V.

AGE OF THE VEDA.

Accurate knowledge of the Veda necessary for a study of Physical Religion.

THE survey of the Vedic literature which I endeavoured to place before you in my last lecture, may seem to have occupied a great deal of our time. But for studies such as we are engaged in, it is absolutely necessary to make our foundation sure. It really makes one shiver if one sees how the Veda is spoken of by some very eminent writers, in their treatises on the origin of mythology and religion. First of all, I hope I shall not hear the Veda any longer spoken of as the Veeda. As I explained to you before, Veda means knowledge, and is derived from the root vid, to see, which we have in Latin *videre*. The vowel in Veda is a diphthong, consisting of a + i. This a + i is pronounced in Sanskrit like ai in aid, and should properly be written ê. It is the same diphthong which in Greek is represented by ο + ι, as in *οἶδα*, I know, which stands for *Ϝοῖδα*. Secondly, though Veda ends in a, it is not a feminine in Sanskrit, but a masculine, and I hope that French and German writers more particularly will no longer speak of the Veda as *she*.

It is not to be expected that every student of the science of mythology and religion should read the Veda in the original. But it is essential that they should know more than the name; that they should have a clear idea what the Vedic literature consists of, how it arose, when it arose, where it arose, how it was handed down, when it was consigned to writing, how it is to be interpreted, and what is the reason why so much of it is still doubtful and unintelligible, and why scholars so frequently differ in their translations of difficult passages. No knowledge is better than knowledge that cannot give an account of itself, and I do not think that a scholarlike study of Physical Religion would be possible without a clear and accurate conception of what the Veda is, which has been truly called the Bible of Physical Religion.

How to fix the Date of the Veda.

As yet the whole of the Vedic literature, such as I described it to you, hangs, so to say, in the air. There was a time, not very long ago, when the whole of Sanskrit literature, the Veda included, was represented as a forgery of the Brâhmans. It seemed too bad to be true that the language of India should be as perfect as Greek, and that the mythology of Greece should have the same roots as the mythology of India. And though this uncompromising scepticism finds but few representatives at present, Sanskrit is still looked upon as an unwelcome guest by many classical scholars, and anything that can be said against it, is welcomed by all who dislike the trouble of learning a new language.

Aryan immigration into India.

Not long ago my friend, Professor Sayce, stated as the result of his Babylonian researches, that the migration of the Âryas towards India could not have taken place before about 600 or 700 B. C. Now consider what a complete upheaval of all our ideas on the ancient history of the Âryas in general, and more especially on the growth of religious thought in India, would be caused if this discovery could be maintained. Between the migration of the Âryas into the land of the Seven Rivers and the composition of hymns, addressed to the rivers of the Penjâb, and containing allusions even to the Ganges, some time must have elapsed. We have then to find room for successive generations of Vedic poets and Vedic princes, for repeated collections of ancient hymns, for a period filled by the composition of the Brâhma*n*as, written in prose and in a dialect different from that of the hymns, and lastly for the rise of that philosophical literature which we find in the Upanishads. If this Upanishad literature is, as I have tried to show, presupposed by Buddhism, and if Buddha lived about 500 B. C., what becomes of the first immigration of the Âryas into India about 600 or 700 B.C.?

Sindhu, cotton, mentioned 3000 B.C.

But while Professor Sayce has given us no arguments in support of this very recent date assigned by him to the first appearance of Âryas in India, he has placed at our disposal some facts which, if true, would seem to prove that Sanskrit must have been the language of India at least 3000 B. C.

We are told[1] that 'in the copy of an old list of clothing one article is mentioned which has to be pronounced sindhu in Assyro-Babylonian, and has the two ideographs "cloth + vegetable fibre." The copy of the list now extant was made for the library of Assur-bani-pal, but the original Babylonian tablet was of a much earlier date, possibly as early as the age of Khammuragas, say about 3000 B. C., though this is not quite certain.'

If we trust to these facts, and if, as Professor Sayce suggests, this vegetable fibre was cotton, and was called sindhu by the Babylonians, because it came from the river Sindhu, i.e. from India, this would prove the presence of Sanskrit-speaking Âryas in India about at least 3000 B. C.

Professor Sayce further identifies the Assyro-Babylonian word sindhu with the Greek *σινδών*, which occurs in Homer, and he thinks that the Hebrew sâtin, a linen shirt, mentioned in Isaiah iii. 23, was borrowed from Greek. I confess I see no similarity, whether in form or meaning, between the Hebrew sâtin and the Greek *σινδών*, particularly as we have in Arabic the word sâtin, meaning a covering in general. But if, as he argues, the Phenicians brought this word from the Sindhu, the Indus, and if both the Greeks and the Babylonians borrowed that word from the Phenicians, the presence of Sanskrit-speaking Âryas on the shores of the Indus would go back to a

[1] *Hibbert Lectures*, by Sayce, p. 138.

far more distant antiquity than we hitherto ventured to assign to it.

It should likewise be considered that cotton is not yet mentioned in the Vedic hymns, nor in the ancient Brâhma*n*as. It appears for the first time in the Sûtras (Â*s*val. *S*rauta Sûtra, IX. 4) as the name of a dress made of karpâsa, cotton. The other names, pi*k*u, pi*k*ula, and tûla are certainly post-Vedic. However, a cloth made of vegetable substances need not necessarily be cotton. It may have been valka, the bark of certain trees, which was used from a very early time in India for making cloth, while in the Veda wool is the principal material used for weaving [1].

This discrepancy between two such dates as 600 B.C. and 3000 B.C., as the time of the migration of the Vedic Âryas into India, will show at all events how necessary it is to defend every approach to the fortress of Vedic chronology, and how essential for our own purposes, to settle once for all the true antiquity and the really historical character of the Veda.

There are but few chronological sheet-anchors which hold the ancient history of India, and we must try to fasten the floating literature of the Veda to one of them, as firmly and securely as we can. In order to do that I must, however, first say a few words more on another class of literary compositions which form the last products of the Vedic age, and which will have to serve as our hawsers to connect the ancient history of India with the *terra firma* of Greek chronology.

The Sûtras.

If you could read some of the Brâhma*n*as, which I

[1] See Appendix IX.

described to you in my last lecture, you would easily understand why, even for the purposes for which they were principally intended, they proved in the long run utterly useless. I defy any one to learn the correct performance of a Vedic sacrifice from these treatises. This explains the rise of a new kind of literature, in style the very opposite of the Brâhma*n*as, in which the performance of the same sacrifices which we saw described in the Brâhma*n*as, is explained in the shortest and the most business-like manner. These works are called Sûtra, which means literally *threads.* Some passages occurring in the Brâhma*n*as and containing short rules are called by the same name, and it is quite clear that these Sûtras, though independent works, are entirely based on ancient Brâhma*n*as. Their style is almost enigmatical by its terseness, their grammar retains but few traces of the Vedic language, though Vedic irregularities are tolerated in them, while the language of the Brâhma*n*as is still entirely Vedic, and contains many ancient forms, even such as do not occur in the Vedic hymns.

The introduction of this new class of literature must have been the result of some social or religious change. The change from the careless diffuseness of the Brâhma*n*as to the studied brevity of the Sûtras must have had a definite purpose.

I can think of two explanations only. It is just possible that a knowledge of the art of writing, which was unknown to the authors of the Brâhma*n*as, may have reached India sooner than we know, and that its inherent difficulties may have produced at first this almost lapidary style of the Sûtras. What is against this supposition is the non-appearance of any allusion to writing in the Sûtras themselves.

We are therefore driven to the other explanation, that the Brâhmans themselves could no longer trust to a traditional knowledge of the different sacrifices; that the text of the Brâhma*n*as, even if learnt by heart, was no longer found sufficient to enable priests to perform their respective duties correctly, and that therefore these new practical manuals were composed, containing no useless speculations, but simply an outline of the duties of the three classes of priests, a thread of rules to be learnt by heart by the priests who had to perform the sacrifices.

These Sûtras are called Kalpa-sûtras, and are divided into two classes, *S*rauta and Smârta. *S*rauta is derived from *s*ruti, hearing, which means revelation. Smârta is derived from sm*ri*ti, memory, which means tradition.

Each class of priests, the labouring, the singing, and the reciting priests, have their own Sûtras, as they had their own Brâhma*n*as and Sa*m*hitâs.

When this Sûtra-style had once become popular, other subjects also were treated in it. The rules of pronunciation, for instance, which were at first taught in metrical form, as in the Rig-veda-prâtisâkhya, were afterwards reduced to the form of Sûtras. The rules of metre also were composed in Sûtras, and not only does the Sûtra-style prevail in the great grammar ascribed to Pâ*n*ini, but the quotations from earlier grammarians also seem to indicate that they were handed down in the same short, pithy sentences.

The Three Literary Periods of the Vedic Age.

We have now finished our survey of the ancient literature of India, as it passes through three distinct stages, each marked by its own style. We saw Vedic Sanskrit at first in the metrical hymns of the Rig-veda; we saw it afterwards in the diffuse prose of the Brâhma*n*as, and we saw it last of all in the strait-jacket of the Sûtras.

We also saw that the Sûtras presupposed the existence of the Brâhma*n*a literature, and that the Brâhma*n*a literature presupposed the existence of the hymns as collected in the Rig-veda-sa*m*hitâ.

If now we ask how we can fix the date of these three periods, it is quite clear that we cannot hope to fix a *terminus a quo*. Whether the Vedic hymns were composed 1000, or 1500, or 2000, or 3000 years B.C., no power on earth will ever determine.

Chronological ***terminus ad quem.***

The question then arises, can we fix on a *terminus ad quem*, can we determine the date of the last Vedic period, that of the Sûtras, and then work our way back to the two preceding literary periods?

Sandrocottus, died 291 B.C.

I believe this is possible. You know that the sheet-anchor of ancient Indian chronology is the date of the contemporary of Alexander the Great, Sandrocottus, who is the *K*andragupta of Indian history. You may also know that this Sandrocottus, who died 291 B.C., was the grandfather of Asoka, who reigned from 259 to 222 B.C., and whose inscriptions we possess engraved on rocks and pillars in numerous places in India. This Asoka tolerated, or even accepted the religion founded by Buddha, and it was during his reign that the second great Buddhist Council was held at Pâ*t*aliputra.

On the strength of the information contained in the Buddhist Canon, as settled at the Council under Asoka, we are enabled to place the rise of Buddhism at about 500 B.C., and the death of its founder at 477 B.C.

These are dates as certain in the eyes of the general historian as we can ever expect to extract from the extant literature of India.

Buddhism, a reaction against the Vedic Religion.

Now Buddhism is not a completely new religion. On the contrary, it represents a reaction against some other already existing religion, and more particularly against some of the extravagant theories of the Brâhmans. In one sense it may really be said to be a practical carrying out of the theories, proclaimed for the first time in the Âra*n*yakas and Upanishads. While the Brâhmans allowed members of the three upper castes to retire from the world *after* they had performed all the duties of their youth and manhood, the Buddhists allowed everybody to become a Bhikshu, a mendicant, whether he had passed this previous apprenticeship or not. Again, while the Brâhmans reserved the right of teaching to themselves, Buddha, who belonged to the caste of the nobles, claimed that right for himself, and for all who were 'enlightened,' i.e. buddha. These are two essential points of difference between Brâhmans and Buddhists, and orthodox Brâhmans constantly harp on them as proving the heterodoxy of Buddha.

But we can not only show that Buddhism was a kind of Protestantism, as compared with Brâhmanism, we can point out also a number of words and thoughts, the growth of which we can watch in the periods of Vedic literature, and which were taken over bodily by the Buddhists, though sometimes with a change of meaning.

The word Upanishad.

For instance, the very name of Upanishad can have been formed and can have grown up towards the end of the Brâhma*n*a period only. Its original meaning was a sitting (sad), below (ni), towards (upa) the teacher[1]. It became the recognised name of the attitude assumed by the pupil when listening to his teacher. It then was fixed as the name of the teaching itself, and at last conveyed the meaning of secret doctrine (âdesa). In that sense which it had slowly acquired in the Brâhma*n*a and Sûtra periods, we find it used again in the sacred canon of the Southern Buddhists, who use upanisâ in the sense of secret and cause. The Northern Buddhists also knew the word upanishad[2]. We may safely conclude therefore that this title and what it signified must have existed previous to the rise of Buddhism, that is, previous to 500 B.C.

[1] *S. B. E.*, vol. i. p. lxxix seq. In Pali also the verb upa-ni-sad occurs with reference to a king and his friends seating themselves at the feet of a teacher. See Mahâvansa, p. 82; Childers, *Pali Dictionary*, s. v.

[2] Vagra*kh*edikâ, § 16, p 35; § 24, p. 42. There it seems to mean approach, comparison.

The word Sûtra.

The same applies to the word Sûtra. We do not know exactly why Sûtra should have become the name of those short sentences to which the scholastic knowledge of the Brâhmans was finally reduced. But that word must have assumed the more general meaning of teaching or lesson, before the Buddhists could have employed it as they do, namely, as the name of the long sermons delivered by Buddha, and collected in one of the three divisions of their sacred canon, the Sutta-pi*t*aka[1].

I could mention other words more or less technical, which have their history in the Brâhma*n*as and Sûtras, and which in that form and with that meaning which they had gradually assumed among the Brâhmans of the Vedic period, were taken over by the Buddhists. But even these two words, Upanishad and Sûtra, will suffice, for it is beyond the limits of probability to suppose that such technical terms as these could have been formed twice and independently one from the other. They were formed by the Brâhmans, and accepted by the Buddhists, though often with a slightly modified meaning.

Relation of Buddhism to Brâhmanism.

Nor must we forget that though Buddhism, as a religious, social, and philosophical system, is a reaction against Brâhmanism, there is an unbroken continuity between the two. We could not understand the antagonism between Buddhism and the ancient religion of India, unless the Vedic religion

[1] See Appendix X.

had first reached that artificial and corrupt stage in which we find it in the Brâhma*n*as. Buddha himself, as represented to us in the canonical writings of the Buddhists, shows no hostility to the Brâhmans in general, nor does he seem to have been fond of arguing against Brâhmanism. If the prevailing religion of India at his time had consisted of the simple Vedic hymns only, Buddha's position would become quite unintelligible. He does not argue against the Vedic gods. He tolerates them in that subordinate capacity in which they were tolerated by the authors of the Upanishads, after they had discovered the higher truth of Brahman, and the identity of their own self with the Highest Self, the Paramâtman. What he attacks is the Brahmanic sacrifice, as it had been developed in the Brâhma*n*as, the privileges arrogated to their caste by the Brâhmans, and the claim of a divine revelation set up for the Veda, particularly for the Brâhma*n*as. It is curious to see how a modern reformer, Dayânanda Sarasvatî, takes a very similar position. He admits the hymns of the Veda as divinely inspired, but he insists on the Brâhma*n*as being the works of men.

If then the very origin of the Buddhistic reform in India would be unintelligible without the latest phase of the Vedic religion, if Upanishads and Sûtras must have existed, if the word Upanishad must have come to mean secret doctrine, before it could be used in the sense of secret and cause, as it is in Buddhism, and if the word Sûtra must have assumed the general meaning of teaching, before it could have been applied to Buddha's sermons, we have found a *terminus ad quem* for our Vedic literature. It must have reached its final shape before the birth of Buddha, that is about 600 B.C. Before that date we must make room for three whole periods of literature, each presupposing the other.

Constructive Chronology.

Here, no doubt, our chronology becomes purely constructive. We can no longer build on solid rock, but must be satisfied to erect our chronological structure, like the palaces of Venice, on piles carefully driven into the shifting sands of historical tradition. If then we place the rise of Buddhism between 500 and 600 B.C., and assign provisionally 200 years to the Sûtra period, and another 200 years to the Brâhma*n*a period, we should arrive at about 1000 B.C. as the date when the collection of the ten books of the ancient hymns must have taken place. How long a time it took for these hymns, some of them very ancient, some of them very modern in character, to grow up, we shall never be able to determine. Some scholars postulate 500, others 1000 or even 2000 years. These are all vague guesses, and cannot be anything else. To us it suffices that the Brâhma*n*as presuppose the Rig-veda as we have it, including even such very late hymns as the Vâlakhilyas in the eighth Ma*nd*ala. It is possible that further critical researches may enable us to distinguish between the present collection of hymns and an older one on which our Rig-veda was founded. But even our Rig-veda, such as it is, with every Ma*nd*ala and every hymn, with every verse and every word counted, must have existed, so far as we know at present, about 1000 B.C., and that is more than can be said of any work of any other Aryan literature.

We have thus thrown our bridge from our own

MSS., say 1000 A.D., to the first arch, represented by the collected Vedic hymns in 1000 B.C. It is a bridge that requires careful testing. But I can honestly say I see no flaw in our chronological argument, and we must leave it as it is, for the present. But I should not be honest towards myself or towards others, if I did not state at the same time that there are hymns in the Rig-veda which make me shiver when I am asked to look upon them as representing the thoughts and language of our humanity three thousand years ago. And yet, how to find a loophole through which what we should consider modern hymns might have crept into the collection of older hymns, I cannot tell. I have tried my best to find it, but I have not succeeded. Perhaps we shall have to confess that, after all, our ideas of what human beings in India ought to have thought 3000 years ago, are evolved from our inner consciousness, and that we must learn to digest facts, though they do not agree with our tastes and our preconceived ideas [1].

Character of the Veda.

I should like now to give you an idea of what the general character of the Vedic hymns is, such as we find them collected in the Rig-veda-sa*m*hitâ, and commented upon in the Brâhma*n*as, in the Prâtisâkhyas, in the Nirukta, and later works. But this is extremely difficult, partly on account of the long period of time during which these hymns were composed, partly on account of the different families or localities where they were collected.

[1] See Appendix XI.

Simplicity of Vedic Hymns.

The Vedic hymns have often been characterised as very simple and primitive. It may be that this simple and primitive character of the Vedic hymns has sometimes been exaggerated, not so much by Vedic scholars as by outsiders, who were led to imagine that what was called simple and primitive meant really what psychologists imagine to have been the very first manifestations of human thought and language. They thought that the Veda would give them what Adam said to Eve, or, as we should say now, what the first anthropoid ape confided to his mate, when his self-consciousness had been roused for the first time, on his discovering that he differed from other apes by the absence of a tail, or when he sighed over the premature falling off of his hair, which left him at last hairless and naked, as the first *Homo sapiens.* These expectations have, no doubt, been disappointed by the publication of the Rig-veda. But the reaction that set in has gone much too far. We are now told that there is nothing simple and primitive in the Vedic hymns, nay, that these verses are no more than the fabrications of priests who wished to accompany certain acts of their complicated sacrifices with sacred hymns.

Let us consider each of these objections by itself. If one class of scholars maintain that they find nothing simple or primitive in the Veda, they ought to tell us, first of all, what they mean by simple and primitive. Surely we may call primitive what requires no antecedents, and simple what is natural, intelligible, and requires no explanation. Of such thoughts I still maintain, as strongly as ever, that we find more in the Rig-veda than in any other book, Aryan or Semitic.

I call many of the hymns addressed to the Dawn, the Sun, the Sky, the Fire, the Waters and Rivers, perfectly simple. If Devas or so-called gods had once been recognised,—and this, as language teaches us, must have been the case before the Âryas separated,—we require no explanation why human beings should have addressed the sun in the morning and evening, asking him to bring light and warmth, on which their very life depended, deprecating his scorching rays, which might destroy their harvest and kill their cattle, and imploring him to return when he had vanished for a time, and had left them helpless in cold and darkness. The phases of the moon, too, might well excite in an observant mind thoughts fit for expression, particularly as we know that it was the moon who first helped men to reckon time, without which no well-regulated social life was possible. Lastly, the return of the seasons and the year would likewise turn the thoughts of husbandmen, hunters, or sailors to powers above them who controlled their life and its occupations, but who themselves could not be controlled either by force or cunning, though they, like animals or men, might be softened, they thought, by kind words and kind deeds.

Nor could the profound and unvarying order that pervades and sustains the whole of nature, escape even the most careless observers. It was perceived by the Vedic poets in the return of day and night, in the changes of the moon, the seasons, and the years. They called that order *Ri*ta, and they soon began to look upon their gods as the guardians of that order (*rita*-pa), while they suspected in storms and floods and other convulsions of nature the working of powers opposed to their gods. The order of nature and belief in their gods were so intimately connected in the minds of the early poets that one of them said (Rv. I. 102, 2), 'Sun and moon move in regular succession, in order that we may see and believe.'

Moral Elements.

The moral relation between men and the Devas or gods was also in its origin of the simplest character. We meet in the Vedic hymns with such homely phrases, addressed to their gods, as 'If you give me this, I shall give you that,' or, 'As you have given me this, I shall give you that.' This was a mere barter as yet between men and gods, and yet the former sentiment might grow in time into a prayer, the latter into a thank-offering. Sometimes the poet expostulates with the gods, and tells them that 'if he were as rich as they are, he would not allow his worshippers to go begging.'

Surely, nothing can be more simple and more natural than all this, provided always that we are dealing with men who had elaborated a perfect language, not with missing links between brute and man.

Early Sacrifices.

Even when sacrificial offerings came in, they consisted at first of nothing but some kinds of food relished by men themselves, such as water, milk, butter, oil, grains, and berries, prepared in different ways as puddings, cakes, etc. Of sacrificial animals we find goats, sheep, oxen; for later and greater sacrifices, horses and even men. There are dark traditions of human sacrifices, but in the recognised ceremonial of the Veda a man is never killed. Incense also is mentioned, and in some sacrifices an intoxicating beverage, the Soma, is very prominent, and must have been known before the Zoroastrians separated from the Vedic people, because it forms a very prominent feature in both religions.

Childish Thoughts in the Veda.

As to almost childish thoughts, surely they abound in the Veda. It is rather hard to have to pick out childish and absurd thoughts, in order to prove the primitive and unsophisticated character of the Veda. But if it must be done, it can be done. The Vedic poets wonder again and again why a dark or a red cow should give white milk[1]. Can we imagine anything more primitive? Yet that thought is not peculiar to India, and some people might feel inclined to refer it to a period previous to the Aryan separation. There is a common saying or riddle in German, which you may hear repeated by children to the present day,

> 'O sagt mir doch, wie geht es zu,
> Dass weiss die Milch der rothen Kuh.'
>
> 'Tell me how does it happen
> That the milk of the red cow is white.'

There is perhaps more excuse for their wondering at another miracle. In I. 68, 2, we read, 'that men were pleased with the power of Agni, that he should

[1] Rv. I. 62, 9; Aufrecht, vol. ii. pref. p. xvii.

be born alive from a dry stick,' ā́t ít te vísve krátum *g*ushanta sú́shkât yát deva *g*îvá*h* *g*ánish*th*â*h*.

Again, can anything be more primitive than the wonderment expressed by Vedic poets, that the sun should not tumble down from the sky? Thus we read, Rv. IV. 13, 5,

'Unsupported, not fastened, how does he (the sun) rising up, not fall down?'

Ánâyata*h* ánibaddha*h* kathā́ ayám nyãṅ uttâná*h* áva padyate ná.

Other nations have wondered why the ocean should receive all the rivers and yet never overflow (Eccles. i. 7). The Vedic poet too discovers signs of the great might of what he calls the wisest Being, in that

'The bright inpouring rivers never fill the ocean with water' (Rv. V. 85, 6).

My object in quoting these passages is simply to show the lowest level of Vedic thought. In no other literature do we find a record of the world's real childhood to be compared with that of the Veda. It is easy to call these utterances childish and absurd. They are childish and absurd. But if we want to study the early childhood, if not the infancy, of the human race; if we think that there is something to be gained from that study, as there is from a study of the scattered boulders of unstratified rocks in geology, then even these childish sayings are welcome to the student of religion, welcome for the simple fact that, whatever their chronological age may be, they cannot easily be matched anywhere else.

More exalted Ideas.

These childish ideas, however, this simple wonderment at the commonest events in nature, soon led on to more exalted ideas. One poet asks (Rv. X. 88, 18),

'How many fires are there, how many suns, how many dawns, and how many waters? I do not say this, O fathers, to worry you; I ask you, O seers, that I may know it.'

Another says:

'What was the wood, and what was the tree from which they have cut out heaven and earth?'

(Rv. X. 31, 7; 81, 4.) Kím svit vánam ká*h* u sá*h* v*ri*kshá*h* âsa yáta*h* dyấvâp*ri*thivî́ ni*h*-tatakshú*h*.

Or again, X. 81, 2:

'What was the stand on which he rested, which was it and how, from whence the All-maker, the all-seeing, created the earth and spread out the sky by his might?'

Kím svit âsît adhish*th*ấnam ârámbha*n*am katamát svit kathấ âsît, yáta*h* bhû́mim *g*anáyan visvákarmâ ví dyấm aúr*n*ot mahinấ visvá*k*akshâ*h*.

We see here how difficult it would be to draw a line between what we call childishness and what we call wisdom from the mouths of babes. If it is true that *il n'y a qu'un pas du sublime au ridicule*, it would seem to be equally true that *il n'y a qu'un pas du ridicule au sublime*. A childish question may call forth an answer full of profound wisdom. But to say that we look in vain for simple and primitive thoughts in the Veda is to set up a standard of simplicity and primitiveness that would apply to cave-dwellers rather and prehistoric monsters, and not to people who, as long as we know them, were in full possession of one of the most perfect of Aryan languages. No doubt there are in the Veda thoughts and sentiments also that might have been uttered in the nineteenth century. But this only serves to show how large a period is covered by those ancient hymns, and how many different minds are reflected in it.

The Sacrificial Character of the Vedic Hymns.

Another view of the Veda, first advanced by Professor Ludwig, has of late been defended with great ingenuity by a French scholar, M. Bergaigne, a man whose death has been a serious loss to our studies. He held that all, or nearly all the Vedic hymns, were modern, artificial, and chiefly composed for the sake of the sacrifice. Other scholars have followed his lead, till at last it has almost become a new doctrine that everywhere in the world sacrifice preceded sacred poetry. Here again we find truth and untruth strangely mixed together.

It is well known that in several cases verses contained in hymns, totally unconnected with the sacrifice, were slightly changed in order to adapt them to the requirements of the sacrificial ceremonial. The first verse, for instance, of the dialogue between Yama and Yamî (Rv. X. 10, 1), is

ó *k*it sákhâyam sakhyắ vav*ri*tyâm,

'May I bring near the friend by friendship.'

In the Sâma-veda, X. 340, the same verse appears as

ắ tvâ sákhâya*h* sakhyắ vav*ri*tyu*h*,

'May the friends bring thee near by friendship,'

that is, 'May the priests bring the god to the sacrifice [1].'

[1] Von Schroeder, *Indiens Literatur*, p. 168; Âpast. Paribh. Sûtra 129.

That many Vedic hymns, however, contain allusions to what may be called sacrificial customs, no one who has ever looked into the Veda can deny. Some of the hymns, and generally those which for other reasons also would be treated as comparatively late, presuppose what we should call a highly developed system of sacrificial technicalities. The distinction, for instance, between a verse (*rik*), and a song (sâman), and a sacrificial formula (ya*g*us), the distinction on which, as we saw, rests the division of the Veda into Rig-veda, Sâma-veda, and Ya*g*ur-veda, is found in one of the hymns, X. 90, and there only. But curiously enough, this very hymn is one of those that occur at the end of an Anuvâka, and contains several other indications of its relatively modern character. Many similar passages, full of sacrificial technicalities, have been pointed out [1] in the Rig-veda, and they certainly show that when these passages were composed, the sacrifice in India had already assumed what seems to us a very advanced, or, if you like, a very degraded and artificial character.

But there are other passages also where the poet says, 'Whosoever sacrifices to Agni with a stick of wood, with a libation, with a bundle of herbs, or with an inclination of his head,' he will be blessed with many blessings (Rv. VIII. 19, 5; 102, 19).

This whole question, so hotly discussed of late, whether sacrifice comes first or prayer, whether the Vedic poets waited till the ceremonial was fully

[1] The most complete collection of sacrificial terms occurring in the hymns of the Rig-veda may be found in Ludwig's *Die Mantralitteratur*, 1878, pp. 353–415. Bergaigne's *Religion Védique* appeared from 1878 to 1883.

developed before they invoked the Dawn, and the Sun, and the Storms to bless them, or whether, on the contrary, their spontaneous prayers suggested the performance of sacrificial acts, repeated at certain times of the day, of the month, of the year, is impossible to solve, because, as it seems to me, it is wrongly put.

'Sacrifice,' as Grimm remarked long ago, 'is only a prayer offered with gifts.' We nowhere hear of a mute sacrifice. What we call sacrifice, the ancients called simply karma, an act. Now in one sense a simple prayer, preceded by a washing of the hands, or accompanied by an inclination of the head, may be called a karma, an act[1]. On the other hand, a man who in lighting the fire on the hearth or in putting one log on the smouldering ashes, bows his head (namas), raises his arms (uttânahasta*h*, Rv. VI. 16, 46), and utters the name of Agni with some kind epithets (ya*g*us), may be said to have addressed a hymn of praise to the god of fire. Prayer and sacrifice may have been originally inseparable, but in human nature I should say that prayer comes always first, sacrifice second.

That the idea of sacrifice did not exist at a very early period, we may gather from the fact that in the common dictionary of the Aryan nations there is no word for it, while Sanskrit and Zend have not only the same name for sacrifice, but share together a great many words which refer to minute technicalities of the ancient ceremonial.

[1] Kalpa, act, in the plural, occurs Rv. IX. 9, 7.

Yag, to sacrifice.

The usual word for sacrificing in Sanskrit is YA*G*, Zend yaz, from which ya*g*ña, sacrifice, ya*g*-us, sacrificial formula, ya*g*âmi, I sacrifice, yâ*g*ya, to be worshipped. This yâ*g*ya has been compared with Greek ἅγιος, sacred, though this is not certain[1]. Why ya*g* should have taken that meaning of sacrificing, or giving to the gods, we cannot tell[2], for it is impossible to trace that root back to any other root of a more general meaning.

Hu, to sacrifice.

Another Sanskrit root which has frequently to be translated by sacrificing is HU. In this case we can clearly see the original intention of the root. It meant to pour out, and was chiefly applied to the act of throwing barley and oil and other substances into the fire[3]. It afterwards took a more general meaning, not so general, however, as to be applicable to animal sacrifices. From it we have in Sanskrit havis, havya, sacrifice, â-hâva, a jug, *g*uhû, a spoon, ho-t*ri*, priest, homa and âhuti, libation. In Greek χυ or χεϝ means simply to pour out, χύ-τρα, an earthenware pot[4]. Θύειν, to sacrifice, might phonetically

[1] The Greek ἄγος or ἅγος does not mean sacrifice, but rather expiation. It cannot be the Sk. âgas, because in Greek the α is short.

[2] Sanskrit theologians connect ya*g* with tya*g*, to give up, to leave, but there is no analogy for this. Comparative philologists used to place bha*g*, to worship, by the side of ya*g*, assigning to bh (bhi) and y (ni or ti) a prepositional origin, but this is a pure hypothesis, which has long been surrendered.

[3] Al-Birûni, ii. p. 96.

[4] Aufrecht in Kuhn's *Zeitschrift*, xiv. p. 268. This root hu, to pour out, exists also in the Latin *futis*, a water-jug, and in *vasa futilia*, which Paulus, *Epit.* p. 89, explains rightly as derived *a fundendo*. *Futilis*, in the sense of futile, may have been conceived either as a man who always pours forth, or as a vessel, leaky, not holding

be traced back to the same source, but its meanings cause difficulty.

Sacrificial Terms.

A third word for sacrifice in Sanskrit is adhvara, which is generally, though I doubt whether correctly, explained as a compound of the negative a and dhvara, flaw. From it, adhvaryu, the name of the officiating priest.

Stress is frequently laid on the sacrificial offering being without a flaw, or free from any blemish. This may account for the meaning of the English *holy*, which is the AS. *hâlig*, derived from *hâl*, that is, *hale* and *whole*. The Greek ἱερός, sacred, holy, had a similar origin. It is identical with the Sk. ishira, which means alive, strong, vigorous, a meaning still perceptible in the Greek of Homer, who speaks of ἱερὸς ἰχθύς (Il. ii. 407), a lively fish, ἱερὸν μένος, a vigorous mind, while in later Greek ἱερός means sacred only, and ἱερεύς, a priest, like adhvar-yu.

This is all that we can discover as to the original conception of a sacrifice among some of the Aryan nations. The equation of ya*g*, to sacrifice, with Greek ἅζομαι, to stand in awe, is difficult, if not impossible, on account of the difference of meaning. Nothing, in fact, justifies us in supposing that the idea of a sacrifice, in our sense of the word, existed among the Âryas before they separated. The concept of gods or devas had, no doubt, been elaborated before their final separation. Words also for metrical language (*kh*andas = scandere, *s*as-man = carmen in cas-

water. *Fundo* is a nasalised form of *fŭd*, and *fud* is a secondary form of *fu*, Sk. hu. The Gothic *giuta* means to pour out.

mena) existed. Such expressions as dâtā́ras vásûnâm or vásuâm in the Veda, dâtârô vohunâm and dâta vaṅhvâm in Zend, and δοτῆρες ἐάων (i.e. ϝεσϝαων) in Homer, would seem to show that the idea of the gods giving gifts to men had been fully realised[1], though not yet the idea of men giving gifts to the gods. If in δοτῆρες ἐάων and dâtā́ras vásuâm we may recognise, as Kuhn suggested, a phrase that had become fixed and idiomatic before the Aryan nations separated, it would have to be kept as a perfect gem in our linguistic museums.

Prayer better than Sacrifice.

In spite of the preponderance which the sacrifice has assumed in India, it is important to observe that the Vedic poets themselves were strongly impressed with the feeling that after all prayer was better than sacrifice. Thus we read, Rv. VIII. 24, 20:

dásmyam vá*k*a*h* ghri*t*ā́t svā́dîya*h* mádhuna*h* *k*a vo*k*ata,

'Utter a powerful speech to Indra, which is sweeter than butter and honey.'

Rv. VI. 16, 47:

ā́ te agne *rik*ā́ havî*h* h*ri*dā́ tash*t*ám bharâmasi, té te bhavantu ukshá*n*a*h* *ri*shabhā́sa*h* vasā́*h* utá.

'We offer to thee, O Agni, an oblation made by the heart with a verse, let this be thy oxen, thy bulls, and thy cows[2].'

Rv. I. 109, 1:

Ví hí ákhyam mánasâ vásya*h* i*kkh*án
Índrâgnî *g*ñâsá*h* utá vâ sa*g*âtā́n,
Ná anyā́ yuvát prámati*h* asti máhyam,
Sá*h* vâm dhíyam vâ*g*ayántîm atakasham.

'I looked about in my mind, O Indra and Agni, wishing for wealth, among acquaintances and kinsfolk. But there is no guardian for me but you, therefore did I compose this song for you.'

[1] Benfey, *Vocativ*, p. 57; M. M., *Selected Essays*, i. p. 224.
[2] It may also mean, 'Let these oxen be thine.'

Rv. III. 53, 2:

> Pitúh ná putráh síkam ắ rabhe te
> Índra svắdishthayâ girắ sakîvah.

'With the sweetest song I lay hold of the hem of thy garment, O Indra, as a son lays hold of his father's garment, O helper.'

The gods are quite as frequently invoked in the hymns to hear as to eat and to drink, and hymns of praise are among the most precious offerings presented to the gods.

The Primitive Sacrifice.

But sacrifices certainly occupy a very prominent part in the Vedic hymns. Only we must distinguish. When *we* hear of sacrifices, we cannot help thinking at once of sacred and solemn acts. But the very names and concepts of sacred and solemn are secondary names and concepts, and presuppose a long development. In Sanskrit a sacrifice is simply called an act, karma, though in time that name assumed the technical meaning of a sacred and solemn act. We must never forget that many of the ancient sacrifices were indeed nothing but the most natural acts, and that some of them are found with slight variations in the most distant parts of the world, and among people entirely unrelated and unconnected.

Morning and Evening Meal.

A morning and evening offering, for instance, is met with among Semitic quite as much as among Aryan nations. It was originally the morning and evening meal, to which in many places a third offering was added, connected with the midday meal. Throwing a few grains of corn on the fire, pouring a few drops of their own drink on the altar, whether in memory of their departed parents, or with a thought of the sun, the giver of light and life, as he rose, and culminated and set every day, was the beginning of the daily sacrifice among the Âryas. These two or three libations in the morning, in the evening, and at noon, were quite familiar to the poets of the Rig-veda. For instance, Rv. IV. 35, 7:

Prâtá*h* sutám apiba*h* haryasva,
Mā̆dhyandinam sávanam kévalam te,
Sám *ri*bhúbhi*h* pibasva ratnadhébhi*h*
Sákhîn yā̆n indra *k*akr*i*shé sukr*i*tyā̆.

'O Indra, thou hast drunk what was poured out in the morning, the midday libation is thine alone; drink now with the liberal *R*ibhus, whom thou hast made friends for their good deeds [1].'

The name savana, libation, occurs in the Veda; but the technical term trishava*n*a, the threefold libation, is not yet found in the hymns of the Rig-veda.

Lighting and keeping of the Fire.

Another most simple and natural act, which in time came to be called a sacrifice, consisted in the making up of the fire on the hearth, at sunrise and sunset, also at noon. It was a useful and necessary act, and would probably soon have to be sanctioned by habit, or enforced by law. It was the beginning of what afterwards became the solemn Agnihotra, or fire-sacrifice. Thus we read, Rv. IV. 2, 8:

Yá*h* tvâ doshā̆ yá*h* ushási prasá*m*sât,
Priyám vâ tvâ kri*n*ávate havishmân.

'He who praises thee, Agni, in the evening or at dawn, Or who makes thee pleased with his oblation.'

[1] See also III. 26, 1, 4, 5; V. 76, 3.

Or again, IV. 12, 1:

> Yá*h* tvā̃m agne inádhate yatásruk
> Trí*h* te ánnam k*r*i*n*ávat sásmin áhan.

'He who lights thee, O Agni, stretching forth his spoon, he who gives thee food three times on the same day.'

But while the simple act of the making-up of the fire, and pouring some fat on it to make it flare up, is often mentioned, the technical term of the Agnihotra sacrifice is not yet met with in the hymns of the Rig-veda.

New and Full Moon.

Again, the observation of the phases of the moon, which was essential in order to remember the months, the fortnights, and the seven days, nay, without which no well-regulated social life was possible, is clearly presupposed by the hymns. But the technical name of the New and Full-moon sacrifice, Darsa-pûr*n*a-mâsa, does not occur in the hymns.

The Three Seasons.

Another probably very primitive sacrifice was the Four-monthly sacrifice, marking the three most important seasons of the year. Here again the technical name *K*âturmâsya is later than the hymns of the Rig-veda.

In all these acts, whether they lasted one moment only, or a whole day, or even many days, we can still discover a simple and natural purpose. They are not sacrifices, in our sense of the word. They prove no more than the existence of festive gatherings in a family or a village, to commemorate and impress on the mind of the young the important divisions of the year, or to make sure of the regular performance of certain essential household duties. After a time, what was natural became artificial, what was simple became complicated; and there cannot be the slightest doubt that in many of the Vedic hymns the poets show themselves already well acquainted with the later complicated phases of the sacrifice in India. Many priests are mentioned with their technical titles; the times and seasons for certain sacrifices are accurately fixed; sacrificial offerings have received their special names, they are restricted to certain deities[1], and the original purpose of the sacrifice is often completely lost in a mass of ritual that seems perfectly meaningless.

The meaning of Solemn.

But what I wish to make quite clear is this, that there is a growth, or a natural development in all this. The mere fact that these simple offerings or these festive gatherings were repeated every day, or every month, or every year, imparted to them a sacred and solemn character. Language itself teaches us that lesson. For how did we get the idea of *solemn?* How did we come to call anything *solemn?* Simply by regular repetition. *Solemn*, the Latin *sollennis*, was derived, as the Romans themselves tell us, from *sollus*, whole, and *annus* for *amnus*, year. It meant therefore originally no more than annual, and then by slow degrees came to supply the new idea of solemn.

[1] The three Savanas, or libations, are chiefly intended for Indra, the Agnihotra for Agni. See Ludwig, *Mantralitteratur*, p. 384.

I should say then that we are perfectly justified, whenever we find in the Veda hymns full of allusions to minute ceremonial technicalities, to class such hymns as secondary or tertiary. But there remains the fact, and in spite of all efforts, I do not see how we can escape from it—that all the 1017 hymns, and even the eleven Vâlakhilya hymns, in which these technicalities occur, must have been collected not later than about 1000 B.C. Can any other Aryan literature match this? If anybody can break through the net of our chronological argument, let him do so. No one would rejoice more than myself. But until that is done, we must learn to bear the slavery of facts.

LECTURE VI.

PHYSICAL RELIGION.

Definition of Physical Religion.

PHYSICAL Religion is generally defined as a worship of the powers of nature. We hear it said of ancient as well as of modern nations, that their gods were the sun or the moon, the sky with its thunder and lightning, the rivers and the sea, the earth, and even the powers under the earth. As Aaron said to the Israelites, the poets and prophets of the heathens are supposed to have said to their people, 'These be thy gods.'

There are some well-known philosophers who go even further, and who, repeating again and again the old mistake of De Brosses and Comte, maintain that the earliest phase of all religion is represented by people believing in stones and bones and fetishes of all kinds as their gods.

God, as a predicate.

As their gods! Does it never strike these theorisers that the whole secret of the origin of religion lies in that predicate, *their gods.* Where did the human mind find that concept and that name? That is the problem which has to be solved; everything else is mere child's play.

We ourselves, the heirs of so many centuries of toil and thought, possess, of course, the name and concept of God, and we can hardly imagine a human mind without that name and concept. But, as a matter of fact, the child's mind is without that name and concept, and such is the difference of meaning assigned by different religions, nay, even by members of the same religion, to the name of God, that a general definition of it has almost become an impossibility. Nevertheless, however our ideas of God may differ, for us to say that the sun or the moon, or a pebble, or the tail of a tiger was God, would be absurd and self-contradictory.

The Greeks also, at least the more enlightened among them, who had arrived at the name and concept of God,—men, I mean, like Socrates and Plato,—could never have brought themselves to say that any one of their mythological deities, such as Hermes or Apollo, was God, *ὁ θεός*. The Greeks, however, had likewise the name and concept of gods in the plural, but even that name, which has a meaning totally different from that of God in the singular, could never have been applied by them to what are called fetishes, bones, feathers, or rags. Most of the Negro tribes, who are so glibly classed as fetish-worshippers, possess a name of God, quite apart from their fetishes; nay, their concept of God is often very pure and simple and true. But they would never apply that name to what we, not they, have called their fetish-gods. All they really do is to preserve with a kind of superstitious awe some casual objects, just as we nail a horse-shoe on our stable-doors, or keep a farthing for luck in our purse. These objects they call *grigri*, or *juju*[1]. This may mean anything, but certainly it does not mean fetish in the sense given to this word by De Brosses and others, neither does it mean God.

It has led to the greatest confusion of thought that our modern languages had to take the singular of the Greek plural, θεοί, the gods, and use it for θεός, God. It is quite true historically that the idea of θεός, God, was evolved from the idea of θεοί, gods; but in passing through that process of intellectual evolution, the meaning of the word became changed as completely as the most insignificant seed is changed when it has blossomed into a full-blown rose. Θεός, God, admits of no plural, θεοί always implies plurality.

The problem of Physical Religion has now assumed a totally different aspect, as treated by the Historical School. Instead of endeavouring to explain how human beings could ever worship the sky as a god, we ask, how did any human being come into possession of the predicate god? We then try to discover what that predicate meant when applied to the sky, or the sun, or the dawn, or the fire. With us the concept of God excludes fire, the dawn, the sun, and the sky; at all events, the two concepts no longer cover each other. What we want to study therefore is that ever-varying circumference of the predicate god, which becomes wider or narrower from century to century, according to the objects which it was made to include, and after a time to exclude again.

[1] *Hibbert Lectures*, p. 103. The names *fitiso*, *fetish*, and *fitisero*, priest, are traced back to Portuguese sailors in Africa by W. J. Müller, *Die Afrikanische Landschaft Fetu*, 1675.

This problem, and a most difficult problem it is, can be studied nowhere so well as in the Veda, that is, in the ancient hymns of the Rig-veda. I doubt whether we should ever have understood the real nature of the problem with which we have to deal, unless we had become acquainted with the Rig-veda.

Deification.

It is quite clear that other nations also passed through the same phases of thought as the Aryan conquerors of India. We see the results of that process everywhere. In Africa, in America, in the Polynesian islands, everywhere we catch glimpses of the process of deification. But the whole of that process is nowhere laid open before our eyes in such fulness and with such perspicuity as in the Veda. Deification, as we can watch it in the Veda, does not mean the application of the name and concept of god to certain phenomena of nature. No, it means the slow and inevitable development of the concept and name of God out of these very phenomena of nature—it means the primitive theogony that takes place in the human mind as living in human language.

It has always been perfectly well known that *Zeus*, for instance, had something to do with the sky, *Poseidon* with the sea, *Hades* with the lower regions. It might have been guessed that *Apollo*, like *Phoebos* and *Helios*, had a solar, *Artemis*, like *Mene*, a lunar character. But all this remained vague, the divine epithet applied to them all remained unintelligible, till the Veda opened to us a stratum of thought and language in which the growth of that predicate could be watched, and its application to various phenomena of nature be clearly understood.

It will be the chief object of this course of lectures to elucidate this process of religious evolution, to place clearly before you, chiefly from the facts supplied by the hymns of the Veda, the gradual and perfectly intelligible development of the predicate god from out of the simplest perceptions and conceptions which the human mind gained from that objective nature by which man found himself surrounded.

The Natural and the Supernatural.

We have now classified the whole of our experience which we derive from nature under two heads, as either *natural* or *supernatural*, *natural* comprising all that seems to us regular, conformable to rule, and intelligible, *supernatural* all that we consider as yet or altogether as beyond the reach of rule and reason. This, however, as you will see, is but the last result of a long succession of intellectual labour. At first sight, nothing seemed less natural than nature. Nature was the greatest surprise, a terror, a marvel, a standing miracle, and it was only on account of their permanence, constancy, and regular recurrence that certain features of that standing miracle were called natural, in the sense of foreseen, common, intelligible. Every advance of natural science meant the wresting of a province from the supernatural, if we may use that word in the sense of what remains as yet a surprise, a terror, a marvel, or a miracle in man's experience of objective nature.

It was that vast domain of surprise, of terror, of marvel, and miracle, the unknown, as distinguished from the known, or, as I like to express it, the infinite, as distinct from the finite, which supplied from the earliest times the impulse to religious thought and language, though in the beginning these thoughts and names had little of what we now call religions about them. You remember that the very name of deva in Sanskrit, of *deus* in Latin, which afterwards became the name of God, meant originally bright, and no more. It came to mean God after a long process of evolution, which took place even before the Aryan separation, and of which we can only just catch the last glimpses in the phraseology of the Vedic poets.

Agni, Fire, as one of the Devas.

How this came about we shall, I think, best learn to understand if we analyse the growth of one of the many Devas or gods who form the Pantheon of the Veda. Many of these Vedic Devas appear likewise under more or less puzzling disguises in the mythology and religion of the other Aryan nations. Some, however, exist in the Veda only as real Devas, while we find no trace of them, as mythological or divine beings, in other countries of the Aryan world. I shall begin my analysis of Physical Religion with a Deva, belonging to this latter class, with the god of fire, called Agni in the Veda, but unknown under that name in any of the other Aryan mythologies, though the word agni, in the sense of fire, occurs in Latin as *ignis*, in Lituanian as *ugnì*, in old Slavonic as *ogni*.

When I say the god of fire, I use an expression which has become familiar to us from classical mythology. We speak of a god of the sky, or of the wind, or of the rain. But you will see that in the

Veda we can watch this god of fire long before he is a god at all; and, on the other hand, we shall be able to trace his further growth till he is no longer a god of fire merely, but a supreme god, a god above all other gods, a creator and ruler of the world.

In fact we shall learn to understand by this one instance the authentic history of that long psychological process which, beginning with the simplest and purely material perceptions, has led the human mind to that highest concept of deity which we have inherited together with our language, as members of the great Aryan, and not of the Semitic family.

Early conceptions of Fire.

If you can for a moment transfer yourselves to that early stage of life to which we must refer not only the origin, but likewise the early phases of Physical Religion, you can easily understand what an impression the first appearance of Fire must have made on the human mind. Fire was not given as something permanent or eternal, like the sky, or the earth, or the water. In whatever way it first appeared, whether through lightning or through the friction of the branches of trees, or through the sparks of flints, it came and went, it had to be guarded, it brought destruction, but at the same time it made life possible in winter, it served as a protection during the night, it became a weapon of defence and offence, and last, not least, it changed man from a devourer of raw flesh into an eater of cooked meat. At a later time it became the means of working metal, of making tools and weapons, it became an indispensable factor in all mechanical and artistic progress, and has remained so ever since. What should we be without fire even now?

The etymological meaning of Agni.

What then did the early Âryas think of it, or, what is the same, how did they name it? Its oldest name in Sanskrit is Agni, and this has been preserved in Latin as *ignis*, in Lituanian as *ugnì*, in old Slavonic as *ogni*. It was therefore a very old name. So far as we can venture to interpret such ancient names, Agni seems to have expressed the idea of quickly moving, from a root AG or A*G*, to drive. The nearest approach would be the Latin *ag-ilis*. Another Sanskrit name for fire is vah-ni, and this, too, coming from the same root which we have in *veho* and *vehemens*, would have meant originally what moves about quickly. In the Veda Agni is called raghupatvan, quickly flying (X. 6, 4).

Names of Fire.

It will be useful to examine some more of the old names of fire, because every one of them, if we can still interpret it etymologically, will enable us to see in how many different ways fire was conceived by the Âryas, how it struck them, what they thought of it.

Dahana means simply the burner.

Anala, from an, to breathe, would seem to mean the breathing, or blowing fire, just as anila is a name for wind. The root AN, to breathe, is the same which we have in *animus*, *anima*, and in Greek ἄνεμος. In the Veda the fire is often said to be breathi.g (abhi-*s*vasan, I. 140, 5).

Pâvaka, a frequent name of Agni, conveys the meaning of cleaning, clearing, illuminating. Some scholars have derived πῦρ and *fire* from the same root.

Tanûnapât is a Vedic name of Agni. It is explained as meaning 'offspring of himself.' It is possible, no doubt, to conceive Agni as self-born. He is called sva-yoni in the Mahâbhârata (19, 13931). But the usual idea in the Veda is that he has a father and mother, namely, the two fire-sticks.

*G*âtavedas, another name for Agni, means all-seeing, all-knowing, like visvavedas.

Vaisvânara seems to convey the meaning of kept by all men, or useful and kind to all, universal.

Another epithet applied to Agni is Bhura*n*yu. Bhura*n*yu means quick, and is formed on the same lines as Agni and Vahni. Derived as it is from a root BHAR, to bear, to carry, it seems to have meant originally, carried along headlong, borne away, or possibly, bearing away, like the Greek φερόμενος. This Sanskrit word bhura*n*yu is almost the same word as the Greek Φορωνεύς, who is supposed to have brought to men the gift of fire, and to have become the founder of cities (Paus. ii. 15, 5)[1].

Fire, named as active.

We ourselves occupy, of course, a totally different position from those who had first to conceive and to name fire. We learn the name mechanically from our parents, and the sound fire is a mere outward sign for what burns and hurts, or warms and cheers us. In after life we may learn to call fire with the

[1] Kuhn, *Mythologische Studien*, i. p. 211.

ancient Greek philosophers one of the four elements; and, later on, a study of natural philosophy may teach us that fire consists of luminous and calorific rays, that it is a natural force, or, it may be, a motion of something unknown which we call ether. But in all this we deal with predicates only, and the underlying substance remains as unknown as the underlying agent whom the, as yet, undivided Âryas called simply Agni, the mover.

At all events we may well understand that the early inhabitants of the earth were puzzled by the fire. There was nothing like it in the whole world —now visible, now invisible, tangible, yet dangerous to touch, destroying whole forests and the habitations of men, and yet most welcome on the hearth, most cheerful in winter.

We can well understand how, after the senses had once taken note of this luminous apparition in its ever-varying aspects, a desire arose in the human mind, and in the human mind only, to know it; to know it, not simply in the sense of seeing or feeling it, but to know it in the sense of conceiving and naming it, which is a very different thing.

How could that be done? I cannot explain here once more the whole of the process of conceiving and naming, or naming and conceiving. You will find that subject treated in my first course of Gifford Lectures, and more fully in my work *On the Science of Thought*, published in 1887.

I can here only state it as a fact that the only instruments by which man could achieve this process of naming were what we call *roots*, and that all these roots, owing to the manner in which they first came into existence, expressed actions, the ordinary actions performed by men in an early state of society. There were roots expressive of striking, pushing, carrying, binding, lifting, squeezing, rubbing, and all the rest, and with these roots all that we now call naming and conceiving, the whole of our language, the whole of our thought, has been elaborated.

This is a fact, simply a fact, and not a mere theory. To doubt it, as has been done of late again, is to doubt the laws of thought. We may differ as to the exact form in which those roots existed from the first. Such doubts are allowable with regard to roots, as elements of speech, they are allowable with regard to letters, as the elements of sound, nay even with regard to the chemical elements, as constituting the whole material world. But to doubt the existence of any of these three classes of elements is either ignorance or unreason.

No one denies that we name and conceive by means of signs. These signs might have been anything, but, as a matter of fact, they were sounds; and again, as a matter of fact, these sounds were what in the Science of Language we call roots. When we examine these roots, as the actual elements of speech, we find that they signify acts, and we conclude that their sound was originally the involuntary *clamor concomitans* of the simplest acts of man. This last conclusion may no doubt be called an hypothesis only, and I have never represented it as anything else; but, till a better hypothesis has been suggested, I retain it as the best working hypothesis.

If then the Âryas possessed a root, such as AG, by which they expressed their own acts of marching, running, jumping, and, at last, moving in general, all they did in naming and conceiving the marching, running, jumping, or quickly moving luminous appearances of fire, was to say to each of them: 'Moving here,' 'Moving there,' or in Sanskrit Ag-ni-s[1].

Agni therefore meant originally the mover, and no more. Many more qualities of the mover might be recalled by the name of Agni, but they were not definitely expressed by that one name. We must remember, however, that by calling him Agni, or the quick mover, the ancient people knew no more who or what that mover was than we do when speaking of fire as an element, or as a force of nature, or, as we do now, as a form of motion. It sounds very learned when we say that 'a mass of matter becomes a source of light and heat in consequence of an extremely rapid vibratory movement of its smallest particles, which is propagated as a series of undulations into the surrounding ether, and is felt by our tactile nerves as heat, and by our optic nerves, if the undulations are sufficiently rapid, as light.'

I confess, from a philosophical point of view, I see little difference between this Ether, and Agni, the god of fire. Both are mythological. Professor Tyndal asks quite rightly: 'Is it in the human mind to imagine motion, without at the same time imagining something moved? Certainly not. The very

[1] From the same root we have in Greek *ἄγω*, to drive, *ἄγρα*, the chase; in Latin *ago*, *agmen*. The Sk. ag*r*a, Gr. *ἀγρός*, Lat. *ager*, Goth. *akr-s*, mean meadow and field, possibly from the cattle being driven over it. The German *Trift* comes likewise from *treiben*. The words for goat also may be referred to this root, if they meant originally quickly moving or agile; Sk. a*g*a, Greek *αἴξ*, Lit. ožys. Consider the *drift* of an argument, and what are you *driving at*.

conception of motion includes that of a moving body. What then is the thing moved in the case of sunlight? The undulatory theory replies that it is a substance of determinate mechanical properties, a body which may or may not be a form of ordinary matter, but to which, whether it is or not, we give the name of Ether.'

May not the ancient Âryas say with the same right: 'Is it in the human mind to imagine motion without at the same time imagining some one that moves?' Certainly not. The very conception of motion includes that of a mover, and, in the end, of a prime mover. Who then is that mover? The ancient Âryas reply that it is a subject of determinate properties, a person who may or may not be like ordinary persons, but to whom, whether he is or not, we give the name of Agni.

Agni as a Human or Animal Agent.

When that step had once been made, when the word Agni, Fire, had once been coined, the temptation was great, nay almost irresistible, as Agni was conceived as an agent, to conceive him also as something like the only other agents known to man, as either an animal or human agent.

We often read in the Veda of the tongue or the tongues of Agni, which are meant for what we call his lambent flames. We read of his bright teeth (*suk*idan, VII. 4, 2), of his jaws, his burning forehead (tapu*h*-mûrdhan, VII. 3, 1), nay, even of his flaming and golden hair (*sokih*-ke*s*a, V. 8, 2; hira*n*yake*s*a, I. 79, 1), and of his golden beard (hiri*s*ma*s*ru, V. 7, 7). His face (anîkam) is mentioned, but that means no more than his appearance, and when he is called winged (I. 58, 5; VIII. 32, 4), or even the hawk of the sky (diva*h* syena*h*, VII. 15, 4), that is simply intended to express, what his very name expresses, his swift movement.

This may help to explain how some nations, particularly the Egyptians[1], were led on to conceive some of their gods in the shape of animals. It arose from a necessity of language. This was not the case, however, in India. Agni and the other gods of the Veda, if they are imagined at all in their bodily shape, are always imagined as human, though never as so intensely human as the gods and goddesses of the Greeks. Beauty, human, superhuman, ideal beauty, is not an Indian conception. When in later times the Indians also invented plastic representations of their gods, they did not shrink from unnatural and monstrous combinations, so long as they helped to convey the character of each god.

All this is perfectly intelligible, and a careful study of language supplies us with the key to almost all the riddles of ancient mythology.

New explanation of Animism, Personification, and Anthropomorphism.

Formerly the attribution of movement, of life, of personality and of other human or animal qualities to the great phenomena of nature, was explained by names such as *Animism, Personification, Anthropomorphism*. It seemed as if people imagined that to name a process was to explain it.

Mr. Herbert Spencer, against Animism.

Here we owe a debt of gratitude to Mr. Herbert

[1] See Appendix XII.

Spencer for having stood up for once as the champion of primitive man. I have often pointed out the bad treatment which these poor primitive creatures receive at the hands of anthropologists. Whatever the anthropologists wish these primitives to do or not to do, to believe or not to believe, they must obey, like silent Karyatides supporting the airy structures of ethnological psychology (*Völkerpsychologie*). If *Animism* is to be supported, they must say, 'Of course, the storm has a soul.' If *Personification* is doubted, they are called in as witnesses that their fetish is very personal indeed. If *Anthropomorphism* has to be proved as a universal feature of early religion, primitive man is dragged in again, and has to confess that the uncouth stone which he worships is certainly a man, and a great deal more than a man.

Whenever I protested against this system of establishing Animism, Personification, and Anthropomorphism as the primeval springs of all religion, I was told that I knew nothing of primitive man, nor of his direct descendants, the modern savages. I have always pleaded guilty of a complete want of acquaintance with primitive man, and have never ventured to speak about savages, whether ancient or modern, unless I knew something, however little, of the nature of their language. Mr. H. Spencer, however, cannot be disposed of so easily. If any one knows the savages, surely he does. But even he has had to protest at last against the theory that the primitive man is a kind of maid-of-all-work, at the beck and call of every anthropologist. 'The assumption,' he writes (*Sociology*, p. 143), 'tacit or avowed, that the primitive man tends to ascribe life to things which are not living, is clearly an untenable assumption.' He defends even the child, which has likewise had to do service again and again for what I called Nursery-psychology, against the charge of animism. When a child says, 'Naughty chair to hurt baby—beat it,' Mr. Herbert Spencer shows that this burst of anger admits of very different explanations, and that no one would be more frightened than the child if the chair, on being beaten, began to kick, to bite, or to cry.

But though Mr. Herbert Spencer does not believe that any human being ever mistook an inanimate for an animate object, for even animals have learnt to make that distinction, he still considers them capable of very wonderful follies. He thinks that they do not distinguish between what they see in dreams and what they see while awake (p. 147), nay, he considers them capable of mistaking their actual shadows for their souls. On this point we shall have to touch at a later time.

At present it suffices to state that all these processes have now been traced back to their *vera causa*, namely, to language, and more particularly to what are called the roots of language. As every one of these roots expressed, owing to their very origin, one of the many acts with which men in an early state of society were most familiar, the objects thus named could not be named and conceived except as agents of such acts or as subjects.

If the Aryan nations wished to speak of fire, they could only speak of it as doing something. If they called it Agni, they meant the agent of fire. Instead of this understood agent, implied in the name of Agni, we hear other nations speak of the heart, the soul, the spirit, the lord, or the god of fire [1]. But all these expressions belong to a later phase of thought, for they presuppose the former elaboration of such concepts as soul, spirit, god, or they are based on metaphor, as in the case of heart.

Prof. Tiele's Theory of the Gods as *facteurs*.

Professor Tiele in his *Le Mythe de Kronos*, 1886, came nearest to my own view on the development of the concept of God. 'The ancient gods,' he says (p. 9), 'are what, according to our abstract manner of speaking, we should call "*des facteurs, des forces, des sources de vie*."' He does not indeed lay stress on the fact that there was in our very language and thought an irresistible necessity of our speaking of the sky, the sun, the fire, if we speak of them at all, as agents. He only warns us against supposing that 'the gods are ever the phenomena of nature themselves, considered as acting persons, but always what he calls souls or spirits, represented as analogous to the soul of man, that impart movement to the celestial bodies and produce all the effects for good or evil which appear in nature.' This is most true, but does it not explain one difficulty by another? Was the soul of man a matter of more easy discovery than the soul of the sky? When we have once arrived at the concept of a spirit, as something substantial, yet different from the material body, the task of the religious and mythological poet is easy enough. In another place (p. 30) Professor Tiele most rightly defines the physical deities, not as '*des objets naturels que l'on a personnifiés*,' but as '*des êtres positifs, des esprits, que l'on a vus à*

[1] Brinton, *Myths of the New World*, pp. 48 seq.

l'œuvre dans la nature, où ils se manifestent par leur action.' All this is perfectly true in our modern languages, which supply us with such terms as *esprits* and *êtres positifs*, ready made, but if we have to account for the more ancient formations and the earliest strata of religious thought, the science of language alone will solve the riddle why the great phenomena of nature were named as agents, as *facteurs*, nay, it will show that what at first seemed a mere freak of fancy was in reality a necessity of language. While I accept Professor Tiele's *facteurs*, I cannot, for the early periods of human thought, accept his *forces* or *sources de vie*. While I gladly accept Mr. H. Spencer's *agents*, I cannot accept his *agencies*[1].

The Agents in Nature.

Facts are stronger than theories, and unless the facts as collected in my *Science of Thought* can be shown to be no facts, the fact remains and will remain for ever, that all objects which were named and conceived at all, were named and conceived at first as agents. The sky was he who covers, the sun he who warms, the moon he who measures night and day, the cloud he who rains, the fire he who moves, the horse he who runs, the bird he who flies, the tree he who grows or shades, even the stone he who cuts. We need not wonder at this, for we ourselves still speak of a cutter, a tender, a sucker, a slipper, of clinkers and splinters, without thinking of the activities ascribed to all these objects by the primitive framers of words.

Though the agents of the different acts of nature

[1] *Sociology*, p. 237.

remained unknown, yet as the agents of the light of the sun or of the rain of the clouds, they were conceived as very real agents. All this was the work, the almost inevitable work of language, provided always that we take language in the sense of the Greek *logos*, comprehending both speech and thought as one.

The Categories of the Understanding.

If we once have accustomed ourselves to speak of thought as something different from language, then, of course, instead of appealing to the necessities of language as a whole, we should, with Kant, have to appeal to the categories of the understanding. We should then have to recognise the category of substance as embodied in the active character of roots. We should thus gain, perhaps, a clearer insight into the abstract process of thought, but we should lose all that is most important to us, namely, the historical growth of the human mind.

I have neither forgotten Kant, nor surrendered my belief in his categories. But the study of language, as the embodiment of thought, has made it clear to me that Kant's categories are abstractions only. They have no existence by themselves. They are not pigeon-holes made of a pine and covered with cloth—they are simply the inside of language.

The Categories of Language.

Justice has at last been done to language. At first Aristotle learnt from language what he very properly called the categories, that is, the predicaments, or what we can predicate of our experience.

Afterwards these categories, though originally abstracted from language, claimed complete independence and became extremely masterful in their relation to language and grammar. At last, however, language has now resumed her proper position as the only possible embodiment of deliberate thought, and the categories, so far from being the moulds in which language was cast, are recognised once more as the inherent forms of thought-language.

We shall thus understand why fire, if it was to be named at all, could at first be named in one way only, namely, as an agent.

Fire, as a Deva.

We may now advance a step further, and ask how it was that Agni in the Veda is not conceived as an agent only, but as a god, or, if not, as yet, as a god in the Greek sense of the word, at least as a Deva. How shall we account for that?

Here we touch at once on the most vital point in our analysis. Certainly in the Veda Agni was called deva, perhaps more frequently than any other god. But fortunately in the Veda we can still discover the original meaning of the word deva. It did not mean divine, for how should such a concept have been suddenly called into being? Deva is derived from the root DIV, and meant originally bright. From the same root we have in Sanskrit diva, sky, divasa, day, in Lat. *dies*, and many more, all originally expressive of light and brightness. In many passages where Agni, or the Dawn, or the Sky, or the Sun are called deva, it is far better to translate deva by bright than by divine, the former conveying a natural meaning in harmony with the whole tenour of the

Vedic hymns, the latter conveying hardly any meaning at all.

But it is true nevertheless that this epithet deva, meaning originally bright, became in time, in the Vedic, nay even in the Aryan period already, the recognised name of those natural agents whom we have been accustomed to call gods. We can watch the evolutionary process before our very eyes. When the different phenomena of nature representing light, such as the morning, the dawn, the sun, the moon, the sky, had been invoked each by its own name, they could all be spoken of by the one epithet which they shared in common, namely deva, bright. In this general concept of those Bright ones, all that was special and peculiar to each was dropt, and there remained only the one epithet deva, to embrace them all. Here then there arose, as if by necessity, a new concept, in which the distinctive features of the various bright beings had all been merged in that of brightness, and in which even the original meaning of brightness, being shared by so many very different beings, had been considerably dimmed or generalised, so that there remained little more than the concept of agent which, as modified by brightness, had been from the beginning contained in the root DIV.

You will now perceive the difference between our saying that the ancient Âryas applied the name of gods to the fire, the sun, or the sky, or our watching the process by which these Âryas were brought to extract or abstract from the concepts of fire, sun, moon, and sky, all being bright beings, the general concept of Deva-hood. But, though we cannot help translating deva by *god*, you will easily understand what a distance there is from Deva-hood to *God-hood.* A Deva is as yet no more than a bright agent, then a kind agent, then a powerful agent, a more than human agent, nay, if you like, a superhuman agent; and then only, by another step, by what may be called a step in the dark, a divine agent.

Greek and Roman Gods.

In Greece the process was slightly different. The Greeks very soon endowed these powerful agents with human qualities, to such an extent that immortality seems almost the only quality which they do not share in common with human beings. In Italy the old gods had less of that anthropomorphic character which they had in Greece. It is, in fact, a distinguishing feature of ancient Roman mythology that there are few family ties that hold the gods together, while the Greek gods are all related with one another most intimately, if not always, most correctly.

The early Christians invented still another concept for these Greek and Roman gods. They did not deny their substantial existence, but they accepted them as living beings, as spirits, as they called them, but as evil spirits. This idea has remained till almost to our own time, when the study of ancient religion and ancient language has enabled us to see what the Devas of the Âryas really were—not evil spirits, not human or superhuman beings, but names given to the most prominent phenomena of nature, which naturally and necessarily implied the idea of agents. With the progress of language and thought *we* are now able to speak instead of agents, of agencies, of forces, forces of nature, as we call them; but what is behind those agencies, what is behind warmth or light or ether, we know as little as the Vedic Rishis knew what was behind their Agni or their other Devas.

Ruskin on the Ancient Gods.

How powerful the influence of words may be, how long they may continue to charm and to mislead even the wisest, we may see from an eloquent passage in Mr. Ruskin's *Praeterita*, vol. iii. p. 172. He tries to explain to himself and to others what he means when he speaks, as he often does, half poet, half philosopher as he is, of gods. 'By gods in the plural,' he writes, 'I mean the totality of spiritual powers, delegated by the Lord of the universe to do, in their several heights, or offices, parts of His will respecting man, or the world that man is imprisoned in; not as myself knowing, or in security believing, that there are such, but in meekness accepting the testimony and belief of all ages, to the presence, in heaven and earth, of angels, principalities, powers, thrones, and the like—with genii, fairies, or spirits ministering and guarding, or destroying and tempting, or aiding good work and inspiring the mightiest. For all these I take the general word "gods," as the best understood in all languages, and the truest and widest in meaning, including the minor ones of seraph, cherub, ghost, wraith, and the like; and myself knowing for indisputable fact, that no true happiness exists, nor is any good work ever done by human creatures, but in the sense or imagination of such presences.'

Does not this confirm the words of Rosmini when he said: 'The deeper we penetrate into this matter, the more do we find that all our intellectual errors, all the pernicious theories, the deceptive sophistries by which individuals and nations have been deluded, can be traced back to the vague and improper use of words[1].'

Evolution of the word Deva.

It is very important that you should clearly apprehend this process by which the word deva, originally meaning bright, assumed in time the meaning of god, in that sense at least in which the Hindus, like the Greeks and Romans, would speak of Agni, the fire, Ushas, the dawn, Dyaus, the sky, as their Devas, or their gods. It is one of the most interesting cases of intellectual evolution, for it shows us how a word, having originally the purely material meaning of brightness, came in the end by the most natural process to mean divine. There was nothing intentional in that process. It was impossible that there should have been a conscious intention to express the divine, for, if there had been such a conscious intention, there would have been already in the human mind a pre-existent name and concept of the divine. The process was one of the most natural evolution. You may say that nothing could be evolved that was not involved in the word deva, and in one sense this is perfectly true. In the idea of agency, which was involved in every root, there lay the germ which, as one outside envelope

[1] *The Ruling Principle of Method, applied to Education by Rosmini.* Translated by Mrs. W. Grey, 1887, p. 262.

after the other was removed, came out in the end in all its simplicity and purity. But it came out nevertheless *after* it had been coloured or determined by these former envelopments. It had passed through an historical process, and had thus grown into an historical concept.

Nor must we suppose that the evolution of the word deva was the only evolution which gave us in the end the idea of divine. That idea was evolved in many different ways, but nowhere can we watch every stage in the evolution so well as in the history of the word deva. Our own word *God* must have passed through a similar evolution, provided it be an old word. But unfortunately nearly all its antecedents are lost, and its etymology is quite unknown.

We have as yet traced the history, or, if you like, the evolution of the word deva to that stage only when it signifies a number of bright, kind, powerful agents, such as Mr. Ruskin declared he could still accept on the testimony and belief of all ages. But its history, as we shall see, does not end there. It gradually rises to the highest concept of deity, to a belief in a God above all gods, a creator, a ruler of the world, a judge, and yet a compassionate father, so that what seems at first a mere matter of linguistic archaeology, will stand before us in the end as the solution of one of the most vital questions of religious philosophy. How many times has the question been asked, Whence comes the idea of God? and how many different answers has it elicited! Some people maintain it is inherent in the human mind, it is an innate idea, or a precept, as it has lately been called. Others assert that it could have come to man by a special revelation only. Others again, like Professor Gruppe, maintain that it is a mere hallucination that took possession of one man, and was then disseminated through well-known channels over the whole world. We do not want any of these guesses. We have a guide that does not leave us in the dark when we are searching for the first germs of the idea of God. Guided by language, we can see as clearly as possible how, in the case of deva, the idea of God grew out of the idea of light, of active light, of an awakening, shining, illuminating, and warming light. We are apt to despise the decayed seed when the majestic oak stands before our eyes, and it may cause a certain dismay in the hearts of some philosophers that the voice of God should first have spoken to man from out the fire. Still as there is no break between deva, bright, as applied to Agni, the fire, and many other powers of nature, and the *Deus Optimus Maximus* of the Romans, nay, as the God whom the Greeks ignorantly worshipped was the same God whom St. Paul declared unto them, we must learn the lesson, and a most valuable lesson it will turn out to be—that the idea of God is the result of an unbroken historical evolution, call it a development, an unveiling, or a purification, but not of a sudden revelation.

Natural Revelation of God.

It seems almost incredible that in our days such a lesson, confirmed as it is by the irrefragable evidence of historical documents, should be objected to as dangerous to the interests of religion, nay, should form the object of virulent attacks.

For some reason or other, our opponents claim for

their own theories the character of orthodoxy, while they try to prejudge the whole question by stigmatising our own argument as heterodox. Now I should like to ask our opponents, first of all, by what authority such metaphysical theories as that of innate ideas can possibly claim the name of orthodox, or where they can point to chapter and verse in support of what they call either a special or a universal primeval revelation, imparting to human beings the first concept and name of God? To a student of the religions of the world, in their immense variety and their constant divisions, the names of orthodox and heterodox, so freely used at all times and on all sides, have lost much both of their charm and their terror. What right have we to find fault with the manner in which the Divine revealed itself, first to the eyes, and then to the mind of man? Is the revelation in nature really so contemptible a thing that we can afford to despise it, or at the utmost treat it as good enough for the heathen world? Our eyes must have grown very dim, our mind very dull, if we can no longer perceive how the heavens declare the glory of God. We have now named and classified the whole of nature, and nothing seems able any longer to surprise, to terrify, to overwhelm us. But if the mind of man had to be roused for the first time, and to be lifted up to the conception of something beyond itself, what language could have been more powerful than that which spoke in mountains and torrents, in clouds and thunderstorms, in skies and dawns, in sun and moon, in day and night, in life and death? Is there no voice, no meaning, is there no revelation in all this? Was it possible to contemplate the movements of the heavenly bodies, the regular return of day and night, of spring and winter, of birth and death, without the deepest emotion?

Of course, people may say now, We know all this, we can account for it all, and philosophy has taught us *Nil admirari.* If that is so, then it may be true indeed that the sluggish mind of man had to be stirred once more by a more than natural revelation. But in the early days of the world, the world was too full of wonders to require any other miracles. The whole world was a miracle and a revelation, there was no need for any special disclosure. At that time the heavens, the waters, the sun and moon, the stars of heaven, the showers and dew, the winds of God, fire and heat, winter and summer, ice and snow, nights and days, lightnings and clouds, the earth, the mountains and hills, the green things upon the earth, the wells, and seas, and floods, —all blessed the Lord, praised Him, and magnified Him for ever.

Can we imagine a more powerful revelation? Is it for us to say that for the children of men to join in praising and magnifying Him who revealed Himself in His own way in all the magnificence, the wisdom, and order of nature, is mere paganism, polytheism, pantheism, and abominable idolatry? I have heard many blasphemies, I have heard none greater than this.

It may be said, however, that the road from nature leads only to nature's *gods*, to a belief in many, not in *one* supreme God. It certainly leads through that gate, but it does not stop there. If we return to the Veda, the oldest record of a polytheistic faith, and if we take up once more the thread where we left it, we shall be able to see how Agni, the god of fire, being at first but one by the side of many other gods, develops into something much higher. He does not remain one out of many gods. He becomes in the end a supreme god, *the* Supreme God, till his very name is thrown away, or is recognised as but one out of many names by which ancient seers in their helpless language called that which is, the One and All. You may remember the passage from the Veda which I quoted before: 'That which is one, the seers call in many ways, they call it Agni, Yama, Mâtarisvan.

The Biography of Agni.

This process, which I call the theogonic process, is so important that we must study it carefully, and step by step, in the case of at least one of the ancient gods. If I select for that purpose the god of fire, Agni, and not Dyaus, Zeus, Jupiter, the supreme god of the Aryan Pantheon, it is because the biography of Dyaus, having been fully worked out by me on former occasions, need not be gone through again in full detail[1]. It is my chief object at present to show how many roads, starting from different beginnings, all converged and met in the end in the same central point, the belief in one Supreme Agent, manifested in all that is and moves and lives, and how the perception of the Infinite was revealed everywhere in what we call the perceptions of the Finite.

[1] *Science of Language*, vol. ii. chap. 11.

LECTURE VII.

THE BIOGRAPHY OF AGNI.

Facts against Theories.

WE begin to-day the biography of Agni, the god of fire, and shall try to follow it from the first chapter to the last. That biography may sometimes seem lengthy and wearisome, but we must go through all its chapters patiently, for the whole question of Natural Religion depends really on the success of our present inquiry. The only successful way of controverting the prevalent theories of the origin of religion is an appeal to facts. I maintain that the ancient records of religion, more particularly in India, supply historical evidences that the human mind was able, by its own inherent powers, to ascend from nature to nature's gods, and, in the end, to the God of nature. If we can prove this, the verdict cannot be doubtful, for even in theological discussion facts are still stronger than theories. In answer to those who have recourse to what they call innate faculties or special revelations, we appeal to historical records, and, where so much is at stake, we must not shrink from wearisome labour. Some of the details in the historical evolution of Agni, fire, may seem unimportant for our purpose, but we have watchful and powerful enemies, and we must not leave any position in our onward march exposed to surprise and capture.

Premature Generalisation.

Nothing does so much mischief in our sphere of work as premature generalisation. It seems that Professor Weber[1] remarked, in one of his early publications, that 'Agni is adored essentially as earthly sacrificial fire, and not as an elemental force.' This statement has been repeated again and again, till at last it was supposed that Agni was really a mere invention of priests, and unknown, at all events, before the development of the sacrificial system in India. It is perfectly true that Agni, as the fire on the altar, takes a very prominent place in the Vedic hymns. Agni, in fact, is, together with Indra, the Deva to whom most hymns are addressed, and in many of them the same praises are repeated and the same epithets used which apply to the sacrificial fire. But there are other passages, less numerous, no doubt, but, for that very reason, more important to us, in which Agni is celebrated without any reference as yet to the fire on the altar.

I shall begin by examining these passages in which Agni is described in his purely physical character.

Agni in his Physical Character.

The first question was, Whence did he come? To this many answers are given. We read, Rv. II. 1, 1:

Tvám agne dyúbhi*h* tvám âsusukshá*n*i*h* tvám adbhyá*h* tvám ásmana*h* pári,

[1] *History of Sanskrit Literature*, p. 40.

Tvám vánebhya*h* tvám óshadhîbhya*h* tvám nri*n*ẫm nri*p*ate *g*âyase *s*ú*k*i*h*.

'Thou, O Agni, art born wishing to shine forth, thou art born from the skies, thou from the waters, thou from the stone, thou from the wood, thou from the herbs, thou, king of men, the bright one.'

Here we learn in one verse all the possible ways in which Agni could have appeared to man. First, from the skies, as the fiery and scorching sun, which by its heat could kindle inflammable substances; secondly, from the waters, that is, from the clouds, as lightning; thirdly, from the stone, which must be meant for the flint, though the striking fire out of flint is not recognised in the Veda as a sacrificial act; fourthly, from the wood and the herbs, that is, from the fire-sticks and from dry leaves which, like our tinder, caught the spark and kept it safe, till, by means of blowing, it would burst forth into flames.

Let us now examine these four kinds of Agni's birth more in detail.

Agni, as the Sun.

That Agni was often taken as the sun, is proved by many passages in the hymns of the Rig-veda. For instance, Rv. VI. 9, 1:

Áha*h* *k*a kri*sh*n*á*m áha*h* ár*g*unam *k*a ví vartete rá*g*asî vedyẫbhi*h*,
Vaisvânará*h* *g*ẫyamâna*h* ná rẫ*g*â áva atirat *g*yótishâ agni*h* támâ*m*si.

'The black day and the red day (night and day) turn heaven and earth by their different colours. Agni strides down across the darkness, beloved by all men, like a born king.'

Here Agni, striding down across the darkness, is evidently meant for the sun itself. In another verse, III. 14, 4, Agni is called Sûrya, sun.

Yát sokíshâ sahasah putra tíshthâh
abhí kshitī́h pratháyan sū́ryah nrī́n.

'(Agni) when thou, O son of strength, stoodst as the sun, spreading wide over men and their dwellings.'

In the Brâhmanas it is stated explicitly that Agni in his third character is the sun[1]. (Yad asya divi tritîyam tad asâv âditya iti hi brâhmanam, Nir. VII. 28.) In other passages, however, the two are distinguished from, though also compared with, one another. Thus the sun is said to spring from the nocturnal Agni. For instance, Rv. X. 88, 6:

Mûrdhā́ bhuváh bhavati náktam agníh tátah sū́ryah gâyate prâtáh udyán.

'Agni is the head of the world by night; from him is born[2] the sun, rising in the morning.'

The two, Agni and the sun, are compared, as when it is said, V. 1, 4, that 'the minds of worshippers turn together towards Agni, as our eyes turn towards the sun.' Or, VII. 8, 4, sū́ryah ná rókate, 'Agni, who shines like the sun.'

And again, VIII. 43, 5:

Eté tyé vríthak agnáyah iddhā́sah sám adrikshata ushásâm iva ketávah.

'These lighted fires are seen scattered, like the splendours of the dawn.'

We often read, particularly in the Brâhmanas, that Agni is the light by night, the sun by day. There is a passage often quoted from the Aitareya-Brâhmana, VIII. 28, 'The sun (Âditya), when setting, enters Agni, and vanishes—Agni, flaring up, enters the air (Vâyu), and vanishes.' And afterwards, 'Agni is born from the air, the sun is born from Agni, fire.'

[1] Bergaigne, *Religion Védique*, i. p. 13.
[2] Cf. X. 88, 16, sîrshatáh gâtám.

Agni, the Sun, or the Fire on the Hearth.

There are other passages where it is doubtful whether the poets thought of the sun rising in the morning and filling the world with splendour, or of the fire on the hearth and the altar, which may likewise be said to rise in the morning and fill the world with light. For instance, Rv. X. 1, 1:

> Ágre b*ri*hán ushásâm ûrdhvá*h* asthât
> ni*h*-*g*aganvā́n támasa*h* *g*yótishâ ā́ agât,
> Agní*h* bhânúnâ rúsatâ sváṅga*h*
> ā́ *g*âtá*h* vísvâ sádmâni aprâ*h*.

'Agni stood up mighty at the head of the dawn, he approached, coming with light out of darkness. Born with beautiful limbs, he has filled all dwellings with his shining light.'

And again, X. 88, 12:

> Vísvasmai agním bhúvanâya devā́*h*
> vaisvânarám ketúm áhnâm ak*ri*n*v*an,
> Ā́ yá*h* tatā́na ushása*h* vibhātī́*h*
> ápo ûr*n*oti táma*h* ar*k*ishâ yán.

'The gods made Agni Vaisvânara the light of days for the whole world, he who stretched out the shining dawns, and drove away the darkness, coming with splendour.'

VII. 78, 3:

Á*g*î*g*anan sū́ryam ya*g*ñám agním apâ*k*ī́nam táma*h* agât á*g*ush*t*am.

'They, the Dawns, created the sun, the sacrifice, the fire; the unloved darkness went away.' (Cf. VII. 99, 4.)

Though the commentators often prefer to apply such passages to the fire on the altar, or to look upon that fire, when lighted in the morning, as a symbol of the rising sun, it is quite clear that the idea of Agni, as manifested in the sun, was perfectly familiar to the Vedic poets.

Sun and Fire in America.

It requires a certain effort with us to understand how two such different percepts as that of the fire, burning on the hearth, and that of the sun, rising in the morning, crossing the sky, and setting in the evening, could be brought into the same mental focus, and be conceived as one and the same object. Here, however, as elsewhere, a comparison of other religions, more particularly of religions which cannot claim any genealogical relationship with the Veda, is very useful in either removing or confirming our doubts and difficulties.

Let us look to the American religions. It is true, there are but few cases where fire and sun have actually received the same name. Brinton, however, in his *Myths of the New World*, p. 143, tells us that the Tezuque of New Mexico use tah both for sun and fire, and that the Kolosh of British America derive at least their names for sun and fire from the same root, fire being kan, sun kakan. But in their accounts of the creation, the sun is always spoken of as fire. It is not represented as anterior to the world, but as manufactured by the old people (Navajos), as kindled and set going by the first of men (Algonkins), or as freed from a dark cave by a kindly deity (Haitians).

J. G. Müller, also, in his *History of the American original Religions*, tells us that fire was kept burning in the temples of the Sun, as a constant representation, it would seem, of the solar deity (pp. 54, 69, 519). Worship of fire, he remarks, was intimately connected with worship of the sun (p. 125). And again: 'The worship of fire continued under the Incas, but it was brought into the most intimate relation with sun-worship. In the temple of the sun, as well as in the house of the virgins of the sun, the eternal fire was always kept burning. At the high festival Raymi, in winter, this fire was lighted, as at Rome, by means of a golden concave mirror. Only if the sky was clouded, did they try, according to the most ancient custom, to get fire by means of rubbing two pieces of wood.'

In Peru, we hear of a fight between two gods, one called Con or Viracocha, the other Pachacamac. The former is said to be the god of water or fertilising rain, the latter of fire, particularly of life-giving fire. This Pachacamac is represented as the son of the sun, thus showing once more the close relation in which, in the imagination of primitive people, sun and fire stood to one another.

Sun and Fire among the Fins.

If now we turn for a moment to the Fins, who, as little as the Americans, can be suspected of having borrowed anything from the Veda, we find there also that Panu, the god of fire, is conceived as a son of the sun. Thus we read in the Kalevala[1], the famous epic poem of the Fins:

> 'O Panu, son of the sun,
> Offspring thou of the dear day,
> Lift the fire up to the sky.
> In the middle of the golden ring,
> Within the rock of copper,
> Carry it as a child to the mother,
> Into the lap of the dear old woman.
> Put it there, to shine by day,
> And to rest at night,
> Let it rise every morning,
> Let it set every evening.'

[1] Rune xxvi, vv. 431–441.

Castrén remarks on this passage, that 'it clearly shows how the ancient Fins looked upon the sun as an enclosed mass of fire, and upon earthly fire as an emanation from the sun, or, to adopt the language of the runes, as a child of the sun-mother. As therefore, sun and fire,' he continues, 'are originally one and the same thing, it is clear that with our ancestors the worship of the Fire coincided with the worship of the Sun, and that Panu, Fire, could not be worshipped as an independent deity, but only as a son of the sun.'

After these parallels, to which many more might be added, we shall be better able to enter into the ideas of our own Aryan, not Finnish, ancestors, when they comprehended under the name of Agni both the fire on the hearth or the altar, and the sun in the sky.

Agni, as Lightning.

We now come to a second class of passages, where Agni is said to be the son of *Dyaus*, the sky (Diva*h* sûnu*h*, or *sisuh*), and likewise to spring from the waters, or to be the child of the waters (apắm gár-bha*h*, Rv. III. 1, 12). Here he must be understood as lightning coming from the clouds. For instance, Rv. VI. 6, 2:

Sá*h* svitâná*h* tanyatú*h* ro*k*anasthắ*h*.

'This Agni, brilliant, thundering in heaven.'

Or again, VII. 3, 6:

Divá*h* ná te tanyatú*h* eti sûshma*h*.

'Thy fierceness comes like the thunder of heaven.'

Rv. X. 45, 4:

> Ákrandat agníh stanáyan iva dyaúh,
>
> 'Agni rattled like the thundering sky.'

Rv. I. 143, 2:

> Sáh gáyamânah paramé vyòmani
> âvíh agníh abhavat mâtarísvane,
> Asyá krátvâ samidhânásya magmánâ
> prá dyấvâ sokíh prithiví arokayat.

'Agni, born in the highest heaven, appeared to Mâtarisvan. His splendour, when he had been kindled by wisdom and strength, lighted up heaven and earth.'

Mâtarisvan.

This Mâtarisvan, to whom Agni appeared as lightning, is frequently mentioned, and we here reach a stratum of mythology, which crops up again and again in the Veda, but which hitherto has resisted all analysis. We do not know what is meant by Mâtarisvan, the name admits of no satisfactory etymology [1], and seems to date from a remoter period of language. We may gather, however, from the passages in which Mâtarisvan occurs that he was meant for the air or for the wind that seemed to carry the fire of lightning from heaven through the air to the earth [2]. I quote again from Rv. I. 143, 2:

> Sáh gáyamânah paramé vyòmani
> âvíh agníh abhavat mâtarísvane.

'Agni, born in the highest heaven, appeared to Mâtarisvan.'

[1] The oldest etymology is that given in Rv. III. 29, 11, mâtarísvâ yát ámimîta mâtári.

[2] 'Among the Creeks also the four winds from the four corners of the earth are believed to have brought the sacred fire and pointed out the seven sacred plants. After having rendered this service to men, the kindly visitors disappeared in the clouds, returning whence they came.' (Brinton, *Myths of the New World*, p. 77.)

In III. 5, 10 Mâtarisvan is said to have lighted Agni, when he was hidden, for the Bh*ri*gus (see also III. 2, 13), and these Bh*ri*gus are often mentioned as having spread Agni among men (I. 58, 6). In VI. 8, 4 Mâtarisvan is called the Messenger of Vivasvat, who brought Agni.

It is but natural that this Mâtarisvan, who is said to have brought down lightning from the sky to man, should have been compared to Prometheus. But though in one point their functions are similar, their names are different, and we shall have to consider hereafter some other well-known attempts to trace the very name of Prometheus in the language of the Veda.

Fire from Flint.

The striking fire out of a stone seems almost unknown in the Rig-veda. In one passage, however, II. 12, 3, Indra is said to have produced Agni from two stones:

Yá*h* ásmano*h* antá*h* agním *g*a*g*ãna.

'He who produced fire from two stones,' or, as others explain, 'from two clouds, acting as stones.'

In either case the mere fact that fire may be struck from a flint seems to have been known in Vedic times.

Fire from Wood.

The fourth process, that of eliciting fire by means of rubbing two fire-sticks and catching the spark in dry herbs, is mentioned again and again. It was evidently considered to require both force and skill. One of the standing epithets of Agni is 'the son of strength' (sûnu*h* sahasa*h*, III. 1, 8), and among ancient families the Bh*ri*gus are often mentioned as having possessed the secret of making and keeping a fire in the house[1]. Thus we read, I. 143, 4:

> Yám eriré bh*ri*gava*h* visvávedasam
> nấbhâ p*ri*thivyấ*h* bhúvanasya ma*g*mánâ.

'The Bh*ri*gus excited or kindled Agni in the centre of the earth by the strength of man.'

And again, II. 4, 2:

> dvitấ adadhu*h* bh*ri*gava*h* vikshú âyó*h*.

'The Bh*ri*gus placed Agni twofold among the tribes of men.'

It is curious that the name Bh*ri*gu should correspond letter by letter to the Φλέγυες of Greek mythology.

Mythological Ideas connected with Fire.

This last process of producing fire by rubbing is a very favourite subject of the Vedic poets. Of the two pieces of wood used for rubbing out fire, one is called the mother, the other the father of Agni. Thus we read, V. 9, 3:

> Utá sma yám *s*i*s*um yathâ návam *g*anish*t*a ará*n*î,
> dhartấram mấnushî*n*âm vi*s*ấm agním svadhvarám.

'He whom the two fire-sticks (ara*n*i) produced, like a new-born babe, Agni, the supporter of the tribes of man, good at the sacrifice.'

This myth of the new-born babe soon assumes greater proportions. Thus it is said, Rv. X. 79, 4:

> Tát vâm *ri*tám rodasî prá bravîmi *g*ấyamâna*h* mâtárâ gárbha*h* atti,
> ná ahám devásya mártya*h* *k*iketa agní*h* aṅgá ví*k*etâ*h* sá*h* prá*k*etâ*h*.

[1] It is curious to observe that in many of the languages of Australia there is but one word both for fire and for wood. See Curr, *The Australian Race*, vol. i. p. 9.

'O Heaven and Earth, I proclaim this truthful fact, that the child, as soon as born, eats his parents. I, a mortal, do not understand this (act) of a god; Agni indeed understands, for he is wise!'

It was considered another wonderful thing, as we saw before, that a living thing, like Agni, should be born from a dry stick, or that, though his mother does not suckle him, he yet should grow so rapidly, and proceed at once to do his work as messenger between gods and men (X. 115, 1). Again (V. 9, 4), he is said to be difficult to catch, like a brood of serpents, and to consume forests, as cattle do on their pasture.

But all this is a beginning only. The subject grows, and is varied in every possible way. You know how often our critics have expressed their inability to believe that the conversation of the Vedic Âryas should have turned on nothing but the trivial events of every day. I can understand their incredulity, so long as they do not open the pages of the Rig-veda. But on every one of these pages they will find facts which are stronger than all theories, and which leave us no doubt that the poetry of the Vedic Âryas turned chiefly on the sun, the moon, the sky, the wind, the storm, and the fire.

The repetition of the same ideas is apt to become tedious, but even this tedious repetition contains a lesson, if it helps to give us a truer idea of the slow but natural growth of the human intellect where we can best watch it,—in the hymns of the Rig-veda; and, if it makes us understand that even a belief in Agents, whether in the fire, or in the sun, or in the sky, need not be considered as mere paganism and idolatry, but as containing healthy seeds, which in time were meant to grow into a rich harvest.

Agni, as Deva, Bright, Amartya, Undying, &c.

We saw how naturally Agni, the fire, could be called deva, bright, without any thought, as yet, of calling him a god. Even when the light of Agni is spoken of as immortal, that need not mean, as yet, any more than that it lasts for ever, if properly kept up. We read, for instance, Rv. VI. 9, 4, idám *g*yóti*h* am*rí*tam mártyeshu, 'See this light immortal among mortals.' Here immortal might still be translated by the never-dying light. The fire, as a masculine, or rather as an agent, was also called, I. 58, 4, a*g*ara, not-aging, and the Vedic poets dwelt again and again on the contrast between the undying Agni and his dying friends. Of other Devas also it was said that they were not, like human beings, subject to decay and death.

Agni, the Immortal among Mortals.

But while the ancient poets brought themselves to think of an impassable gulf between the mortals on one side and the immortals on the other, this gulf vanished again in the case of Agni. He, immortal as he was, dwelt among men. He was the guest (átithi, II. 4, 1) of men, often called the immortal among mortals (am*rí*ta*h* mártyeshu, VIII. 71, 11).

Now this expression, 'immortal among mortals,' seems at first sight of no great consequence. But like many of these ancient phrases, it contains germs waiting for a most important development in the future. We may recognise in that simple expression of an immortal, dwelling among mortals, being the guest, the friend, the benefactor of mortals, the first attempt at bridging over the gulf which human language and human thought had themselves created between the mortal and the immortal, between the visible and the invisible, between the finite and the infinite. Such ideas appear at first in a very simple and almost unconscious form, they present themselves without being looked for, but they remain fixed in the mind, they gain from year to year in strength and depth, and they form at last a fertile soil from which in later ages may spring up the most sublime conceptions of the unity between the mortal and the immortal, between the visible and the invisible, between the finite and the infinite, such as are expressed in the dark words of Heraclitus, *ἀθάνατοι θνητοί, θνητοὶ ἀθάνατοι*. There is a continuity in all our thoughts, and there is nothing more important for a true appreciation of our intellectual organisation than the discovery of the coarse threads that form the woof of our most abstract thoughts.

Agni, the Friend, Helper, Father.

If Agni had once been recognised as a friend or as a welcome guest in the house, there soon followed a shower of other epithets expressive of man's appreciation of Agni's benefits. I can mention here a few only. He is called master of the house, gr*i*hapati*h*, I. 12, 6; lord of the people, vispati*h*, I. 12, 2; leader, puraetâ, III. 11, 5; king, râ*g*â, I. 59, 5. In I. 31, 10 we read:

Tvám agne prámati*h* tvám pitấ asi na*h*, tvám vayaskr*i*t táva *g*âmáya*h* vayám.

'Thou, O Agni, art our providence, our father; thou givest us vigour, we are thy kindred.'

II. 1, 9:

Tvám putráh bhavasi yáh te ávidhat.

'Thou art a son to him who worships thee.'

VI. 1, 5:

Pitā̆ mâtā̆ sádam ít mā̆nushâ*n*âm.

'Thou art always father and mother for men.'

X. 7, 3:

Agním manye pitáram agním âpím
agním bhrā̆taram sádam it sákhâyam;
agnéh ánîkam b*r*ihatáh saparyam
diví *s*ukrám ya*g*atám sū̆ryasya.

'I hold Agni to be my father, I hold him to be my kinsman, my brother, and always my friend. I worshipped the face of the mighty Agni, the holy light of the sun in heaven.'

Agni, Helper in Battle.

But Agni was not only beneficial in the house, he was also a powerful helper in battle, the destroyer of enemies, whether human or superhuman. It is easy to imagine what an advantage the possession of fire must have proved in primitive warfare. How easy it was with a well flung torch to set a whole forest on fire, or to smoke out enemies who had taken refuge in a cave.

Fireless Races.

The enemies of the Âryas in the Vedic times are called Dasyu[1], or even Rakshas and Yâtudhâna, giants and devils. These wild tribes are often called an-agni-tra, those who do not keep the fire. Thus we read, I. 189, 3:

Ágne tvám asmát yuyodhi
ámîvâ*h*, ánagnitrâ*h* abhí ámanta k*r*ish*t*í*h*,
púna*h* asmábhyam suvitā̆ya deva
kshā̆m vísvebhi*h* am*r*itebhi*h* ya*g*atra.

[1] *Letter on the Turanian Languages*, pp. 83 sq.

'Agni, drive away from us the enemies,—tribes who keep no fire came to attack us. Come again to the earth for our welfare, sacred god with all the immortals.'

These fireless races are also called kravya-ad, eating raw flesh (κρεοφάγοι), and âmấd (X. 87, 7) (ὠμοφάγοι). They are even suspected of feeding on human flesh, X. 87, 16 (yá*h* paúrusheye*n*a kravíshâ samaṅkté). They are described very much in the same way in which lower races are described even now by those who covet their land. Thus, in Rv. VII. 104, two of the warlike gods of the Vedic people, Indra and Soma, are invoked by Vasish*th*a to help him and his people to destroy those who do not worship his gods, who do not speak the truth, and who keep no fire in their houses.

1. Índrâsomâ tápatam ráksha*h* ub*g*átam
ní arpayatam v*r*isha*n*â tama*h*-v*r*idha*h*;
párâ *s*ri*n*îtam a*k*ita*h* ní oshatam
hatám nudéthâm ní *s*i*s*îtam atrí*n*a*h*.

2. Índrâsomâ sấm aghá*s*a*m*sam abhí aghám
tápu*h* yayastu *k*arú*h* agnivấn iva,
brahmadvíshe kravya-áde ghorá*k*akshase
dvésha*h* dhattam anavâyám kimîdíne.

3. Índrâsomâ du*h*-k*r*ita*h* vavré antá*h*
anârambha*n*é támasi prá vidhyatam,
yáthâ ná áta*h* púna*h* éka*h* *k*aná udáyat
tát vâm astu sáhase manyumát *s*áva*h*.

4. Índrâsomâ vartáyatam divá*h* vadhám
sám p*r*ithivyấ*h* aghá*s*a*m*sâya tárha*n*am,
út takshatam svaryấm párvatebhya*h*
yéna ráksha*h* vav*r*idhânám ni*g*úrvatha*h*.

1. 'O Indra and Soma, burn the devils (Rakshas), hold them under, throw them down, they who grow in darkness. Tear them off, the madmen, burn them, kill them, hurl them away, slay the gluttons.

2. 'O Indra and Soma, up together against the cursing demon! May he burn and hiss like an oblation on the fire. Put your everlasting hatred upon the villain who hates the Brahman, who eats flesh, and who looks abominable.

3. 'O Indra and Soma, hurl the evil-doer into the pit, into un-

fathomed darkness, that no one may come out again—such may be your wrathful strength to hold out.

4. 'O Indra and Soma, hurl from the sky and from the earth the bolt to fell the cursing demon. Shape the rattling lightning from out the clouds to crush the growing devil.'

The descriptions given of these enemies are so real that we can hardly doubt that they refer to the aboriginal inhabitants of India whose descendants survive to the present day, speaking non-Aryan dialects. The poets of the Veda often distinguish between their Aryan and non-Aryan enemies. They praise their gods for having destroyed their enemies, both Aryan and barbarian (dâsâ *k*a v*ri*trâ hatam, âryâ*ni* *k*a), and we frequently find such expressions as 'Kill our Aryan enemies and the Dâsa enemies, yea, kill all our enemies.'

In my letter to Bunsen '*On the Turanian Languages*,' published in 1854 in his '*Christianity and Mankind*,' vol. iii, I pointed out that these indigenous races were black-skinned, while the Âryas prided themselves on their bright colour. They were called kravyâd, eating raw flesh; anagnitra, not keeping fire; v*ri*sha-sipra, bull-nosed; a-nâsa, flat-nosed or noseless, &c. These enemies had strongholds, and their wealth consisted chiefly in cattle.

Sometimes, no doubt, these enemies are represented as demons and devils, as enemies of the gods rather than of men. But that again is perfectly natural, and need not surprise us after we have read more recent descriptions of savage races occupying land which is coveted by the white man. You remember that even Darwin spoke of certain tribes in South America as being more like devils than human beings. On the contrary, these warlike hymns, which describe the enemies whom the advancing Âryas had to conquer, contain some of the few glimpses of real history, and are all the more valuable at present, when we have so often been told that the Vedic hymns were nothing but the lucubrations of priests, when performing their intricate ceremonies. It must be clear that the work on which Vasish*th*a is bent in this hymn has little to do with intricate ceremonial; it is the simple and always recurring work of men killing men, of the stronger depriving the weaker of his land, his servants, and his cattle—what we now more euphemistically call 'the struggle for life,' and 'the survival of the fittest.'

Agricultural Âryas.

From the glimpses which we catch from the hymns of the Veda, it is safe to conclude that the Âryas who settled in North-Western India were agricultural tribes. Their very name ârya, as I have tried to show (*Encycl. Brit.*, s.v. Ârya), meant ploughers, from ar, to plough, to ear. Even before the great Âryan separation, agriculture must have been known, for Greek *ἄρουρα*, as Benfey has shown and Meyer has not disproved, corresponds to the Sk. and Zend urvarâ, a cultivated field. The Âryas in India call themselves k*ri*sh*t*is, tribes, and that too is derived from karsh, to plough[1].

The poets of the Veda begin to complain that the land is not large enough for them. Thus we read, Rv. VI. 47, 20:

'O gods, we have come to a country without meadows, the earth which is wide, has become narrow.'

[1] See *Biographies of Words*, p. 174.

The wealth of these Indian Âryas consisted chiefly in cattle, in cows, horses, sheep, goats, and in men. Corn was cut with sickles and afterwards thrashed. Their settlements were called v*r*i*g*ana, clearings, grâma, villages; while outside the grâma was the ara*n*ya, the heath or the forest which belonged to no one. Towns, in our sense, did not exist, though strongholds and camps are mentioned.

Each family had its house and hearth. Several families together formed a vis, *vicus*, or grâma, *pagus*, and several of such settlements seem to have formed a *g*ana, i.e. kin or clan. We hear of the vispati, the lord of a vis, of grâma*n*îs, leaders of villages, and of kings, râ*g*an, who are also called gopâ *g*anasya, shepherds of a clan. We even hear of leagues of five *g*anas or clans. We read of kings, both hereditary and elective. They led the armies, and received booty and tribute. We also hear of public assemblies, samitis or vidathas, held in a sabhâ, a public hall. The king was present. Discussions took place, and likewise social amusements.

The cultivated land seems to have belonged to the village, but booty in war seems to have constituted the first private property.

In the struggles between the Âryan invaders and the dark-skinned natives the possession of Agni or fire, as an ally, was in those distant days as great an advantage as the possession of armour or gunpowder in later days, and we may well understand, therefore, that Agni or fire should have been celebrated, till he became a familiar name, as a protector, a leader, a ruler, a powerful something, whether he was called deva, bright, or amartya, immortal.

What Agni was, or what he did, was often called a miracle (vápus).

Rv. IV. 7, 9:

> K*r*ish*n*âm te éma rúsata*h* purá*h* bhấ*h* *k*arish*n*ú ar*k*í*h* vápushâm ít ékam.

'Thy path is black, but there is light before thee when thou shinest;—thy flame moves swiftly—this is one of (many) wonders.'

Agni, destroying Forests.

More particularly his power of destroying or devouring whole forests imparts to Agni in the eyes of the Âryas a terrible character. We saw before how his flames were represented as tongues, licking (I. 140, 9) what they meant to consume. These tongues of Agni are called brilliant (II. 9, 1), and sharp (tigma, IV. 7, 10). They are also conceived as teeth, golden (V. 2, 3) and bright (VII. 4, 2), as tusks strong like metal (X. 87, 2), as jaws strong (III. 29, 13), sharp (I. 79, 6), and burning (I. 36, 16). In VIII. 43, 3, we read:

> Dadbhí*h* vánâni bapsati.

'He eats the forests with his teeth.'

In I. 143, 5:

> Ná yá*h* várâya marûtâm iva svaná*h*
> sénâ iva s*r*ish*t*ấ divyấ yáthâ asáni*h*,
> agní*h* *g*ámbhai*h* tigitaí*h* atti bhárvati
> yodhá*h* ná sátrûn sá*h* vánâ ní riñ*g*ate.

'He who cannot be resisted, like the blast of the Maruts, like a hurled weapon, like the heavenly thunder-bolt, Agni eats with his sharpened jaws, he champs, he prostrates forests, like a warrior his enemies.'

I. 58, 4–5:

> Ví vấta*g*ûta*h* ataséshu tish*th*ate
> v*r*ithâ *g*uhúbhi*h* s*r*i*n*yâ tuvi-sváni*h*;

trishú yát agne vanínah vrishayáse
krishnám te éma rúsat-urme agara.
Tápuh-gambhah váne ấ vấta-koditah
yûthé ná sahvấn áva vâti vámsagah;
abhivrágan ákshitam pấgasâ rágah
sthâtúh karátham bhayate patatrínah.

'Roused by the wind, he moves about among the shrubs everywhere with his tongues, and resounding with his sickle. When thou in a moment doest violence to the trees in the forest, thy path is black, O thou never-aging Agni, thou whose waves are brilliant.

'With fiery jaws, roused by the wind, he blows down on the forest like a powerful bull on his herd, moving with splendour towards the eternal sky. What moves and stands trembles before the bird[1].'

VIII. 43, 6–8:

6. Krishnâ rágâmsi patsutáh prayấne
gâtávedasah agníh yát ródhati kshámi.
7. Dhâsím krinvânáh óshadhîh bápsat
agníh ná vâyati púnah yán tárunîh ápi.
8. Gihvấbhih áha námnamat arkíshâ
gañganâbhávan agníh váneshu rokate.

'The clouds are black under his feet at his advance, when Agni descends to the earth,

'Making the herbs his food Agni never tires, eating, coming again and again, even the tall herbs.

'Turning about with his tongues of fire, as if laughing with his light, Agni flares up in the forests.'

I. 65, 8:

Yát vấta-gûtah vánâ ví ásthât
agníh ha dâti róma prithivyấh.

'When roused by the wind he strides about on to the forests, Agni shaves off the hair of the earth.'

His horses also when let loose are said to shave the earth (VI. 6, 4), and much the same is meant when Agni is said to lick the garment of the earth (I. 140, 9).

[1] See, however, I. 94, 11.

Agni's Horses.

Agni's horses are frequently mentioned, and they appear in different colours, as red (arusha and rohita, I. 94, 10), as dark (syâva, II. 10, 2), as bright (harit, I. 130, 2), and as brilliant white (sukra, VI. 6, 4). All this is quite intelligible, nor is the next step so very bold which leads the poets to speak of Agni himself as a horse. I know that some philosophers would see in this at once a sign of what they call zoolatry, whereas to the student of language such expressions, particularly if they occur as in the Veda but casually, are nothing but poetical metaphor. If the poet has once brought himself to say that Agni chews like a horse (VI. 3, 4), or that he shakes his tail like the horse of a chariot (II. 4, 4), why should he not say as he does in IV. 15, 1:

Agní*h* hótâ na*h* adhvaré
vâ*g*î sán pári nîyate
devá*h* devéshu ya*gñ*íya*h*.

'Agni, our priest, is led about at the sacrifice, being a horse.'

The leading about is an expression that applies to horses being led round or exercised, and the words, 'being a horse,' are no more than a metaphor. They mean that, as he is supposed to be a horse, therefore he is led about at the sacrifice. And this is exactly what has often to be done with the fire also, which at a sacrifice is carried about from one altar to another. This is not zoolatry, it is nothing but the natural play of language.

Agni, as Sacrificial Fire.

Hitherto it must be clear that all that has been said of Agni in the Veda applies to fire, such as it is, without any necessary reference as yet to the sacrificial fire.

This, as we shall see, occupies, no doubt, a very large place in the poetry of the ancient Rishis, but all that is said about it tells us very little of what we really care to know, the historical genesis of the concept of fire and its elevation to a divine rank.

That the Vedic poets were not entirely overawed by this sacrificial or sacred character of Agni, is best shown by their painting the same Agni occasionally in the most hideous colours. We saw how they spoke with horror of the black inhabitants of India as flesh-eaters, kravyâd. But they could not help seeing that Agni, the fire, also was a kind of flesh-eater. He not only served to cook the meat, whether for feasts or for sacrifices, he also devoured it, and he became particularly terrible in the eyes of the Vedic poets, when used for cremating the corpses of animals or men. In one hymn of the tenth Ma*nd*ala (X. 87) he is asked to sharpen his two iron tusks, and to put the enemies into his mouth to devour them. He is implored to heat the edges of his shafts and to send them into the heart of the Rakshas, and to break their outstretched arms. He is supposed to tear their skin, to mince their members, and to throw their bodies before shrieking vultures, to be eaten by them.

However, we have only to open the Veda in order to see that the sacrificial character of Agni is certainly very predominant in our collection of hymns. It began, as we saw, with the very natural feeling towards Agni, that is, towards the fire, which was carefully preserved on the hearth of every house. Agni, the fire on the hearth, was the centre of the family. Whoever belonged to a family, shared the same fire, and whoever was driven away from that fire was what the Romans called *aqua et igni interdictus*[1]. The fire on the hearth was looked upon as a friend and benefactor, round whom the members of a family, old and young, gathered in the morning and the evening. At meals, again, and at more solemn festivals, the fire was always present, and when libations and offerings were introduced, either in memory of the departed or in gratitude to the powers above, the fire on the hearth was the most convenient place to receive them. The people of Mexico threw the first morsel of their meals into the fire, they did not know why[2]. Many Tungusian, Mongolian, and Turkish tribes would never dare to eat meat without first throwing a piece on the fire of the hearth[3]. Here then we see what we call by the grand names of sacrifices and ceremonial, springing up in the most natural manner. The people, while feasting and enjoying themselves, thought in their childish way that something should be given up to their departed friends, and that the bright friends also whose presence they thought they had discovered in the genial sky, in the seasonable rain, or in the cheerful breezes of the morning, should not be forgotten. Everything else followed without any effort. The fire burning on the hearth, when it flared up with the fat or butter that had been poured upon it, was supposed to be carrying the offerings to the sky in clouds of smoke and fire.

[1] Thus Festus, p. 78, explains *extrarius* as *qui extra focum sacramentum jusque sit;* cf. Leist, *Jus Gentium*, p. 608. According to the judicial law, the same idea is expressed by declaring that a man who does not keep his fires becomes like a Sûdra, Vasish*th*a III. 1; or that to desert one's fires is as great a crime as to desert one's father, mother, son, or wife, Vish*n*u XXXVII. 6.

[2] J. G. Müller, *Geschichte der Amerikanischen Urreligionen*, p. 626.

[3] Castrén, *Finnische Mythologie*, p. 57.

Or when it consumed itself the more substantial gifts, the fire was looked upon as the representative of gods or ancestors, accepting and enjoying what had been offered to them (Rv. II. 1, 13).

Agni, the Messenger between Gods and Men.

Here comes in the very natural idea that Agni is the messenger between gods and men, the swift carrier travelling between heaven and earth. At first he is conceived as carrying prayers and offerings to the abode of the gods; but very soon he is also supposed to bring the gods down from their abodes to the abodes of men, and more particularly, to the places where sacrifices were performed. Thus we read, Rv. X. 70, 11:

Á agne vaha vâru*n*am ish*t*áye na*h*
índram divá*h* marúta*h* antárikshât.

'O Agni, bring hither Varu*n*a to our offering, bring Indra from the sky, the Maruts from the air.'

Agni, as Priest.

All this is still more or less natural, but after Agni has once been raised to the rank of messenger, he soon assumes the office of priest in all its endless varieties. The Vedic poets never weary of this subject. Agni is called the priest, and with the refinements of the priestly offices, every special office also is assigned to him. He is called the Hot*ri*, the priest who pours out the libation; he is the *R*itvi*g*, the priest who performs at the great seasons of the year[1]; he is the Purohita, the domestic priest; he is the Brahman, the superintending priest, who sees that no mistakes may be made in the performance of the sacrifice, or, if they have been made, corrects them. Even the more special

[1] Rv. X. 2, 1: Vidvấn *ri*tûn *ri*tupate ya*g*a ihá.

ceremonial offices of the minor priests are all assigned to him, and nothing gives us so strong an impression of what we should call the modern character of the Vedic hymns as these trivial and paltry ritualistic devices which are actually transferred from the human priesthood to the gods. Still, in this case also we must live and learn, and it is not for us to say that ancient sages were utterly incapable of follies which we are too much inclined to consider as peculiar to our own age.

However, as Agni, the sacrificial fire, was identified with the sacrificer and the priest, he participated likewise in all the good qualities of his prototypes, and was represented as kind, as wise, as enlightened, and as omniscient (visvavít, X. 91, 3). Thus he is called, VI. 14, 2, prá*k*etâ*h*, wise; VII. 4, 4, ayám kaví*h* ákavíshu prá*k*etâ*h*, the sage wise among the foolish; VI. 14, 2, vedhástama*h* *ri*shi*h*, the wisest poet. If any mistake has been committed, Agni is supposed to be able and willing to correct it. For instance, X. 2, 4–5:

4. Yát va*h* vayám praminấma vratấni
vidúshâm devâ*h* ávidush*t*arâsa*h*,
agní*h* tát vísvam ấ pri*n*âti vidvấn
yébhi*h* devấn *ri*túbhi*h* kalpáyâti.

5. Yát pâkatrấ mánasâ dînádakshâ*h*
ná ya*gñ*ásya manvaté mártyâsa*h*,
agní*h* tát hótâ kratuvít vi*g*ânán
yá*g*ish*th*a*h* devấn *ri*tusá*h* ya*g*âti.

'If we, O gods, impair your statutes, we ignorant among the wise, Agni makes it all good, he who knows at what seasons to place the gods.

'Whatever of the sacrifice weak mortals with their feeble intellect do not comprehend, Agni, the Hot*ri* priest, who knows all rites, comprehends it, and he will worship the gods at the proper seasons.'

Hymn to Agni.

In order to give you an idea what an ordinary Vedic hymn to Agni is like, I shall read you now the first hymn of the Rig-veda which is addressed to Agni. It is a poor hymn in many respects. First of all, it belongs to the first Ma*nd*ala, which, as I pointed out before, contains many hymns merely put together for the sake of the sacrifice, and possibly of a later date. It repeats the ordinary praises and invocations of Agni which we find elsewhere in the Veda, and treats Agni simply as the sacrificial fire, as the divine priest by the side of the ordinary human priests. Yet it contains a few expressions which are of value to us, because expressive of a genuine human feeling, particularly the last verse, where Agni is implored to be 'easy of approach as a father is to his son.'

Hymn to Agni,

ascribed to Madhu*kkh*andas of the family of Visvâmitra, written in Gâyatrî metre.

1. Agním î*l*e puróhitam ya*gñ*ásya devám *ri*tví*g*am, hótâra*m* ratnadhấtamam.

'I implore Agni, the chief priest, the divine minister of the sacrifice, the Hot*ri* priest, the best giver of wealth.'

The verb î*l*e is not only 'I praise,' but 'I implore;' and the Nirukta explains it by adhyesha*n*â, solicitation, or pû*g*â, worship. Thus, Rv. III. 48, 3, we read upasthấya mâtáram ánnam ai*tt*a, he (the new-born Indra) having approached his mother asked for food; unless we prefer to translate, he having approached, asked his mother for food, making both accusatives dependent on the verb. Cf. Rv. VII. 93, 4. The verb î*d* is construed with the accusative of the god implored, with the dative of the object for which, and the instrumental of the means by which, he is implored; cf. Rv. VIII. 71, 14, agním î*l*ishva ávase gấthâbhi*h*. Stress ought to be laid on devam, divine, the adjective to *ritvig*, minister, Agni being here called the divine minister as contrasted with the ministering priests.

2. Agní*h* pū́rvebhi*h* *rí*shibhi*h* ī́*d*yo nū́tanai*h* utá,
sá*h* devā́n ā́ ihá vakshati.

'Agni, worthy to be implored by former poets and by new, may he bring the gods hither!'

Remarkable only for its allusion to former poets or Rishis, an expression which frequently occurs.

3. Agnínâ rayím a*s*navat pósham eva divé-dive,
ya*s*ásam vī́rávattamam.

'Through Agni man gained wealth, satisfying even day by day, glorious wealth of vigorous kindred.'

The imperfect asnavat implies that man always gained wealth through their sacrifices. The third person singular is used without a noun, in the sense of 'one gains.' The adjective vîravattama is well explained by Sâya*n*a, and well translated by Benfey, *heldenreichsten*. It implies that the wealth consists in a large number of sons, and relations, and slaves, who constituted the wealth and strength of the ancient Aryan settlers in India.

4. Ágne yám ya*g*ñám adhvarám vi*s*váta*h* paribhū́*h* ási,
sá*h* ít devéshu ga*kk*hati.

'Agni, the offering which thou encirclest on all sides, unhurt, that alone goes to the gods.'

The adjective adhvara, unhurt, belongs to ya*gñ*a, an offering. There is no necessity for translating adhvara by 'without fraud,' as Benfey does. Adhvara means originally 'without hurt,' from a, and dhvara, root dhvar. The idea that whatever is offered to the gods must be free from hurt and blemish is common to Aryan and Semitic nations. In Homer the victim must be τέλειος, perfect (Friedrich, *Realien*, p. 444), and ἱερὰ τέλεια, are perfect sacrifices, performed with all rites. Moses (Leviticus iii. 1) commands: 'And if his oblation be a sacrifice of peace offering, if he offer it of the herd; whether it be a male or a female, he shall offer it *without blemish* before the Lord.' In the ritual Sûtras of the Brâhmans the same idea is constantly expressed, and the whole chapter on Prâya*sk*itta or penance refers to remedies against accidents happening during a sacrifice. Agni, in particular, is implored not to injure the offering. (Rv. X. 16, 1; see also *History of Anc. S. L.*, p. 553 seq., and Nirukta, ed Roth, p. xl.) From being originally an adjective constantly applied to sacrifices, adhvara, masc., came to be used by itself in the sense of sacrifice, and adhvaryu became the name of the ministering priest.

5. Agní*h* hótâ kavíkratu*h* satyá*h* *k*itrá*s*ravastama*h*,
devá*h* devébhi*h* ấ gamat.

'Agni, the Hot*ri* priest, the wise counsellor[1], the truthful, the most glorious, may he, the god, come with the gods!'

[1] It is next to impossible to render these pregnant Sanskrit words. There is in most of them the etymological background discernible without great effort, and not too distant from the real and traditional meaning. In kavikratu we have kavi, a poet, a sage, and kratu, counsel, agreeing with the German *Rath*, as meaning both thought and deed. Wise counsellor renders only half of the Sanskrit term; wise-minded is not much better. On *Rath* and its supposed connection with râdhas, see Kuhn, *Zeitschrift*, vi. 390.

6. Yát angá dâ*s*úshe tvám ágne bhadrám karishyási,
táva ít tát satyám angira*h*.

'Whatever wealth thou, Agni, shalt bestow on the sacrificer, thine it will be[1], forsooth, O Angiras[2].

[1] The idea of bargaining with the gods is frequent in the Veda.

[2] Angiras is a name of Agni, but it also became a name of a family or clan, the Angiras. Its original meaning seems to have been bright or shining, and popular etymology naturally, and it seems rightly, connected it with angâra, cinders. As there were two kinds of Angiras, namely, the bright rays of light personified in various aspects of nature, and represented by Agni, the chief of the Angiras (*g*yésh*th*am ángirasâm, the oldest of the Angiras, Rv. I. 127, 2), and secondly the clan of the Angiras, many of them distinguished as priests and poets, the race of the Angiras is often derived from Agni, and the two are often confounded.

7. Úpa tvâ agne divé-dive dóshâ-vasta*h* dhiyấ vayám,
náma*h* bhárant*ah* ấ imasi.

'To thee, O Agni, we come day by day, bringing praise in mind, O illuminator of darkness.'

To bring praise in mind is to pray. Doshâvastar occurs three times in the Rig-veda. In our passage the commentator explains it as an adverb, by night and by day. Rv. IV. 4, 9, he allows both meanings, either by night and by day, or illuminator and dispeller of darkness. In VII. 15, 15, he only gives the second interpretation, because divâ naktam, by day and by night, occurs in the same verse. The true meaning therefore seems the second, irradiator of night or of darkness, from doshâ, darkness, and vastar, a vocative of vastri, lightener. With this the accent too agrees. Rv. VII. 1, 6, the expression doshā́ vástoh occurs, meaning by night and by day. Cf. Rv. VIII. 25, 21; V. 32, 11, &c.

8. Rā́gantam adhvarā́nâm gopā́m ritásya dī́divim,
várdhamânam své dáme.

'To thee, the lord of sacrifices, the bright guardian of the law, who art growing in thy own house.'

Dîdivi occurs but once in the Rig-veda. It is formed from div or dyu, to shine, like gâgrivih. Cf. Unâdi-sûtras IV. 54-56. It might be a substantive as well as an adjective. As, however, the phrases râgantam adhvarânâm and gopâm ritasya are stereotyped phrases, we could not well connect dîdivim with ritasya, as it were, the lord or ruler of law; but must take it as an adjective. (Râgantam adhvarânâm, Rv. I. 45, 4; I. 27, 1 (sam); VIII. 8, 18 (asvinau).) If it were not for this, the interpretation of Sâyana might be adopted: 'To thee, the brilliant, the guardian of sacrifices, the revealer of order.'

Rita means what is settled, ordered, what is right and holy. This is the primitive meaning which can be perceived in all its manifold applications.

9. Sáh nah pitā́ iva sûnáve ágne sûpâyanáh bhava,
sákasva nah svastáye.

'Thou, then, O Agni, be gracious to us like as a father to his son; stay with us for our welfare!'

Sûpâyana, gracious, literally of easy access. The comparison of the god Agni with a father being gracious to his son, the worshipper, is remarkable. The number of such simple and genuine sentiments is small in the Veda.

The next hymn is less formal, though again full of references to the ceremonial. Verse 6, however, is probably a later addition.

Mandala I, Sûkta 94.

1. Let us skilfully build up this hymn of praise, like a chariot, for the worthy Gâtavedas (the omniscient Agni); for his protection is blissful to our homestead:—O Agni, let us not suffer in thy friendship!

2. He for whom thou sacrificest, succeeds, he dwells unhurt, he gathers strength. He prospers, and evil does not touch him:—O Agni, let us not suffer in thy friendship!

3. May we be able to light thee, fulfil thou our prayers; in thee the gods consume the poured-out libation. Bring thou hither the Âdityas, for we long for them:—O Agni, let us not suffer in thy friendship!

4. Let us bring wood, let us prepare the libations, thinking of thee at every phase of the moon. Fulfil our prayers that we may live longer:—O Agni, let us not suffer in thy friendship!

5. He is the guardian of men[1], his creatures—all that is two-footed and four-footed—move about freely by night. Thou art the bright and great shine of the dawn:—O Agni, let us not suffer in thy friendship!

[6. Thou art the Adhvaryu priest, and the old Hot*ri* priest, thou art the Prasâst*ri* and Pot*ri* priest, and the Purohita by birth; knowing all duties of the priests, thou prosperest, O wise one:—O Agni, let us not suffer in thy friendship!]

7. Thou who art always alike[2], beautiful to behold on every side, thou blazest forth, like lightning, though being far off; thou glancest forth even above the darkness of the night:—O Agni, let us not suffer in thy friendship!

8. O gods, let the chariot of the sacrificer come first, let our curse overcome the wicked. Accept and

[1] Cf. I. 96, 4.

[2] It might be better to read yá*h* visvá*tah* suprátîka*h* susa*m*d*risah*; see I. 143, 3.

prosper this our speech:—O Agni, let us not suffer in thy friendship!

9. Strike away with thy weapons the evil-wishers, and the wicked, the devourers, whether they be far or near; then make it easy for thy praiser to sacrifice:—O Agni, let us not suffer in thy friendship!

10. When thou hast yoked the two red mares to the chariot, quick like the wind, then thy roar is like a bull's, and thou stirrest the trees with thy smoke-bannered flame:—O Agni, let us not suffer in thy friendship!

11. Then the birds also tremble before thy shout; when thy grass-devouring sparks are scattered about, the road is made easy for thee and thy chariot:—O Agni, let us not suffer in thy friendship!

12. This is the marvellous fury of the storm winds, for the support of Mitra and Varu*n*a. O have pity on us, let their (kind) mind return to us:—O Agni, let us not suffer in thy friendship!

13. Thou art the god of gods, the marvellous friend, thou art the Vasu of Vasus, beautiful at the sacrifice. O let us abide under thy far-reaching protection:—O Agni, let us not suffer in thy friendship!

14. This is thy blessing that, when once kindled in his house and fed with Soma, thou bestirrest thyself as the most gracious friend, and givest treasure and wealth to thy worshipper:—O Agni, let us not suffer in thy friendship!

15. May we be of those to whom thou, O wealthy god, grantest sinlessness, O Aditi, at all times, and whom thou fillest with happy strength, and with wealth of offspring.

16. O thou, Agni, who knowest true welfare,

lengthen our life, O god. May Mitra and Varu*n*a achieve this for us, also Aditi, Sindhu, the Earth and the Sky!

We have now finished the biography of Agni as a purely mythological god. In our next lecture I shall try to show, how Agni is slowly being divested of all that is mythological, and stands before us in the end with the name of Agni, but with the nature of true Divinity.

LECTURE VIII.

AGNI AS DIVESTED OF HIS MATERIAL CHARACTER.

Later Development of Agni.

WE saw in our last lecture how Agni, the fire, grew as it were before our eyes, from a mere spark of light to the dignity of a kind and omniscient being, a Deva, or, if you like, a god. Nowhere in the annals of the human intellect have we an opportunity of watching this natural theogonic process in such fulness as in India, for I need not tell you that the specimens which I was able to place before you, form but an insignificant portion of what the Vedic poets have to say about Agni. The most important lesson which the evidence, so far as we have examined it, should teach us is this, that there is nothing that is not perfectly natural and intelligible in the development of this concept up to the stage which we have now reached, where Agni stands before us in every respect the equal of such beings as we are accustomed to call gods, I mean Apollo in Greece, or Mercury in Italy, or Odin in Germany. We saw that Agni, like other gods, could boast of many fathers and mothers, and, like other gods in Greece and Italy, he also has acquired a wife, Agnâyî (Rv. I. 22, 12; V. 46, 8), though we do not know much more of her than her name. Agni, so far, has become what we should call a mythological god.

But his career does not end there; on the contrary, it becomes more and more interesting and important to us, as showing how the natural theogonic process which we have hitherto watched, does not stop there, but forms the foundation only, and the only safe foundation from which in later times the highest, the truest, nay, from which something exactly like our own conception of the Deity has sprung.

If you remember the many things that were said of Agni, the various names by which he was called, the different phenomena of nature in which his presence was suspected, you will find it easy to understand how behind these various apparitions a more and more general character grew up, a being that was Agni, but was nevertheless distinct from all these individual manifestations. We saw how Agni was perceived in the fire on the altar, in the spark produced by a powerful friction of fire-sticks, in the lightning that sprang from the sky and the clouds and consumed vast forests, like a horse champing his hay, and finally in the immortal light of the sun.

Now, it is clear that Agni, who was all these things, could also be divested of every one of these attributes, and yet remain Agni. This led to two trains of thought. Agni was either identified with other Devas who likewise represented the sun, the sky, and the lightning, or he was more and more divested of his purely material attributes, and recognised as a supreme deity, in every sense of the word.

Agni identical with other Gods.

The first process, that of identification, is very prominent in the Veda. It could hardly be otherwise but that, after nature had been peopled with ever so many Devas, some of them should encroach on each other's domains, and be no longer distinguishable one from the other. This has been very well brought out by Professor von Schroeder in his book on the *Literature and Culture of India* (p. 77). 'It should be pointed out,' he says, 'that many of the Vedic gods coincide from the beginning in their spheres of action, and cover one another almost entirely in their character and functions, so that each may be said to represent but a slightly varying conception of the same phenomenon. Thus Dyaus was the sky as shining, but Varu*n*a also was originally the sky, as all-embracing. Sûrya was the sun, but Savitar also was the sun, as imparting movement and life to all creatures. Pûshan also was the sun, as giving prosperity to the flocks, and light and leading to the wanderer on his journey. Vish*n*u lastly was the sun, as striding across the regions of the sky. Indra was the powerful lord, the begetter of storm, thunder, lightning, and rain. But the same is said of Par*g*anya, and B*ri*haspati also performs much the same work. Rudra is the storm, the Maruts are the storms, Vâta is the wind, and so is Vâyu. It seems clear that this peculiarity of the Vedic gods is closely connected with what has been called their *henotheistic* character, and that it contributed to its formation.'

Henotheism.

What Professor von Schroeder here calls the henotheistic character is, indeed, a very important and instructive feature in the development of all religious thought, though it is nowhere so prominent as in the religion of the Veda. It was formerly supposed that there were only three forms of religion possible, *Polytheism*, *Monotheism*, and *Atheism*. But in the Veda, and elsewhere also, it has become necessary to distinguish Polytheism from a previous stage, which may best be called Henotheism. What we mean by Polytheism is a belief in many gods, who, by the very fact that they are many and stand side by side, are limited in their divine character. They generally form together a kind of Pantheon, and are mostly, though not always, represented as subject to a supreme god. Polytheism therefore implies the admission of a number of beings who all claim a kind of equality, so far as their divine character is concerned, who are conceived, in fact, as members of one class, and whose divinity is consequently a limited divinity, or, if we hold that divinity cannot be limited, no true divinity at all.

But there are, as I said just now, clear traces of a totally different phase of religious thought in the Veda. No doubt, the number of gods invoked in the hymns of the Rig-veda is very considerable, and in this sense the Vedic religion may be called polytheistic. In many hymns where different gods are invoked together, the conception of divinity shared by them all, is as limited as in Homer. But there are other hymns in which the poet seems to know, for the time being, of one single god only. That single god is to him the only god, and in the momentary vision of the poets his divinity is not limited by the thought of any other god. This phase of thought, this worship, not of many, nor of one only god, but of a single god, I called *Henotheism,* a name which is now accepted by the most competent authorities as representing an important phase in the development of religious ideas [1]. It may be that India, where social life was chiefly developed in families, clans, and village-communities, favoured the growth and permanence of this worship of single deities more than any other country; but, from a psychological point of view, it seems as if all polytheism must have passed through this previous phase, and as if everywhere, whether consciously or unconsciously, the progress must have been from the single to the many, and finally to the one.

But apart from all theories, the fact remains that in the religious childhood of India, as represented to us in the hymns of the Veda, we can see this henotheistic tendency fully developed. We can see a poet, or a family, or a clan, or a village believing in this or that god as for the time and for certain purposes the only god, yet quite ready, under new circumstances, to invoke the help of another god who again stands supreme, or, more correctly, stands alone, before the mind of the suppliant, as his only helper in distress.

[1] It is to be regretted that other scholars should have used the name henotheistic in a different sense from that which I assigned to it. Nothing causes so much confusion as the equivocal use of technical terms, and the framer of a new term has generally had the right of defining it.

Henotheism in Finland.

The same henotheistic character was pointed out by Castrén in his *Lectures on Finnish Mythology*. He described it fully, though he did not give it any definite name. 'In general,' he writes, 'the single deities of the Finnish mythology do not, as in Greek and Roman mythology, seem dependent on each other. Each god, however small he may be, acts in his own sphere as a free and independent power, or, if we use the language of the runes, as host in his own house. As among mortals, so among immortals, one host is rich and powerful, possessed of wide-stretching lands, large flocks, numerous man- and maid-servants, while another has but a small property, a small family or none at all. Yet within their own walls each enjoys the same independence. The god of a star rules only over an insignificant spot in the sky, but on that spot he is his own host and master.'

Early Scepticism.

I must protest against the supposition that I had ever represented the whole of the Vedic religion as henotheistic. I seldom speak of the whole of the Vedic religion, for the simple reason that it does not form a whole, but represents to us in its numerous hymns several phases of the early religious thought of India. That is the very thing which makes the Veda so instructive to students of religion. There are hymns in which the gods have been counted and represented as all alike, none greater, none smaller. There are others in which one god is praised as greater than another god, nay, as greater than all other gods.

It could not be otherwise. The great natural phenomena of which the gods were supposed to be the secret agents, though they might seem all powerful by themselves, showed also clear traces of their mutual limitations. When the fire was seen quenched by water, or the sun was seen hidden in the clouds or sunk into the sea, the poet could only repeat what he saw, that Agni was hidden in the water, that the sun was swallowed by the clouds. We saw how these ideas were expressed mythologically, but they acted also in a different direction. They provoked the first doubts in the omnipotence, nay in the very existence of certain gods of nature.

We find traces of this early scepticism in the well-known dialogue ascribed to Abraham and Nimrod [1]. Here it is said that fire should not be worshipped, because water can quench it; nor water, because the clouds can carry it; nor the clouds, because the winds tear them; nor the winds, because even men can withstand them [2].

The same scepticism appears in the remarkable story of the Inca Tupac Yupanqui, as told by Garcilasso (viii. 8). Though it may have been embellished by the Jesuit Blas Valera, on whose authority Garcilasso tells it, it seems to have had an historical foundation. That Inca, though himself reputed a son of the sun, began to doubt the divine omnipotence of his divine ancestor [3].

At a great religious council, held at the consecration of the newly-built temple of the Sun at Cazco, about

[1] Beer, *Leben Abrahams*, p. xi.

[2] See Whitley Stokes, *Academy*, No. 933, p. 207.

[3] Réville, *Les Religions du Mexique*, p. 321; Brinton, *Myths of the New World*, p. 55.

1440, he rose before the assembled multitude to deny the divinity of the Sun. 'Many say,' he began, 'that the Sun is the maker of all things. But he who makes should abide by what he has made. Now many things happen when the Sun is absent; therefore he cannot be the universal Creator. And that he is alive at all, is doubtful, for his journeys do not tire him. Were he a living thing, he would grow weary like ourselves; were he fire, he would visit other parts of the heavens. He is like a tethered beast who makes a daily round; he is like an arrow which must go whither it is sent, not whither it wishes. I tell you that he, our Father and Maker, the Sun, must have a lord and master more powerful than himself, who constrains him to his daily circuit without pause or rest.'

Surely, this speech forms one of the brightest moments in the whole history of religion, and our bold Inca deserves a place by the side of Luther at the Diet of Worms.

Exchange of Gods.

If I have succeeded in making the henotheistic phase of religious thought clear to you, you will understand how rightly Professor von Schroeder remarked that the later identification of several gods, which is also very prominent in the Veda, is closely connected with this henotheistic tendency. If two families or two villages, each having their own name for the god of fire, came into closer contact, nothing was more natural for them than to say, What you call the morning sun we call the dawn; what you call Agni, fire, we call Dyaus, light; what you call

Sûrya, the sun, we call Savit*ri*, the enlivener. If Agni, as we saw, meant light and fire and warmth in its various manifestations, no wonder that the Vedic poets identified Agni with the various names under which light and fire and warmth had assumed a certain individuality in their ancient religious phraseology. Thus we read, Rv. V. 3, 1–2:

Tvám agne váru*n*a*h* *g*âyase yát
tvám mitrá*h* bhavasi yát sámiddha*h*,
tvé vísve sahasa*h* putra devā́*h*
tvám índra*h* dâsúshe mártyâya.

Tvám aryamā́ bhavasi yát kanī́nâm
nā́ma svadhâvan gū́hyam bibharshi,
añ*g*ánti mitrám sûdhitam ná góbhi*h*
yát dámpatî sámanasâ k*r*i*n*óshi.

'Thou, O Agni, art Varu*n*a, when thou art born; thou art Mitra, when thou art kindled; in thee, O son of strength, are *all* the gods; thou art Indra to the generous mortal.

'Thou art Aryaman, when with the girls, thou bearest a secret name. When thou makest the husband and wife to be of one mind, they anoint thee with butter as a welcome friend.'

Or again in the Atharva-veda[1] (XIII. 3, 13) we read:

Sá*h* váru*n*a*h* sâyám agní*h* bhavati
sá*h* mitrá*h* bhavati prâtá*h* udyán;
sá*h* savitā́ bhûtvā́ ántarikshe*n*a yâti
sá*h* índra*h* bhûtvā́ tapati madhyatá*h* divám.

'In the evening Agni becomes Varu*n*a; he becomes Mitra when rising in the morning; having become Savit*ri* he passes through the sky; having become Indra he warms the heaven in the centre.'

In another place the idea that Agni is or comprehends all other gods is expressed metaphorically, Rv. V. 13, 6:

Ágne nemí*h* arā́n iva devā́n tvám paribhū́*h* asi.

'O Agni, thou surroundest the gods, as a felly the spokes of a wheel.'

[1] *Hibbert Lectures*, p. 297.

In other hymns[1] this idea of identifying Agni with every possible god is carried to excess, and may be merely the fancy of individual poets.

Dual Deities.

But that the common character of certain gods was clearly perceived by the people at large, we can see best in a number of dual names which have become the recognised titles of certain deities[2]. Thus we find hymns addressed to Agni and Indra as one deity, called Indrâgnî; to Agni and Soma, then called Agnîshomau—a process similar, probably, to that which in Greek led to such combined names as *Phoebos Apollon* and *Pallas Athene*, where two originally distinct names were likewise recognised as, to all intents and purposes, identical names, and the gods as identical gods.

Reconciliation of the Solar and Meteoric Theories.

A clear recognition of this religious syncretism, or rather of the common foundation of three such gods as those of the sun, the lightning, and the fire, may help us to remove a difficulty which has hitherto divided Comparative Mythologists into two hostile, or, at all events, separate camps. The two schools, called the *solar* and *meteorological*, were often driven to explain the same myth as developed originally from solar phenomena, such as the sudden effulgence of the dawn, the fight of the sun against the darkness of the night, and the victorious return of the light of the morning; or from meteoric events, such as the sudden

[1] Rv. II. 1.

[2] *Hibbert Lectures*, p. 297.

effulgence of the lightning, the fight of the storm-god against the dark clouds, and the victorious return of the blue sky at the end of a thunder-storm.

These two systems of mythological interpretation, which for a time seemed irreconcilable, may after all find their common justification in the fact which we discovered in our analysis of the growth of Agni, recognised as present not only in the sun, but in the lightning also, both being manifestations of the same bright power, both performing similar deeds, though under different circumstances. Professor Tiele, in his excellent essay, *Le Mythe de Kronos*, 1886 (p. 17), has shown very clearly that there are deities who are at the same time gods of the dawn, the sun, and the thunder.

Supremacy of Agni.

But besides this process of identification which led to such conceptions as the Visve Devâs, the All-gods, and in the end to the more or less well-founded suspicion that all the names of the gods were names of one nameless power, there was another result, springing from what I explained before as the henotheistic tendency of the Vedic Rishis, namely, the exaltation of one or other of these single gods to the rank of a supreme deity.

This last stage in the development of divine beings is again very fully represented in the case of Agni. Other gods also share the same fate[1]. Indra, for instance, is constantly celebrated as the strongest and most heroic of gods, and in one of the hymns addressed to him, every verse ends with the words, visvasmâd Indra uttara*h*, 'Indra is greater than

[1] *Hibbert Lectures*, p. 293.

all.' Of Varu*n*a it is said that he is lord of all, of heaven and earth, that he is king of gods and men, that he rules the world, that he knows the past and the future, and that he rewards the virtuous and punishes the evil-doer. Nor is this character of supremacy ascribed to such mighty gods only as Indra and Varu*n*a. Soma, a god of whose original character we perceive but few traces in the Veda, and who has become identified simply with an intoxicating drink used at the sacrifice, is nevertheless praised as the king of heaven and earth, of men and gods, the giver of life, nay, the giver of immortality.

Let us now return to Agni. Let us remember that Agni was at first simply *ignis*, the fire. It was a name for certain luminous manifestations, comprehended under the name of Agni, which, so far as we know, meant originally not much more than *agile*, quickly moving.

The General Name of Deity.

Let us remember also that, in accordance with the fact that most words are formed from roots, and most roots are expressive of human acts, Agni, the agile, had to be conceived and named as an agent, an actor, though nothing was said as to who that actor was. It was enough that he was known and named from one of his manifestations as a quick mover or runner. Other names and epithets were added from time to time to make him better known and better named in every one of his modes of acting and modes of being, but he always remained Agni, the quick.

We saw also that one of his earliest epithets was deva, bright, and that he shared that epithet with many other unknown agents, the sun, the sky, the dawn, and others, who were all called Devas, the bright. Now it is clear that when a number of different objects are comprehended under the same name, that name becomes *ipso facto* a general name. These general names mark a most important period in the growth of language, and, what is the same, in the growth of the human mind. Individual objects, when brought under a general name, are divested for the time of their distinguishing features, and named or known by one prominent feature only, which they all share in common, and which is expressed by the general name. On the other hand, the general name, applied to them all, becomes likewise less definite than it was when applied to one object only, so that in the end it expresses not much more than some very general quality shared in common by a number of otherwise quite different beings.

When Agni, fire, was called deva, bright, there could be little doubt what was meant. But when the sun, the sky, the dawn, the day, the spring, and the rivers were all called deva, the brightness they shared in common had become, if I may say so, a very diluted brightness. On the other hand, the different objects or agents, now comprehended under the name of Devas, had so far to surrender their respective characters, or their peculiar modes of agency, that when they had all alike become conceived as Devas, deva could mean hardly more than sunny, cheerful, kind, and beneficent. If then Agni, fire, and Dyaus, the sky, and Ushas, the dawn, and all the rest were all called Devas, or sunny, cheerful, kind, and beneficent agents, unknown agents, powerful agents, never ceasing, never dying, immortal agents,—had not the word Deva then reached very nearly the general or abstract meaning of gods, at least of what we call the gods of the ancient world?

Evolution of Concepts.

So far, I think, it will be admitted that nothing of what is called supernatural, no miracles in the modern sense of that word, no superhuman revelation were required to account for the simple and perfectly intelligible evolution of the concept of deity. What should we give if in any realm of nature we could watch that wonderful process of evolution, of growth or development, so clearly as here in the realm of thought? If some students of physical science come to us and tell us of the great discovery of evolution in the nineteenth century, and express a hope that we also, we poor metaphysicians, and psychologists, and philologists should become evolutionists, one hardly knows what to say.

What have we been doing all this time but trying to understand how things have become what they are, how from a few roots language, by an uninterrupted growth, developed into the endless varieties, now scattered all over the world; how from a few simple concepts the infinitude of thought was evolved which represents the intellectual wealth of mankind; and how philosophers, as distant from one another as Kant and Thales, are nevertheless held together by an unseen chain in the historical march that led them nearer and nearer to the truth.

Really, to be told, as we were lately by Professor

Romanes in his *Origin of Human Faculty*, p. 240, that 'the idea that language was the result of natural growth could not be appreciated in its full significance, before the advent of the general theory of evolution,' that 'till the middle of the present century the possibility of language having been the result of a natural growth, was not sufficiently recognised,' and that it was 'the same year that witnessed the publication of the *Origin of Species* (1859) which gave to science the first issue of Steinthal's *Zeitschrift für Völkerpsychologie und Sprachwissenschaft*,' is enough to take away one's breath[1]. It is nearly as bad as when Mr. M. Conway tells us that not a single society for the protection of animals existed before the publication of Darwin's book. *The Origin of Species* appeared in 1859; the Society for Prevention of Cruelty to Animals was founded in 1824. The idea of evolution was more fully recognised and more clearly defined by the students of language than it has ever been by the students of nature, and they certainly did not wait for the advent in 1859, before explaining what was meant by genealogical, what by morphological classification; what was meant by dialects (varieties), by families of speech (genera); what was meant by the constant elimination of useless words, which is but another and a more correct name for natural selection. If Professor Romanes says, *Even* Professor Max Müller insists that 'no student of the science of language can be anything but an evolutionist, for, wherever he looks, he sees nothing but evolution going on all around him,' what

[1] Wilhelm von Humboldt died in 1835. His great work on the *Kawi-sprache*, with the introduction, *Über die Verschiedenheit des menschlichen Sprachbaues*, appeared in 1836-40.

is the meaning of that *even?* *Even* before Professor Romanes joined the ranks of evolutionists, I had in the warmest terms greeted the discoveries of Darwin, as a biologist, because they lent such strong support to the theories put forward long ago by comparative philologists, and they enabled them to see many things far more clearly by their analogies with his theories. Unfortunately, Darwin had been misinformed as to the results obtained by the Science of Language, having consulted some personal friends whom he trusted, and who were not quite competent to give the necessary information. It was in the interest of the true theory of evolution, in support of true against false Darwinism, that I published my criticism of Darwin's Views on Language, not as an opponent of the theory of evolution. That theory has no stronger fortress than the Science of Language, of Thought, and of Religion. For it is here that evolution stands before us as a simple fact, and not, as is so often the case in nature, as a mere hope and desire. We have here no missing links, but one perfect and unbroken chain.

The Highest Concept of Deity.

And now we have another and a much more important step to make. Many philosophers, many historians, many students of the evolution of the human mind would readily grant that the human mind, unassisted by any but the great natural miracles by which it finds itself surrounded from the first moments of its conscious life, might have reached the concept of gods, such as we find it in the ancient religions of the world, in what have often been called natural religions as distinct from supernatural religions. But they would demur, if asked to admit that the highest concept of God, such as we find it among Jews, Christians, and possibly among Mohammedans, was within the reach of unassisted human reason. We need not inquire why they should have so strong a wish that it should be so, and why others should wish with the same intensity that it should not be so. If it can be shown that the highest and purest concept of deity has been the result of a natural and perfectly intelligible evolution, all we have to do is to study the facts which history has preserved to us, and then to draw our own conclusions. Let those who hold that the highest concept of deity is unattainable without a special revelation, put down those attributes of deity which they believe are outside the ken of natural religion. Let us then put by the side of them the divine attributes which are the property of natural religion, and if there remain any that cannot be matched, let us then freely admit that these were unattainable by man as placed in this world, though it is a world of unceasing miracle and of never-ending revelation.

There is one powerful prejudice against which all believers in evolution have to guard. When we see the last result of an evolution we are loth to identify it with its simple and often apparently very mean beginnings. When we see the mouth of the Thames, which can be as wild and as terrific as the ocean itself, we can hardly believe that it began with the few trickling rills on the south-eastern slope of the Cotswolds. When we look up to the towering branches of an ancient oak tree, we cannot realise how it should have sprung from one of those small decaying acorns that lie scattered round its roots. And when we admire the beauty of a full-grown man, we almost shrink from the idea that not many years ago that noblest work of nature was nothing but a plastic cell, undistinguishable, to our eyes at least, from any other cell that might in time develop into a dog or an ape.

It is the same with our words. Their original meaning is often so commonplace and so material that nothing but downright facts can force us to believe that, for instance, such abstract terms as to *perceive* and to *conceive* are derived from *capio*, to lay hands on a thing. But because *aspiration* and *inspiration* come from the same source as *respiration* and *perspiration*, they lose nothing of that sublime meaning with which in the course of time they have been invested. If, therefore, we should find that the highest and purest concept of divinity had slowly been elaborated out of the primitive material concept of fire, that would in no way lower the divine concept. On the contrary, it would only serve to impress upon our minds the same lesson which nature teaches us again and again, namely, that the highest achievements are often connected by a continuous growth with the meanest beginnings, and that we are not to call common or unclean what has been cleansed by the spirit.

Agni, as Creator, Ruler, Judge.

With these warnings as a preface, let us now watch the latest phases in the growth of Agni. We saw him in the Veda as one of many single gods, afterwards as identified with other gods whose nature and functions he shared. We shall now see him, still with the name of Agni, though with little of his original physical character left, as the Supreme God.

From an Indian point of view, the idea of a creator of the world is by no means the highest idea of deity. Some Indian philosophers regard the character of a creator, whether explained as a maker, or architect, or operator of any kind, as even incompatible with their sublimest idea of God. But in the Veda, Agni is still distinctly conceived as the creator. In I. 96, 4, it is he who is called *g*anitā́ ródasyo*h*, the progenitor of heaven and earth; and in VII. 5, 7 it is said that he produced all things, bhúvanâ *g*anáyan. Sometimes this act of creation is represented as a spreading out of heaven and earth, as in III. 6, 5, táva krátvâ ródasî ā́ tatantha; or as a stretching out of heaven and earth like the stretching out of skins, VI. 8, 3, ví *k*árma*n*î iva dhishá*n*e avartayat, 'he unfolded heaven and earth, like two skins.' At other times it is said that Agni supported earth and heaven, I. 67, 5, and that he kept heaven and earth asunder, VI. 8, 3[1].

Being the maker, the creator, the progenitor of the world, he is likewise the supreme lord (samrâ*g*), the king of men (rā́*g*â k*ri*sh*t*înā́m mā́nushî*n*âm, I. 59, 5). Not only does his greatness exceed that of heaven, I. 59, 5, but his wisdom also is infinite. He knows all worlds, III. 55, 10, and his laws cannot be broken (II. 8, 3; VI. 7, 5).

Nor are his moral character and his kindness towards

[1] Cf. Isaiah xlii. 5, 'Thus saith God the Lord, he that created the heavens, and stretched them out; he that spread forth the earth and that which cometh out of it.' xl. 22, 'He that stretcheth out the heavens as a curtain, and spreadeth them out as a tent to dwell in.'

sinful man forgotten. For in IV. 12, 4 he is invoked in the following terms:

Yát *k*it hí te purushatrấ yavish*th*a
á*k*ittibhi*h* *k*akrimá kát *k*it ấga*h*,
k*ri*dhí sú asmấn ádite*h* ánâgân
ví énâ*m*si sisratha*h* víshvak agne.

'If we have committed any sin against thee through human weakness, through thoughtlessness, make us sinless before Aditi, O Agni, loosen our misdeeds from us on every side.'

And those who worship him and obey his commands do not prosper here on earth only, but it is believed that he can also impart to them immortality; I. 31, 7:

Tvám tám agne am*ri*tatvé
uttamé mártam dadhâsi.

'Thou placest that mortal in the highest immortality.'

Now, I ask, can we ourselves form a much more sublime conception of the deity than what we see the conception of Agni to have become in the Veda? Of Agni, the fire, there is little, nay, there is nothing left in that supreme god whose laws must be obeyed, and who can at the same time forgive those who have broken his laws, nay, who can promise to those who worship him, eternal life.

It is quite true that by the side of these sublime conceptions, we find also the most homely and childish ideas entertained of Agni by some of the Vedic poets. But that is not now the question. There is an ebb and flow in all religions. At present we want to know the highest mark which the tide of Vedic religion has ever reached, in order to understand what the human mind, left face to face with the natural revelation of this world, can achieve. Trusting to the fragments that have been preserved to us in the Veda, to the remains of the most childish as well as the most exalted thoughts, we may say that natural religion, or the natural faculties of man under the dominion of the natural impressions of the world around us, can lead, nay, has led man step by step to the highest conception of deity, a conception that can hardly be surpassed by any of those well-known definitions of deity which so-called supernatural religions have hitherto claimed as their exclusive property.

What I have just stated are either facts or no facts, but if they are facts, they should be accepted and inwardly digested in the same spirit in which St. Paul accepted and inwardly digested the facts that met his eyes when standing before the very altars of the heathen world. 'Whom ye ignorantly worship,' he said, 'Him declare I unto you,'—not a new god, not a god different in origin from their own, but the same god who had been ignorantly worshipped in the childhood of the world, who is ignorantly worshipped even now, but for whom the human heart and the human mind have always sought, in the bounds of their habitation, if haply they might feel after him and find him, though he is not far from every one of us.

The Dark Side of Vedic Religion.

Let us now look at the dark side of Indian religion. There could be no greater mistake than to attempt to hide it, for that dark side also has many lessons to teach us.

In the later Sanskrit literature, and in the epic poetry already, there is a decided falling off in the high conception of Agni, as the supreme deity, such as we saw it in the Veda. Or, at all events, there is a most puzzling mixture of different conceptions of Agni. In some places he is described as a man, or, if you like, as a god with dark yellow eyes (pingâksha), a red neck (lohitagrîva), and seven tongues, that is, flames. He appears in full armour with bow and disc (*k*akra), driving along on a chariot drawn by seven red horses. He is one of the eight Vasus, generally the first among them. These Vasus are the bright gods, Agni, fire; Soma, moon; Ahas, day; Anila, wind; Pratyûsha, dawn; Prabhâsa, light; Dhara (earth?); and Dhruva (sky?). His father is Brahmâ, his mother *S*â*nd*ilî. Other fathers and mothers of his are also mentioned, according to the different ways in which fire takes its origin. Sometimes Anila, wind, is called his father; sometimes Âpas, the waters, the clouds, his mothers. He is sometimes called his own father, because he was produced from himself and by himself (tanûnapât, svayoni, etc.). According to an old tradition Agni is represented as the brother of Dyaus, the sky, and the uncle of Indra, who, though perhaps mightier and more popular than Agni, is nevertheless a younger god. Indra is not a Vasu, but a Vâsava, a descendant of Vasu, probably of Dyaus. He is more the god of the Brâhmans, while Indra is more the god of the Kshatriyas.

Agni has even his love-affairs, like any of the Greek gods. In the Rig-veda already, I. 66, 8, he is called *g*ârá*h* kanî́nâm páti*h* *g*ánînâm, the lover of girls, the husband of wives. His wife Svâhâ often complains about his fancies for other ladies. He fell in love, for instance, with Mahishmatî [1], the daughter of king Nîla, and, as a consequence, the fire on the altars of the palace would never burn except when blown by

[1] Mahâbhârata II. 30, 1130.

the sweet breath of the young princess. The king is much incensed, but as Agni refuses altogether to burn in the palace, except on condition of receiving the princess as his wife, the king has to yield, and Agni becomes his son-in-law and his protector.

The same story happens a second time, when Agni refuses to burn at the sacrifice of king Duryodhana, unless he gives him his daughter Sudarsanâ. Here also the king has to yield, and Agni, in the form of a Brâhma*n*a, marries the young princess.

But in spite of this mythological and dramatic colouring which Agni has received, more particularly in the Purâ*n*as and in the ordinary superstitions of the day, the memory of his divine and supreme character has never entirely perished. Agni is known in the Mahâbhârata[1] also as omnipresent and omniscient, as the witness of all our acts, whether good or evil. He is conceived, not only as visible, but likewise as invisible, and dwelling within all things that have life. He is not only the lord of all things, of the world, of gods and men, but the creation of the world is ascribed to him, and it is said of him that he who created the world will, when the time comes (prâpte kâle), destroy it also (Mahâbhârata I. 232, 8417):

S*ri*sh*t*vâ lokâns trîn imân havyavâha,
kâle prâpte pa*k*asi puna*h* samiddha*h*,
tva*m* sarvasya bhuvanasya prasûtis
tvam evâgne bhavasi puna*h* pratish*th*â.

'O Havyavâha, thou, having created these three worlds, ripenest them (lit. cookest them) again when thou hast been kindled at the right time. Thou art the origin of the whole world, and thou alone art again its refuge.'

The purifying power of Agni is frequently put forward, and though he is said to hate all crimes, yet

[1] Holtzmann, *Agni nach den Vorstellungen des Mahâbhârata*, 1878, p. 5.

his favour can be gained even by the sinner by prayer and truthfulness. There is a prayer in the Mahâbhârata (II. 30, 1152) addressed by Sahadeva to Agni, where we can see the most curious mixture of his mythological and divine characters, and gain a valuable insight into the chaotic state of religious ideas in the later ages of Hinduism.

'O thou whose path is black, this undertaking is for thy sake, adoration be to thee! Thou art the mouth of the gods, thou art the sacrifice, O purifier! Thou art called the purifier (pâvaka) because thou purifiest, thou art the carrier (havyavâhana) because thou carriest the sacrificial offerings. The Vedas were produced for thy sake, and therefore thou art *G*âtavedas[1]. O Vibhâvasu, thou art *K*itrabhânu (with brilliant light), Suresa, the lord of gods, Anala (fire), the doorkeeper of heaven, the eater of offerings, the flaming, the crested. Thou art Vaisvânara (belonging to all men), with dark yellow eyes, the monkey, possessed of great splendour, the father of Kumâra (god of war), the holy, the son of Rudra (Rudragarbha), the maker of gold. May Agni give me splendour, Vâyu breath, the Earth strength, and the Waters happiness! O thou son of the waters, powerful *G*âtavedas, lord of gods, mouth of the gods, O Agni, do thou purify me by thy truth! O thou, who art always well worshipped at the sacrifices by Rishis, Brâhma*n*as, gods or demons, do thou purify me by thy truth! O thou, with smoke as thy banner, crested, destroyer of sin, born of wind, always abiding within living things, do thou purify me by thy truth!'

[1] An impossible etymology, resting on a misunderstanding of Agni's Vedic name *G*âtavedas, i.e. knowing all that exists, like visva-vedas, knowing all things.

Such ideas as we here find mixed up together, may seem to us quite incompatible.

Anthropomorphism.

But we must not forget that the anthropomorphic tendencies in man are well-nigh irresistible. The old commandment, 'Thou shalt not make to thyself any graven image, nor the likeness of anything that is in heaven above, or in the earth beneath, or in the water under the earth,' has been broken by nearly all religions, if not by making likenesses, at least by conceiving the Deity in the likeness of man. In the ancient Vedic religion there is no sign as yet of graven images, and though many human qualities are attributed to the gods, they never assumed that plastic human character which they have in Greece. Still, the anthropomorphic tendency was there, particularly in later times.

The Sage Nârada.

There is a curious legend, preserved by Al-Birûnî (I. 116), of an Indian sage, called Nârada, a son of Brahman. He had but one desire, that of seeing God, and used to walk about, holding a stick. If he threw it down it became a serpent, and he was able to work other miracles with it. One day, being engrossed in meditation on the object of his hopes, he saw a fire from afar. He went towards it, and then a voice spoke to him out of the fire: 'What you demand and wish is impossible. You cannot see me save thus.' When Nârada looked in that direction, he saw a fiery appearance in something like a human shape. Henceforward it has been the custom to erect idols of certain shapes!

There is a deep meaning in this story, a consciousness of our human weakness to conceive God except in the likeness of man. However, the story may be late, and the writer may possibly have been acquainted with the story of Moses.

Influence of Children on Religion.

No doubt, the childish legends about the gods may originally have grown up among the uneducated classes; they may have been intended for children only who could not be fed on stronger food. But what we have learnt in our childhood is surrounded by a halo which often lasts for life, and what is old and has been handed down from mother to child, retains a sacredness of its own, often beyond the reach of reflection or argument. We must never forget that all religions, particularly in their earliest stages, represent the thoughts of the highest and the lowest layers of society, and that many a story told at first in good faith by an old grandmother, may in time become a sacred narrative.

If all the stories that are told by the common people in Roman Catholic countries about St. Peter, as the doorkeeper of heaven, and his very free-and-easy conversations with God, the Father; if all the miracles of the childhood of Christ, contained in the spurious Gospels; if all the circumstances attending the supposed apparitions of the Virgin in ancient, in mediaeval, and even in modern times, had been reduced to writing, we should then have something corresponding to the silly stories about Agni and other gods which we find in India in the epic poems and in the Purâ*n*as. However, as the level of civilisation and good taste is higher in Europe than it is in India, it is certainly true that in Europe the corruption of religion has never gone so far as in India. There are some portions of the Bible which, I believe, most Christians would not be sorry to miss. But that is nothing in comparison to the absurd and even revolting stories occurring in Sanskrit books which are called sacred. In that respect it is quite true that there is no comparison between our own sacred book, the New Testament, and the Sacred Books of the East. Nevertheless, the study of these Sacred Books of the East is full of lessons, and full of warnings. If we see Agni, the god of fire and light, conceived as the highest god, as the soul of the world (âtman), he being in the universe and the universe in him [1], and then read of the same Agni as in love with a young princess, we can learn by an extreme case, how religion, being the common property of the young and the old, of the wise and the foolish, is exposed to dangers from which nothing but perfect freedom of thought and perfect freedom of speech, granted to all its followers, can save it. But we can also learn another lesson, namely, that every religion, being the property of the young and the old, the wise and the foolish, must always be a kind of compromise, and that, while protesting against real corruptions and degradations, we must learn to bear with those whose language differs from our own, and trust that in spite of the tares that have sprung up during the night, some grains of wheat will ripen towards the harvest in every honest heart.

[1] Holtzmann, l. c., p. 9.

LECTURE IX.

USEFULNESS OF THE VEDIC RELIGION FOR A COMPARATIVE STUDY OF OTHER RELIGIONS.

Agni, Fire, in other Religions.

IT would hardly be possible anywhere but in India to discover so complete a collection of fragments with which to reconstruct what I call the biography of the god of fire. Of the early period to which the formation of the name of Agni must be assigned, and of the successive phases of its application to the various manifestations of the beneficial and baneful power of fire, we have no records anywhere but in the Veda. But it must not be supposed that it was in India only that the god of fire and other gods sprang from the simplest observations of the phenomena of nature, and that other nations, more particularly the Semitic, began at once with abstract names of deity. No language can have abstract names without something to abstract them from. The great advantage which the Veda offers to us consists in its enabling us to watch the very process of abstraction more fully and more minutely than it can be watched anywhere else.

In the hymns of the Rig-veda there is as yet no

definite system of belief. There is no doubt a uniformity of thought, but there is at the same time the greatest variety of individual expression. We saw how in some of the hymns Agni was really no more as yet than the name of fire, whether burning on the hearth, or destroying forests, or descending from the sky in the shape of lightning. But we also saw how in other hymns there remained nothing but the name of Agni, while what was meant by it was the omnipotent creator and the omniscient ruler of the world. I think I may say therefore that nowhere in the whole world does ancient literature enable us to study this development of religious thought so fully and so uninterruptedly as in ancient India.

No Religious Literature in Greece and Italy.

In Greece and in Italy there are some, but not many indications left, that might have opened the eyes of classical scholars as to the real theogony of the Olympian gods. But the continuous stratification of religious thought, which is so instructive, and in its teachings so irresistible in the Veda, was broken up in Italy and Greece, and little is left to us beyond the detritus forming part of a tertiary surface.

If we turn our eyes to other countries which claim to be in possession of a very ancient literature, and try to study there also what may be called the geology of theology, we seldom find the documents we really care for, documents exhibiting the actual growth, not the final upshot of religious thought.

Religion in Egypt.

In Egypt, for instance, there is plenty of religious literature, and plenty of local variety, but every cluster of mythology and religion, whether in Upper or in Lower Egypt, whether under the earliest or under the latest dynasties, seems already finished, systematised, and complete.

Brugsch on Egyptian Religion.

I may quote the words of one of the best Egyptian scholars, Professor Brugsch, who in the introduction to his last work, *The Religion of the Old Egyptians* (1888), writes:

'The opinion which has lately been very unreservedly pronounced, that the Egyptians possessed a kind of village-religion, which assumed different forms in different parts of the country, and was at last reduced to some kind of uniformity by the sophistical wisdom of the priests, is refuted by the texts of the pyramids, in which we perceive both the unity of a general fundamental system and the differences, in details only, of local cults. No one would deny that the mythology of the Egyptians, like that of the Greeks and Romans and other civilised nations of antiquity, arose from simple conceptions closely connected at first with the sky and the general nature of the country; but as far as monuments of mythological meaning can carry us back in the valley of the Nile, nowhere do they display the faintest traces of those first beginnings, least of all in the later legends and stories of the gods. Everywhere we are met by a well-established system, and local traditions seem only like variegated illustrations of one and the same fundamental conception within a system.'

No religion has been represented to us under such different forms as the religion of Egypt. From the days of Herodotus and Manetho to our own days every kind of theory has been proposed as to its origin, its nature, and its purpose. Those who know least of the language and literature of that mysterious country have always been most emphatic in their opinions on Egyptian religion. We have been told with equal assurance that the gods of the Egyptians were deified men or deified animals, that their religion was fetishism and totemism, and that nowhere could sacrificial worship be traced back so clearly to a primitive worship of ancestors as in the original home of mummies and pyramids. That elements of all these beliefs may be discovered in Egypt need not surprise us, considering that they are found in nearly all religions, even in those that have not been spread over so large an area and preserved through so many ages as that of Egypt.

But scholarship surely has its rights, and however much we may admire the achievements of the inner consciousness, surely men who have devoted their lives to the study of Egyptian philology, and to whom hieroglyphic, hieratic, and demotic texts are as familiar as Greek and Latin, have a right to be listened to, particularly if they are entirely free from predilections in favour of any philosophical system.

Le Page Renouf on the Gods of Egypt.

I have quoted the opinion of Professor Brugsch as to the real character of the ancient religion of Egypt. I cannot resist quoting likewise the opinion of Mr. Le Page Renouf, an eminent student of hieroglyphics, wedded to no system of philosophy, nor suspected of any religious bias. And I do so the more readily, because I am afraid that his words, being contained in the Preface to the *Book of the Dead*, *Facsimile of the Papyrus of Ani*, 1890, have reached but few except students of hieroglyphics.

'The beginnings of the Egyptian religion,' he writes (p. 7), 'are anterior, probably by many centuries, to the earliest documents, and we can only speak with certainty of it from a time when the nation had already attained a very high degree of civilisation. A period when the religion was confined to fetishism or to the worship of ancestors is historically unknown. Although many of the gods are mere names to us, we have very accurate knowledge of all the important ones, and those which are not yet understood are certainly of the same nature.

'No competent scholar has the least doubt that the Earth and Sky, the Sun, Moon, and Stars (and certain constellations in particular), Light and Darkness, and the very hours of the day and of the night, were considered as gods; and that the gods most frequently mentioned, Seb, Nu, Nut, Râ, Tmu, Horus, are personifications of physical phenomena. And no greater names than these can be found.'

And again: 'The mythology of Egypt had its origin exactly like the mythologies of other nations known to us. All proper names were originally appellatives; and every name is derived from *one* only of the attributes or characteristics of an object. And as every object has several attributes, or may be considered from various points of view, it is susceptible of various names. Hence arise in some languages the many synonyms (often poetical or metaphorical) for such objects as island, river, horse, serpent, camel, sword, gold. It is evident that in countries where the powers of nature are the objects of worship, the same power is liable to be called by very different names. This is especially likely to be the case when the population is distributed over a large extent of country, with local worships under the superintendence of priesthoods independent of each other. The myths arising either from the name of the god, or from the phenomena which he personified, would necessarily vary according to locality. And this diversity would continue even when, at a later period of intercourse between the different parts of the country, many of the local worships and mythologies had come into general acceptance. No attempt was then made at harmonising contradictions, and all attempts which have more recently been made to exhibit a consistent system, whether of Greek, Indian, or Egyptian mythology, spring from a radical misconception of the nature of a myth. When we know *who* the gods really are, the myths about them are perfectly intelligible.'

Unless these statements, emanating from real scholars, can be proved to be erroneous, it seems that we have a right to say that, as in India so in Egypt, the concept of something divine arose first from a contemplation of the wonderful activities of nature, and that when other objects were deified, this meant that they were, more or less consciously, placed within the boundaries of the same concept[1]. If the Egyptians could not mummify without having their *mum*, or some similar substance answering the same purpose, neither could they deify, unless they were

[1] *Hibbert Lectures*, p. 265.

beforehand in possession of a *deus*, or something divine.

Religion in Babylon and Assyria.

We should have expected most valuable light on the origin and the growth of religious conceptions from Babylon and Nineveh. But, in spite of the wonderful discoveries that have been made among the recently disinterred ruins of palaces with their archives, and temples with their libraries, all is for the present chaotic and shifting. The very best scholars confess that they cannot tell what may be Accadian or Sumerian, and what may be Babylonian or Assyrian, in the religious phraseology of the inscriptions, while the very names and gender of the gods vary from year to year. Much, no doubt, will in time be brought to light by the indefatigable discoverers and decipherers of Mesopotamian antiquities; but the student of religion who should venture to support his theories by facts taken from cuneiform sources, would find that these supports have to be renewed or changed from year to year[1]. I say this from personal experience, and without any disparagement;—on the contrary, I think we ought to recognise in it the best proof of the rapid progress of cuneiform studies.

[1] A very excellent *résumé* of what was known of the ancient Babylonian religion in 1887 may be seen in Prof. Sayce's *Hibbert Lectures*. These lectures are particularly useful because they are honest in acknowledging the present state of knowledge, with its inevitable uncertainties. On p. 6 we read: 'Unfortunately, in the present state of our knowledge, it is sometimes impossible to tell to which of these two classes of texts a document belongs, and yet upon the right determination of the question may depend also the right determination of the development of Babylonian religion.' On p. 105 we are told that it is doubtful whether the principal deity of Babylon, Bel Merodach, was Accadian or Semitic, whether Marudak (Merodach) was an Accadian or a Semitic name (p. 106).

Where to study the Historical Growth of Religious Ideas.

It would be easy to collect from Egyptian and Babylonian sources some striking parallels to the development of Agni, which we have traced in the Veda, but we must leave this for a later lecture. Among uncivilised nations also the worship of fire in its various phases, from the lowest to the highest, can be and has been studied by some of our best anthropologists. But here, even more than in Egypt and Babylon and other countries which possess literary documents of various dates, the opportunities of studying the problem which occupies us at present are totally wanting. We find there also nothing but results. We see the last surface of religious belief, but we have no means of piercing one inch beneath that surface. Fortified by our experience, derived chiefly from the Veda, we may guess at the antecedents of the actual beliefs of uncivilised races. We may apply the general principle of 'like results, like causes.' But we shall have to do this with the greatest caution, for the human mind, which is, after all, the only soil of religious ideas, is least amenable to generalisation, and in the growth of religion, though the determining influence of the masses must not be forgotten, the power of the individual is immense, and often withdraws itself from all calculation.

The Old Testament.

We should naturally have expected the most useful information as to the natural growth of the concept of deity in the various books of the Old Testament. They profess to give us an account of the earliest intercourse between man and God, from the days when we are told that Adam and Eve heard the voice of the Lord God walking in the garden in the cool of the day (Gen. iii. 8), to the time when Moses was told that no man can see God and live (Ex. xxxiii. 20).

But you know how difficult, nay, how impossible it is, in the present state of Biblical criticism, to use the single books of the Old Testament for historical purposes. I need hardly remind you that by the students of the Science of Religion the Old Testament can only be looked upon as a strictly historical book by the side of other historical books. It can claim no privilege before the tribunal of history, nay, to claim such a privilege would be to really deprive it of the high position which it justly holds among the most valuable monuments of the distant past. But, at present, the authorship of the single books which form the Old Testament, and more particularly the dates at which they were reduced to writing, form the subject of keen controversy, not among critics hostile to religion, whether Jewish or Christian, but among theologians who treat these questions in the most independent, but, at the same time, the most candid and judicial spirit. By this treatment many difficulties, which in former times disturbed the minds of thoughtful theologians, have been removed, and the Old Testament has resumed its rightful place among the most valuable monuments of antiquity. It is now often invoked to confirm the evidence of cuneiform and hieroglyphic inscriptions, instead of having to invoke the testimony of these inscriptions in its own support. But all this was possible on one condition only, namely, that the Old Testament should be treated simply as an historical book, willing to submit to all the tests of historical criticism to which other historical books have submitted.

But what the student of the history, that is, of the continuous growth of religion, looks for in vain in the books of the Old Testament are the successive stages in the development of religious concepts. He does not know which books he may consider as more ancient or more modern than other books. He asks in vain how much of the religious ideas reflected in certain of these books may be due to ancient tradition, how much to the mind of the latest writer. In the third chapter of Exodus God is revealed to Moses on Mount Horeb, not only as the supreme, but as the only God. But we are now told by competent scholars that Exodus could not have been written down till probably a thousand years later than Moses. How then can we rely on it as an accurate picture of the thoughts of Moses and his contemporaries? It has been said with great truth[1] that 'it is almost impossible to believe that a people who had been emancipated from superstition at the time of the Exodus, say 1491, and had again and again proved the evils of idolatry and been driven to repentance, and who had been all along taught to conceive God as the one universal spirit, existing only in truth and righteousness, and justice, and mercy, should be found at the time of Josiah, in 621, nearly nine hundred years later, steeped in every superstition, and permitting among themselves the perpetration of all the crimes, known to the false and barbarous forms of worship.' Still, if the writings of the Old Testament were con-

[1] A. O. Butler, *What Moses saw and heard*, p. 83.

sidered as contemporaneous with the events which they relate, this retrogressive movement in the religion of the Jews would have to be accepted.

Most of these difficulties, however, are removed, or, at all events, considerably lessened, if we accept the results of modern Hebrew scholarship, and remember that though the Old Testament may contain very ancient traditions, they probably were not reduced to writing till the middle of the fifth century B. C., and may have been modified by and mixed up with ideas belonging to the age of Ezra.

This is not the place to discuss questions of Hebrew scholarship, and yet it is of extreme importance for us to know whether we may, or, in fact, whether we must take into account the books of the Old Testament in studying the growth of religious ideas. What would the student of religion give, if he could really feel sure that he was reading in the books of Moses the thoughts of humanity 1500 B. C. All our ideas of the historical growth of religious ideas, among Semitic nations at least, would have to be modified, whereas at present, unless we can fix the date of each individual book of the Old Testament, our only safe course is to leave this most important collection of sacred documents aside, the very collection from which formerly all our ideas of the ancient history of religion used to be formed.

It sometimes happens, however, that researches carried on for quite different purposes, suddenly cross the path of other inquiries, and help in settling questions with which they were originally unconnected. The same has happened in our case.

Invention of Alphabetic Writing.

Thanks to the genius of De Rougé, and the subsequent labours of Lenormant and Brugsch, there can be no doubt—at least, I cannot see how there could be—that what we call the Phenician letters, and what the Greeks also very honestly called the Phenician letters, were derived from hieratic hieroglyphics. I cannot at present explain the whole process by which out of a large number of hieroglyphic signs about twenty-two were selected to serve as alphabetic letters, as consonants and vowels. Nor has it been possible to fix the exact date at which this process took place, though such evidence as there is points, according to De Rougé, to about 1000 B. C. But it is a matter of history that we have no evidence of alphabetic writing, even for the purpose of inscriptions, much less for the purpose of the composition of books, till about the time of king Mesha, whose famous inscription dates from the ninth century B. C.[1]

Between the use of writing for monumental or even for commercial and epistolary purposes, and the use of writing for literary purposes, however, there is everywhere a gulf of centuries. In fact we may say, so far as our knowledge extends at present, that there is no historical evidence of any *book* in alphabetic writing before the seventh century B. C.

[1] I do not take account here of the ancient inscriptions discovered by Euting, Glaser, and others in Arabia. Their dates are as yet too much a matter of controversy. Dr. Glaser refers the Minaean alphabet to 2000 to 3000 B.C. Professor D. H. Müller places it from 600 B.C. to 600 A.D. On the other hand Dr. Müller takes the Lihyân alphabet to be more primitive than the Sabaeo-Minaean, while Dr. Glaser makes it post-Christian, 150 to 475 A.D. Under these circumstances it is surely wise to wait. See *Allgemeine Zeitung*, Nos. 36, 37. 1890.

To suppose therefore that Moses could have *written* a book in Hebrew, and with a Semitic alphabet, would be to antedate the writing of books by nearly a thousand years, and the employment of alphabetic writing in general by more than 500 years.

If Moses wrote at all, if he actually held a book and read it in the audience of the people (Exod. xxiv. 7), he could only, learned as he was in all the learning of the Egyptians, have written in hieroglyphics, but certainly not in the Phenician alphabet. The very tables of the law could not have been traced with any but hieroglyphic or hieratic letters, for the simple reason that our Phenician alphabet, so far as we know at present, did not exist before 1000 B.C., if so early. Of course, the arguments which are used in support of this conclusion may be controverted. One single inscription, in Phenician or Semitic letters, found in Egypt or Arabia might by its date upset our conclusions as to the date of the invention of alphabetic writing. But what will hardly ever be upset is our conviction that books in alphabetic letters were a far more recent invention, and existed nowhere before the seventh century B. C.

The Sixth Century B. C.

It has been truly said that a more interesting history of the world might be written if, instead of being divided according to the domination of particular dynasties or the supremacy of particular races, it were cut off into departments, indicated by the influence of particular discoveries upon the destinies of mankind[1]. You would have the epochs marked

[1] See speech by Lord Salisbury, in *Times*, Nov. 4, 1889.

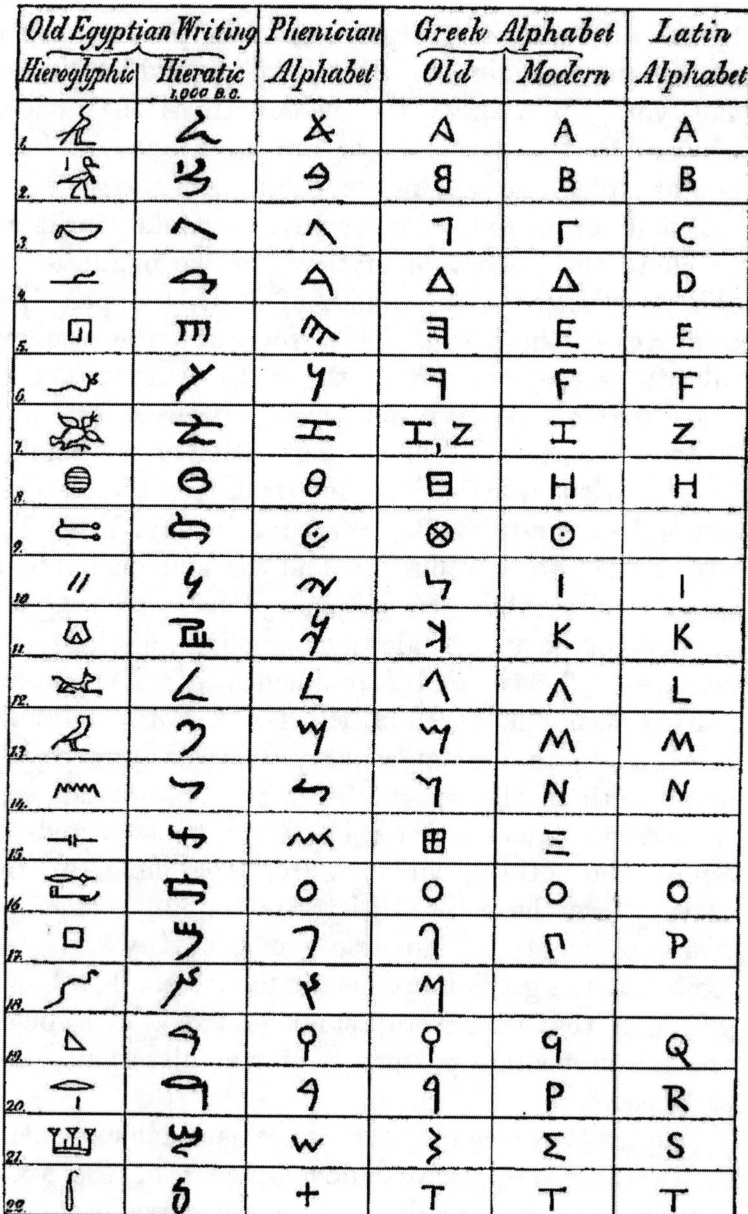

From Brugsch.

by the discovery of gunpowder, of the printing press, of the steam engine, of electricity in modern times; and you would have in ancient times the epochs marked by the discovery of fire, of bronze, of iron, and of alphabetic writing for literary purposes.

But if the introduction of written books marks an epoch in the history of civilisation, we ought to be able to discover clear traces of it in the principal countries of the world. Now you know the wonderful intellectual activity of the sixth century B.C. in every part of the civilised world. Between 600 and 500 B.C. we have in Asia the foundation of the Persian Empire, with Cyrus and Darius Hydaspes, the restorer of the Zoroastrian faith. We have in Asia Minor the rise of the Ionian republics, and the sudden burst of Greek philosophy, Greek poetry, nay even Greek history. Not only Thales (solar eclipse, 585), Anaximander (612–546) and Anaximenes, but Pythagoras († 510), Xenophanes, Herakleitos, and Parmenides all belonged to that great century. Greek lyric poetry burst forth in the songs of Theognis, Simonides, and Anakreon; ancient laws began to be collected by Solon and others, and towards the close of the century we hear of Pisistratus († 528) collecting manuscripts of the Homeric songs, as they had been recited at the great Panathenaic festivals. The Logographi of that time were actual *writers* of chronicles, and the immediate precursors of real historians, such as Herodotus.

Though it is a mere guess, it seems to me extremely likely that this literary development of the sixth century B.C. was really due to the introduction of alphabetic writing for literary purposes from Egypt and Phenicia to Asia Minor and Europe. I doubt whether we can trace the writing down of any of the sacred books of the East to an earlier date than that century, though they, no doubt, existed for centuries before that time, preserved by oral tradition.

The Zoroastrian texts may have been collected at the time of Darius. The Veda was probably not reduced to writing till much later, and the same applies to the Buddhist canon. In China writing, according to their fashion, may have been known long before, but the collection of the canonical books of Confucius and Laotze belongs again to the sixth century.

The Old Testament as an Historical Book.

If then we turn to the books of the Old Testament, we find that they were finally collected by Ezra, 458 B.C., who lived about seventy-five years after Darius, the collector of the Zoroastrian code. We must remember that Ezra had been brought up in Babylon during the reign of Artaxerxes. To suppose that portions of the Old Testament existed in the form of books at the time of Moses would run counter to all history. The Jews, we must remember, were far from being a more literary people than their neighbours, and to suppose that they alone should have possessed a book-literature at a time when all their neighbours had to be satisfied with oral tradition, or with hieroglyphic inscriptions, hieratic papyri, and cuneiform cylinders, is more than at present any historian can admit[1].

But though in using the books of the Old Testament we must always be on our guard against intellectual

[1] See Appendix XIII.

anachronisms, due to the inevitable colouring which the mind of the collector and final redactor may have thrown on the character of a book, the traditions, as finally collected by Ezra, and before him by the High Priest, Hilkiah, hardly allow us to doubt that a belief in one Supreme God, even if at first it was only a henotheistic, and not yet a monotheistic belief, took possession of the leading spirits of the Jewish race at a very early time. All tradition assigns that belief in One God, the Most High, to Abraham. According to the Old Testament, Abraham, though he did not deny the existence of the gods worshipped by the neighbouring tribes, yet looked upon them as different from, and as decidedly inferior to, his own God. His monotheism was, no doubt, narrow. His God was the friend of Abraham, as Abraham was the friend of God. Yet the concept of God formed by Abraham was a concept that could grow and that did grow. Neither Moses, nor the Prophets, nor Christ himself, nor even Mohammed, had to introduce a new God. Their God was always called the God of Abraham, even when freed from all that was still local and narrow and superstitious in the faith of that patriarch.

Monotheistic Instinct of the Semitic Race.

It is well known that some excellent Semitic scholars, and more particularly Renan, find the explanation of this early monotheistic belief of the Father of the Faithful in what they call the monotheistic instinct of the whole Semitic race. That theory, however, even if it explained anything, is flatly contradicted by all the facts that have come to light in the early history of the Semitic nations.

If there was any religious instinct in them, it was a polytheistic instinct, as we see in the monuments of Babylon and Nineveh, in the traditions of Arabia, and even in the constant backslidings of the Jews.

Abraham.

Many years ago, in one of my earliest essays on Semitic Monotheism (1860), I tried to show, in opposition to Renan's view, that the Jewish belief in One Supreme God must be traced back, like all great ideas, to one person, namely to Abraham, and that, in his case, it could not be ascribed to a national instinct, which rather would have led him in the very opposite direction, but on the contrary, to his personal opposition to the national instinct, or to what I ventured to call, in the truest sense of the word, a special revelation. For that expression I have been taken to task again and again during the last thirty years, though I thought I had made it very clear in all my writings what I meant by a special revelation, not a theophany, but 'a profound insight, an inspired vision of truth, so deep and so living as to make it a reality like that of the outward world[1],' nay, more than that of the outward world. Such a revelation can, by its very nature, be granted to one man only, can be preached by one man only, with the full faith in its reality, and this man, as far as the religion of Jews, Christians, and Mohammedans is concerned, was Abraham.

But although Abraham may have attained at a very early time to his sublime conception of the One God,

[1] These are the words in which my defence was undertaken by J. F. Clarke in his *Ten Great Religions*, p. 403.

the Most High God, freed from the purely physical characteristics which adhere to the gods of other nations, we can see very clearly that in this sublime conception he stood almost alone, and that the gods of the Jews, and of the Semitic nations in general, had once been gods of nature, quite as much as the gods of India.

If we saw the account of the appearance of Jehovah on mount Sinai in the sacred books of any other religion, we should have little doubt that the God, as there described, was originally a god of fire and thunder. 'In the morning,' we read, 'there were thunders and lightnings, and a thick cloud upon the mount. And mount Sinai was altogether on a smoke, because the Lord descended upon it in fire: and the smoke thereof ascended as the smoke of a furnace, and the whole mount quaked greatly.'

Elijah.

What is told of Elijah and of his vision on mount Horeb is like an epitome of the whole growth of the Jewish religion in general. We read that 'the Lord passed by, and a great and strong wind rent the mountains, and brake in pieces the rocks before the Lord; but the Lord was not in the wind.

And after the wind an earthquake; but the Lord was not in the earthquake.

'And after the earthquake a fire; but the Lord was not in the fire.

'And after the fire a still, small voice.'

What we should have expected in any other sacred book, at the end of this description of a storm, would have been the loud, strong voice of the thunder, following after the storm, and the earthquake, and the fire of lightning. But the still small voice shows that Elijah saw more than the mere physical features of the storm, and that the voice which he heard was meant for a higher voice that speaks not only in the storm, the earthquake, and the fire, but in the heart of man.

The God of Fire in the Old Testament.

The highest authorities on the religious antiquities of the Semitic peoples, and of the Jewish people in particular, have expressed their conviction that the physical characteristics of their principal God point to an original god of fire, taking fire in the same wide sense in which it was taken in India, not only as the fire on earth, but as the fire of heaven, the fire manifested in storm and lightning, nay, the fire as the life of nature and of man. In this way only, they think, can we account for the poetical phraseology still found in many places of the Old Testament. For instance, Psalm xviii. 8:

> 'There went up a smoke out of his nostrils,
> And fire out of his mouth devoured;
> Coals were kindled by it.
> He bowed the heavens also, and came down,
> And thick darkness was under his feet.'

Or again, Psalm xxix. 3:

> 'The voice of the Lord is upon the waters,
> The glory of God thundereth,
> Even the Lord, upon many waters.'

But though we can clearly perceive in these and similar passages that there were physical ingredients in the character of the supreme God of the Jews, nowhere but in the hymns of the Veda can we watch the gradual elimination of these physical ingredients, and the historical unfolding of the true idea of God out of these primitive germs. I know full well that to some any attempt to trace back the name and concept of Jehovah to the same hidden sources from which other nations derived their first intimation of deity, may seem almost sacrilegious. They forget the difference between the human concept of the deity and the deity itself, which is beyond the reach of all human concepts. But the historian reads deeper lessons in the growth of these human concepts, as they spring up everywhere in the minds of men who have been seekers after truth—seeking the Lord, if haply they might feel after him and find him;—and when he can show the slow, but healthy growth of the noblest and sublimest thoughts out of small and apparently insignificant beginnings, he rejoices as the labourer rejoices over his golden harvest; nay, he often wonders what is more truly wonderful, the butterfly that soars up to heaven on its silvery wings, or the grub that hides within its mean chrysalis such marvellous possibilities.

LECTURE X.

FIRE AS CONCEIVED IN OTHER RELIGIONS.

Fire widely Worshipped.

THOUGH we cannot hope to find in other religions any documents in which to study, as we can in the Veda, the successive stages through which the worship of fire passed from its simplest beginnings, as the fire on the hearth, to its highest stage, as the creator and ruler of the world, we may at all events try to collect some fragments of the worship of Fire, preserved in other religions, whether united genealogically with the Vedic religion or independent in their origin.

Next to the worship of the sun, there is probably no religious worship so widely diffused as that of Fire. 'Since there has been fire, it has been worshipped,' is a saying of Bashshar Ibn Burd, quoted by Al-Birûnî (vol. ii. p. 131). But we must distinguish. Fire has been worshipped for very different reasons, and the very name of worship comprehends many heterogeneous kinds of reverence, esteem, gratitude, and even prudential considerations, which were called forth by the benefits and services rendered by fire to the different races of man. Nevertheless, I believe we shall find that there is nothing, or very little, in the religious, philosophical, and mythological conceptions of fire, whether entertained by civilised or uncivilised, by ancient or modern races, that does not find some analogy, and, to a great extent, some explanation, in the rich religious, philosophical, and mythological phraseology of India.

Fire in the Avesta.

The nearest relations of the ancient Âryas of India were no doubt the Âryas of Media and Persia, of whose religion we obtain some interesting, though fragmentary, information from the Zend-avesta. The idea, once so prevalent, that their religion consisted entirely of Fire-worship has long been surrendered by scholars, though it crops up again and again in popular writings. From the first acquaintance with the original texts of their sacred writings, it became clear that Fire occupied only a subordinate place in their religious system.

If we call the religion of Zoroaster fire-worship, we must apply the same name to the religion of India, nay even to the religion of the Jews. Almost every religion which recognises burnt offerings, exhibits at the same time a more or less prominent reverence for the sacrificial fire itself. To outsiders in particular, and to casual observers, the fires burning on the altars of temples or on the hearth of every house seem to be the principal manifestation of religious worship and of religious faith. Thus it happened that, like the religion of Persia, that of India also was often represented as fire-worship. Al-Birûnî, for instance (vol. i. p. 128; vol. ii. p. 139), declares that the Rig-veda treats of the sacrifices to the fire, as if it treated of nothing else. He is, however, more correct when he states (vol. ii. p. 131) 'that the Hindus highly venerate the fire, and offer flowers to it,' though we ought to remember that there are many things besides flowers which were sacrificed in and to the fire.

Ormazd, not Fire.

In the Zend-avesta Agni, as a separate god of fire, occupies in fact a far less prominent place than in the Veda. The real object of veneration with Zoroaster and his followers was Ahura-mazda, whom we call Ormazd. Ahura-mazda was a deity whose deepest roots we shall discover in the concepts of heaven, light, and wisdom. He was not Fire, though he is often represented as the father of Fire. This shows his close relationship with the Vedic Dyaus, the sky, who was likewise conceived as the father of Agni.

Âtar, Fire.

The name of fire in Zend, however, is not Agni, but Âtar, a word which in Sanskrit is supposed to exist in the name Athar-van, one of the early sages who kept the fire, the supposed ancestor of the family of the Âtharvans, to whom, as we saw, the Atharva-veda was attributed. It is sometimes used also as a name of Agni himself. The word âtar has no etymology, so far as we know [1], whether in Sanskrit or in Zend.

[1] Darmesteter, *Ormazd et Ahriman*, p. 55, note. That athar in athar-van is the same word as âtar may be conceded. In Zend âthravan has long, athaurun short a. The Vedic atharî also, and atharyu, may be connected with athar, and possibly the

It seemed strange to students of the Parsi religion that Âtar, fire, should be the son of Ahura-mazda, and that his mother, the wife of Ahura-mazda, should be water. From what we now know, however, from the Rig-veda, this becomes perfectly intelligible. Fire is the son of the sky, whether in his character of the sun or of lightning, and he is the son of the waters, whether as rising from the clouds in the morning, or as issuing from the clouds as lightning in a thunderstorm [1].

Âtar's Fight with Azi Dahâka.

This Âtar or fire in the Avesta represents in some respects both Agni and Indra, for the battle against Azi Dahâka, the fiendish snake, is waged in the Avesta by Âtar alone, who frightens the fiend away and recovers the light (*hv*arenô). Trita, who in the Veda takes sometimes the place of the conqueror of the fiend, is called Âptya, the descendant of the waters, which shows his close connection with Agni, as Apâm napât, the offspring of the waters or the clouds, that is, the lightning. In the Avesta this Trita appears as Thraêtaona Âthwya, who kills Azi Dahâka in the four-cornered Varena, originally a name of the sky, corresponding to Greek οὐρανός, and Sanskrit Varu*n*a.

This battle between Agni or Trita and Ahi in the Veda, between Âtar or Thraêtaona and Azi Dahâka

Greek ἀθραγένη, a tree of which tinder was made. 'Αθήρ also in the sense of the point of a weapon might be related, but not so 'Αθήνη, which comes from a very different source.

[1] Apâm napât is distinguished in the Avesta from Âtar, but is often mentioned in close connection with him; see Vispered, VII. 5.

in the Avesta, which was originally a purely mythological representation of the battle between light and darkness, whether in a thunderstorm or in the diurnal struggle between day and night, became after a time a mere legend. And it was one of Burnouf's most brilliant discoveries that in what was formerly accepted as genuine Persian history, namely the overthrow of king Jemshîd by the usurper Zohâk, and the overthrow of Zohâk by Ferîdûn, he recognised once more our old Vedic friends, Trita, Ahi, and Yama, brought down from the sky to the earth, and changed from divine and mythological powers into human and historical characters[1].

Plurality of Âtar.

When by the side of the one Âtar we find also many âtars (*S. B. E.* xxiii. 8) mentioned in the Avesta, we have only to remember that in the Veda also there were many agnis or fires, in which the presence of Agni was discovered and acknowledged. This subdivision of Fire was carried on even further in the Avesta than in the Veda. In the Veda we can distinguish three fires, sometimes called Agni nirmathya, fire obtained by rubbing, Agni aushasya, fire rising with the dawn, solar fire, and Agni vaidyuta, the fire of lightning. In the Avesta (Yasna XVII) we meet with five fires:—(1) the fire that was before Ahura-mazda, (2) the fire that dwells in animal bodies, (3) the fire in trees and plants, (4) the fire in the clouds, (5) the domestic fire, (6) the Nairya-sangha

[1] On the changes of Thraêtaona into Ferîdûn, of Yima Khshâeta into Jemshîd, and of Azi Dahâka into Zohâk, see *Selected Essays*, i. p. 479.

fire, also called the Behram fire, which is to be kept burning in temples[1].

Besides the three principal fires in the Veda, the fire obtained by rubbing, the fire of lightning, and the fire in the sun, two more are often mentioned, the *gâth*ara, that which resides in the stomach and cooks or digests food, and another that is supposed to reside in plants. This identity of the fire on the hearth with the fire in the human body was expressed with great definiteness by a Shawnee prophet. 'Know,' he said, 'that the life in your body and the fire on your hearth are one and the same thing, and that both proceed from one source[2].' When, however, Agni is invoked as residing in all things, and also as a witness abiding in our own body, this is not meant for the *gâth*arâgni, but involves a higher conception of Agni as an omnipresent power. Thus we read, Râm. VI. 101, 30:—

Tvam agne sarvabhûtânâm sarîrântar ago*k*ara*h*, Tvam sâkshî nâma dehasthas, trâhi mâm devasattama.

'Thou, O Agni, art invisible inside the body of all creatures, thou art called the witness in the body, save me, O best of gods.'

The Agni residing in the plants, may be the warmth that ripens them (Rv. X. 88, 10, sá*h* óshadhî*h* pa*k*ati visvárûpâ*h*); but more frequently he is conceived as dwelling within trees and plants, because he can be called forth from them by friction. He is called, VI. 3, 3, vane*g*â*h*, born in the wood; II. 1, 14, gárbha*h* vîrúdhâm, the child of the plants; and he is often represented as hidden in certain trees which were used for producing fire.

[1] *S. B. E.* xxxi. p. 258.
[2] *Narrative of John Tanner*, p. 161; Brinton, *Myths of the New World*, p. 144.

The three sacrificial fires are the Gârhapatya, Dakshi*n*a, and Âhavanîya, to which the Âvasathya and Sabhya are sometimes added so as to make five.

Âtar, Son of Ormazd.

But Âtar had also a divine personality of his own. His constant name is the son of Ahura-mazda. He is called a warrior, driving on a blazing chariot (*S. B. E.* xxiii. p. 153), a benefactor, a source of glory and a source of healing (l.c., p. 15). In the Âtas Nyâgis (l. c., p. 359) we read not only of sacrifices and invocations offered unto Âtar, but he himself is called worthy of sacrifice and invocation. He is implored to burn for ever in the house, until the time of the good and powerful restoration of the world. It is said to be well with a man who worships Âtar with sacrifices, holding in his hand the sacred wood, the baresma, and the meat. For Âtar can bestow not only fulness of life and welfare, but also knowledge, sagacity, quickness of tongue, a good memory, an understanding that goes on growing and that is not acquired through learning. In a prayer addressed to him the poet says: 'Give me, O Âtar, son of Ahura-mazda, however unworthy I am, now and for ever, a seat in the bright, all-happy, blissful abode of the holy ones. May I obtain the good reward, a good renown, a long cheerfulness of soul.' And Âtar is supposed to bestow the following blessing on his worshippers: 'May herds of oxen grow for thee, and increase of sons; may thy mind and thy soul be master of its vow, and mayest thou live on in the joy of the soul all the nights of thy life' (xxiii. p. 360; and xxxi. p. 313).

Difference between Âtar and Agni.

Remember all this is addressed to Âtar, originally simply a name of fire. It is much the same as what we saw addressed to Agni in the Veda. But there are differences also between the Vedic Agni and the Avestic Âtar. We saw that Agni in the Veda was made a sarvabhaksha, a devourer of all things, that he resented the affront, but that in the end everything was supposed to be purified by fire. Thus the Vedic Indians burnt their dead in the fire, and afterwards buried the ashes. To the Zoroastrians both these acts would have seemed sacrilegious, for such was their belief in the holiness of fire and of the earth, that they would have considered both polluted by any contact with unclean things[1]. The very breath of man or of woman, which, as we saw, Agni was so fond of, was believed by the Zoroastrians to contaminate the fire[2], and hence the Paitidâna[3], a kind of veil worn by the priest, and reaching from the nose to the chin, the modern Penom[4].

[1] *S. B. E.* iv. p. 80.

[2] It should be remembered, however, that Manu also (IV. 53) forbids blowing the fire with one's mouth. He likewise disapproves of throwing impure substances into the fire, warming one's feet at it, or stepping over it. Some authorities, however, say that the *S*rauta fire may be kindled by blowing, because it is particularly ordained so in the Vâ*g*asaneyaka, but that the domestic fire is not to be thus treated. See Âpastamba Sûtras, translated by Bühler, *S. B. E.* ii. p. 56; I. 15, 20; Vasish*th*a XII. 27–29.

[3] l. c., p. 164.

[4] A curious coincidence shows itself in the ceremonial of the Slaves, as described by Saxo Grammaticus. The priest has to clean the sacellum with a broom, and while doing this must never allow his breath to escape. When he can retain his breath no longer, he has to go out and then to return to his work in the temple, so that the deity may not be contaminated by human breath. See Lippert, *Die Religionen der Europäischen Culturvölker*, p. 93.

Is the Avestic Religion dualistic?

It is generally supposed that the religion of the Avesta differs from that of the Veda by being dualistic[1]. In one sense this is perfectly true. The Zoroastrians recognise an evil spirit, Angra Mainyu, by the side of the good spirit, Ahura-mazda. In some respects these two spirits are equals. The good spirit did not create the evil spirit, nor can he altogether prevent the mischief that is wrought by the evil spirit. The Zoroastrian religion, having a decidedly moral character, recognises in this struggle between good and evil the eternal law of reward and punishment, good always begetting good and evil evil. In the same manner as the good spirit opposes the evil spirit, every man is expected to fight against evil in every shape. Zoroaster himself was supposed to have been appointed by Ahura-mazda to defend the good people, it may be the agricultural population, against the attacks of their enemies, the worshippers of the Daêvas. The oldest prayers in the Avesta are supposed to have been addressed by Zoroaster to Ahura-mazda, imploring his help, and mourning over the sufferings of his people.

All this is perfectly true, but if we once know from the Veda what the fight between good and evil, between light and darkness meant in the beginning, we shall understand why after all, in the dualism of the Avesta, the good spirit is always supreme, as Indra is supreme over V*ri*tra, Agni over Ahi, Âtar over A*z*i Dahâka. The fact that Indra or Agni or Âtar has an enemy, that light is sometimes over-

[1] See West, *S. B. E.*, vol. v. p. lxix; Mills, *S. B. E.*, vol. xxxi. Introd.

whelmed by darkness, does not annihilate the belief in the supremacy of one of these two contending powers. The gods are always conceived as different in kind from their opponents. The gods are worshipped, the demons are feared. If therefore we call the ancient religion of Zoroaster dualistic, the same name might be applied to the Vedic religion, so far as it recognises V*ri*tra and other powers of darkness as dangerous opponents of the bright beings. Indeed, I doubt whether there is any religion which is dualistic in the sense of recognising two divine antagonistic powers as perfect equals. Even so-called Satanic races who offer sacrifices to evil spirits only, and seem to neglect the good spirits, do so because they can trust the latter, but are afraid of the former. Wherever there is a belief in a devil, the devil may be very powerful, but he can never become supreme. He is by its very nature a negative, not a positive concept. No doubt, the powers of evil in the Avesta are different from the powers of darkness in the Veda. They have assumed a decidedly moral character. But they are the same in origin, and it is owing to this that they never have, never could have attained to perfect equality with the Good and Wise Spirit, Ahura-mazda.

The most important lesson which we may learn from the Avesta, particularly when we do not lose sight of its antecedents in the Veda, is that we may see how physical religion leads on almost unconsciously to moral religion. It is the distinction between night and day, between darkness and light, that foreshadows and predetermines the distinction between what is lovely and unlovely, between what is evil and good, between what belongs to the powers of darkness and the powers of light. Nature, as the voice of the God of Nature, awakens in the heart of man the first conception of that eternal Dualism which is manifested in night and day, in darkness and light, and in the works of darkness and in the works of light. And as night is the negation of day, not day of night, as darkness is the negation of light, not light of darkness, a deep conviction was left in the mind of man, that evil also is the negation of good, not good of evil. The light of the sun might be absent for a time, but it was hidden only, it could never be destroyed, and as every morning proclaimed the victory of light, the ancient worshippers of nature and of the gods of nature never doubted that the final victory must belong to the powers of light, that V*ri*tra must succumb, that Ahriman must be vanquished, and that light and truth and righteousness must prevail in the end.

Fire in Egypt.

But it is not only the religion of Persia which receives its true explanation from India, it is not only the Zoroastrian Âtar whose true historical antecedents are preserved to us in the hymns addressed to the Vedic Agni. In this case there is really a genealogical relationship between the two religions and between the two deities. But even where there can be no thought of such a genealogical relationship, we shall often find in the most distant countries the most striking similarities with the conceptions of fire as elaborated by the Vedic Indians.

In some cases mythological ideas which seemed utterly irrational become at once intelligible by a mere comparison with Vedic ideas. We saw how many different characters were ascribed to Agni in the hymns of the Veda. In one hymn he was clearly the fire on the hearth, the protector of the family; in another the lightning, the destroyer of the demons of darkness; in another again the sun, the light of the world, the giver of life and strength. Being all this, and representing such different powers, he soon was conceived as something different from each and all of these manifestations, something behind and above them all, and thus was raised at last to that divine supremacy which, as we saw, marks the highest stage which religious speculation has reached at any time. If we have clearly understood this process, and then turn our eyes to Egypt, we shall find it repeated there in almost every detail.

Modern Character of the Egyptian Religion.

Only while in Egypt we can no longer discover the motives that led to this syncretism, these motives are fully disclosed to us in the hymns of the Veda. It is strange, but it is recognised as a fact by the best scholars, that in Egypt, where the actual monuments are apparently so much older than in India, we seldom, if ever, can discover the deepest roots and feeders of religion. Professor Chantepie de la Saussaye, in his able *résumé* of the recent researches of Egyptologists, remarks (§ 51): 'Our knowledge of the first dynasties has been greatly enlarged by Maspero's discoveries during the last years, but we have not come any nearer to the original sources of Egyptian civilisation. Our knowledge does not reach beyond Menes, who governed a fully organised kingdom. The religion also of the oldest periods was quite complete, at least we find there almost all the elements of religious thought, but we cannot discover their beginnings. Everything, even architecture and plastic art, is already so fully developed that we must look for a more ancient antiquity, and that is entirely withdrawn from our sight.'

Under these circumstances a comparative study of religions can alone throw light on those periods in the development of the Egyptian religion which lie confessedly beyond the earliest monuments. Though we cannot admit a common historical ground from which the religions of Egypt and India branched off, we can admit a common human foundation in which they had their deepest roots. Even if the Veda did not allow us an insight into the workings of the Indian mind which produced, for instance, that strange syncretism of a terrestrial, celestial, and atmospheric Agni, the mere fact that the same puzzle presented itself to the Indians and to the Egyptians would lead us to look for a common cause, simply in their common human nature, and thus facilitate the solution of the riddle. But if in India we still find the key left, as it were, in the lock, we have a perfect right to try whether the same key will not turn the bolts in the Egyptian lock. If it does, we have done all that we can do. If we have not perfect certainty, we have at all events high probability that the problem can be, and has been successfully solved in Egypt as well as in India. I quote once more from M. Chantepie de la Saussaye: 'We first draw attention,' he writes (§ 49), 'to the general identification of the gods with one another. We perceive at once how impossible it is to distinguish from each other the attributes of the individual gods or the spheres of their activity. From this arises the assertion made by many Egyptologists that fundamentally the Egyptian gods all meant the same thing; the gods represented the sun, the goddesses the mothers or something else. This is most certainly not the case. But at a very early date the gods were almost all represented as being gods of light. Hence the combined names of Amon-Ra, Ra-Osiris, and many more. This is the reason why it is so difficult to fathom the nature of the gods from the texts. Originally Ptah was probably not a sun-god. Still he is most distinctly called the sun-disc. The fact that Set appears in the boat of the sun, does not determine his original nature.' All this, as we saw before, would be applicable to the Vedic religion as well as to the religion of Egypt. Let us now consider some individual gods in Egypt that show some similarity with Agni.

Ra.

When we read the account given, for instance, of Ra, we almost imagine that we are reading an account of Agni, in his character as sun-god. Nearly all the gods are identified with Ra. He is the sun-god, the creator and ruler of the world. He daily conquers his enemies, particularly the dark cloud-serpent Apep (Sk. Ahi). His nearest relatives are Shu and Tefnut, the children of the sun (Asvinau, divo napâtau). Ra is identified with Tmu, the setting sun (Yama), and with Harmachis, the daily sun travelling from East to West (Vish*n*u).

Osiris.

In Osiris, again, most Egyptian scholars have now discovered a solar deity. He is the oldest child of Seb, goddess of the earth (P*ri*thivî), and Nut, goddess of heaven (Dyaus). He is married to his sister Isis (Yama and Yamî[1]), killed by his brother Set, but avenged by his son Horus. Osiris becomes lord of the lower world and judge of the dead (Yama); and his worshippers look forward after death to admission into his kingdom. As Agni is Yama and Yama Agni, so Ra is called the soul of Osiris, Osiris the soul of Ra (l. c., § 47).

Ptah.

Another Egyptian deity, Ptah (the opener?), is often identified with Osiris. Both are represented in the form of mummies, and like Osiris, Ptah also is invoked in the end as the creator of heaven, of earth, and of man. Ptah represents, in fact, another phase of the sun, the sun that has set and become invisible, but that returns again at the end of the night, or at the end of winter[2].

And while Ptah thus receives light from Agni, both being the light by night as distinguished from the sun, the light by day, Ptah also reflects light on Agni, at least in one of his special developments.

We saw how Agni, the sacrificial fire, was not only used by the priest as a means of conveying offering to the gods, but was very soon, by a very natural transition

[1] On a curious coincidence between the twins Yama and Yamî, and the twins Yame and Yama in Peru, see Brinton, *Myths of the New World*, p. 155.

[2] Brugsch, *Religion der alten Aegypter*, p. 237.

of thought, conceived as himself a priest. In a very similar manner, the fire which was used by the smith for melting metal and fashioning it into tools and weapons, was likewise conceived as himself a smith and an artificer. We see this change very clearly in the Greek Hephaestos, in the Roman Vulcan, and in the Egyptian Ptah. For Ptah is not only the nocturnal sun, Ptah is the former and artificer, the worker of metals from gold to iron [1], he is the lord of artists, and to him is naturally ascribed the forging of the vault of heaven and of the sun. By another (l. c., p. 512) step he advances to the dignity of a maker of the world, father of the beginnings, creator of the egg, and father of the gods. Nay, like Agni, he is said to have generated himself (p. 514).

Tvash*tri* in the Veda.

A similar concatenation of ideas seems to have led to the conception of a Vedic deity, otherwise difficult to explain, namely Tvash*tri*. Tvash*tri* means the artificer, the maker and shaper, but it is clear that originally this name belonged to Agni. In some of the Vedic hymns Tvash*tri* is still used as a synonym of Agni (I. 95, 2; 5); in others he is identified with Savit*ri* visvarûpa, the sun of many forms (III. 55, 19; X. 10, 5). His character in the Veda is by no means coherent and intelligible, but if we admit Agni, the solar fire, as his foundation, we can account for his more special character as the fire applied to every kind of workmanship, as the forger of the thunderbolt, the maker of the sky, and lastly, as the creator of the

[1] Brugsch, l. c., p. 508.

whole world (Vâ*g*. Sa*m*h. XXIX. 9), and the giver of life (Rv. X. 18, 6). In the end, his original character as Agni was so entirely forgotten that in one passage Tvash*tri* is actually represented as having fashioned Agni also (Rv. X. 46, 9).

But though the Egyptian Ptah explains some characteristic features in the Vedic Tvash*tri*, there is much that still remains mysterious in the legends told about this Indian Hephaestos, particularly the marriage of his daughter (Sara*n*yû), and the murder of his three-headed son, Visvarûpa (X. 10, 5 ; X. 8, 9).

Fire in Greece, Hephaestos.

If now we turn our eyes from Egypt to Greece and Rome, we find hardly anything for which we are not fully prepared. Anything like pyrolatry or worship of fire, as a mere element, is foreign to the character of the Greeks. All their gods had become thoroughly personal and almost human long before we know anything about them. Hence, though we can discover an elementary background in Hephaestós, his personal character preponderates so decidedly that it has almost obliterated every trace of his origin. According to Homer (Il. i. 577 ; Od. viii. 312), Hephaestos was the son of Zeus and Hera, just as Agni was the son of Dyaus and of the waters. These waters represented not only the clouds, but the whole bright atmosphere, where fire, as light or lightning, was supposed to dwell. *Here* (Ἥρη) corresponds to a Sanskrit form *Svârâ, a feminine of Svar, sky, from which also Ἥλιος, the sun. *Here*, though recognised as the principal wife of Zeus, represented but one out of the many phenomena of nature with which Zeus, the highest god of heaven, was supposed to have produced offspring. We have only to remember that in the Veda Dyaus was often assigned to Agni as his father, and the waters and the dawn as his mothers [1], in order to understand the Homeric conception that Hephaestos was the child of Zeus and Here. The idea that Hephaestos had no father, but that Here, out of spite, brought him forth by herself, as Zeus had given birth by himself to Athene, is but one of the many half-poetical, half-philosophical, and often purely imaginative expansions of mythology which abound in Greece more than anywhere else. The statue of Here, mentioned by Herodotus (vi. 82), which represented her as emitting fire from her breast, is the truest image of her as the bright atmosphere, sending forth lightning from the clouds. As Agni is often called the child of the waters, without any mention of a father, Hephaestos may possibly, in that sense also, have been called the offspring of Here. Even the lameness of Hephaestos may find its explanation in the fact that Agni in the Veda is called footless (apâd), and that his movement is unsteady and vacillating. The violent catastrophe when Zeus hurls Hephaestos from the sky, is again a mythological rendering of Zeus hurling his thunderbolt upon the earth, while the myth that it took Hephaestos a whole day to fall from the sky to the earth, and that he touched the island of Lemnos with the setting sun, may contain a recollection of the identity of Agni, as

[1] It is true that Dyâvâ-*pri*thivyau, Heaven and Earth, are often mentioned as the parents of Agni, but this would not justify us in taking Here, with Welcker (*Götterlehre*, i. p. 363), as originally a goddess of the earth.

lightning, with Agni, as the setting sun. Even the hiding of Hephaestos during nine years may be a faint echo of the many stories told in the Veda of Agni wishing to absent himself and hiding in the waters (cf. Il. xviii. 398). In the mind of Homer, however, the elementary antecedents of Hephaestos exist no longer. With him he is the crafty smith or carpenter or artist, and it is difficult to say whether Charis or Aphrodite was assigned to him as his wife, because originally she represented the Dawn, or whether this myth was merely intended to indicate the grace and charm of the art of Hephaestos.

The name of Ἥφαιστος is difficult to explain. I thought[1] it might be traced back to the Vedic yávish*th*a, a constant epithet of Agni, meaning the youngest, or the always young. Thus we read, Rv. II. 4, 5:

*g*u*g*urvā̆n yá*h* múhur ā̆ yúvâ bhū́t.

'Agni, when he had grown old, became always young again.'

Rv. I. 144, 4:

dívâ ná náktam palitá*h* yúvâ a*g*ani.

'By night, as by day, having become grey, he was born young.'

But there are phonetic difficulties, as I pointed out, which make this derivation doubtful[2].

[1] Kuhn's *Zeitschrift*, xviii.

[2] The question is whether Hephaistos is the original form, or Ἐφίστος, Ἐπίστος, i.e. Ἐφέστιος (Welcker, *Griech. Götterlehre*, i. p. 665). Ἐφέστιος might have been meant for ἐπὶ or πρὸς ταῖς ἑστίαις. But in that case we should have to admit two names, as Ἥφαιστος could not be a corruption of Ἐφίστιος. It should be remembered also that an earthenware image of Hephaestos, which in Athens stood near every hearth, was called ἐπιστάτης. Aristoph. Aves, 436.

Fire in Italy, Vulcanus.

The deity which in Italy corresponds to the Greek Hephaestos and the Vedic Agni is *Vulcanus*. His name is very clear. It is connected with Sk. ulkâ, a firebrand, a meteor. This word occurs in the Rigveda IV. 4, 2:

ásam*d*ita*h* ví s*r*i*g*a víshvak ulk*ắh*.

'Unfettered scatter about thy sparks.'

The fuller form of ulkâ would be *varkâ, instead of which we find vár*k*as, light, lustre, vigour.

Rv. III. 22, 2:

Ágne yát te diví vár*k*a*h* p*r*ithivyắm
yát óshadhîshu apsú ắ ya*g*atra,
yéna antáriksham urú âtatántha
tvesh*áh* s*áh* bhânú*h* ar*n*av*áh* n*r*i*k*ákshâ*h*.

'O Agni, the lustre which is thine in heaven, in earth, in plants, and in the waters, O worshipful, wherewith thou hast stretched out the sky wide, that light is brilliant, waving, all-seeing.'

Vulcan was therefore a god of fire, but in Italy he became pre-eminently the representative of subterraneous or volcanic fire, and then, possibly by Greek influence, the clever craftsman.

Philosophical Aspects of Fire in Greece.

But while in the Greek and Roman religious mythology the representatives of fire occupy a rather subordinate place as compared with the position assigned to fire in India and Persia, in Egypt and Babylon, we find that in Greece the concept of fire led from very early times to philosophical speculation. It is a mistake to draw a very sharp line of demarcation in ancient times between religion and philosophy. The religious sentiments of the Greeks, or, at least, of the more thoughtful among the Greeks, were far more profoundly swayed by the teachings of Thales, Pythagoras, and Herakleitos than by the Homeric poems. It is too often forgotten that Herakleitos considered himself a far higher authority on religion than Homer, whose theology he stigmatised as flippant infidelity[1], while Pythagoras declared that he saw (and, no doubt, he wished to see) the soul of Homer in Hades hanging on a tree and surrounded by serpents, as a punishment for the unseemly things which he had said of the gods.

There certainly is more of what we mean by religion in Herakleitos than in Homer, and I believe that our right appreciation of early Greek philosophers has been much impeded by our forgetting that those early philosophers were religious even more than philosophical teachers. Even Aristotle (Metaph. i. 3), to whom most of us owe our first acquaintance with the ancient sages of Greece, treats them far too much as mere philosophers, and discusses their doctrines, as Hegel did in later times, far too much from his own philosophical point of view[2].

The Fire of Herakleitos.

With Herakleitos fire, the *πῦρ ἀείζωον*, or *αἰώνιον*, the ever-living or immortal fire, was not merely an *ἀρχή* in the Aristotelian sense of the word, or what we call one of the four elements. It was the primordial being, the origin of all things, a higher conception than that of the gods of the populace whom Herakleitos tolerated, though he did not believe in

[1] *Lectures on the Science of Language*, vol. ii. p. 424.

[2] Gladisch, *Die Vorsokratische Philosophie*, in *Jahrb. für Klass. Philologie*, 1879, p. 721.

them. 'Neither one of the gods, he declares [1], nor of men has made this world, the same for all, but it always was and will be, ever-living fire, catching forms and consuming them.' When Herakleitos used the word fire, we should now probably use motion, warmth, or life. In one place he actually used *κεραυνός*, lightning, instead of *πῦρ*, when he declares that lightning rules everything, *τὰ δὲ πάντα οἰακίζει κεραυνός*. From another of his sayings it seems clear that he recognises his fire in the sun also, though he speaks of it as never setting. 'For how,' he says, 'could anybody hide himself from that which never sets?'

Zoroaster.

There is no doubt a distant similarity between the eternal fire of Herakleitos and the fire as conceived by the followers of Zoroaster. But the dissimilarities are far greater than the similarities, and the idea advanced by certain historians of Greek philosophy, particularly by Gladisch [2], that Herakleitos borrowed his opinions from the Persians, is uncalled for, and unsupported by any historical evidence. What was possible in Persia was possible in Greece, and the idea that fire was the beginning of all things, is no more opposed to Greek ideas than the teaching of Thales or that of Anaximenes that water or air were the beginnings of all things.

Fire and Water in the Brâhma*n*as.

We find the same ideas in the Vedic Brâhma*n*as also, but we should not therefore say that Herakleitos

[1] Zeller, *Die Philosophie der Griechen*, vol. i. p. 537.
[2] *Herakleitos und Zoroaster*, 1869.

borrowed his ideas from India. In the Brâhma*n*as we read that in the beginning there was water, or there was fire, or there was Brahman, or there was being and not-being. Thus the Taittirîya-Sa*m*hitâ VII. 1, 5, 1 says: Ấpo vấ idám ágre salilám âsît, tásmin pra*g*ấpatir vâyúr bhûtvấ-*k*arat. 'In the beginning this (world) was water, the sea, and Pra*g*âpati, the Lord of creation, moved on it, having become wind.' How like this is to the language of Genesis, 'And the Spirit of God moved on the face of the waters'—and yet, who would say that the writer of Genesis borrowed from the Taittirîya-Sa*m*hitâ, or *vice versâ?*

In other cosmogonic accounts which we find scattered about in the Brâhma*n*as, the old cosmogony has generally been modified into some kind of emanation from, or creation by Brahman or Pra*g*âpati, the Lord of creatures. But when we leave out this first link, Brahman or Pra*g*âpati, we find a large number of cosmogonic theories, probably much older than the Brâhma*n*as, and older than the first conception of such abstract deities as Brahman or Pra*g*âpati. In some passages it seemed as if it had not been quite forgotten that the place which was assigned to Brahman and Pra*g*âpati was originally held by Agni. We read, for instance, in the *S*atapatha-Brâhma*n*a VI. 1, 1, 5:

> Sa ya*h* sa purusha*h* Pra*g*âpatir abhavad, ayam eva sa yo-yam Agnis *k*îyate.
>
> 'He who became Pra*g*âpati is the same as Agni, kindled on the hearth.'

But, as a rule, Brahman or Pra*g*âpati comes first, and afterwards fire and water and all the rest. In the

Taittirîya-Sa*m*hitâ, for instance, VII. 1, 1, 4, the successive stages in the development of the world, beginning with Pra*g*âpati, are represented (1) by Agni, the Brâhma*n*a (the priest), and the goat; (2) by Indra, the Râ*g*anya (the warrior), and the sheep; (3) by the Visvedevas, the Vaisya, and the cow; (4) by the *S*ûdra and the horse.

In the hymns also similar cosmogonic guesses are uttered from time to time, though we must remember that ideas about the beginning of all things are generally late, and that hymns containing cosmogonic theories cannot be counted among the earliest relics of Vedic poetry. Thus we read, Rv. X. 190:

> *Ri*tám *k*a satyám *k*âbhî́ddhât tápasó*s*dhya*g*âyata,
> táto rấtry a*g*âyata tátah samudró ar*n*avá*h*.
> Samudrấd ar*n*avấd ádhi sa*m*vatsaró a*g*âyata,
> ahorâtrấ*n*i vidádhad vísvasya misható vasî́.
> Sûryâ*k*andramásau dhâtấ yathâpûrvám akalpayat,
> dívam *k*a p*ri*thivî́m *k*ântáriksham átho svấ*h*.

'The right and true was born from kindled heat, then the night was born and the surging sea. From the surging sea the annual sun was born, he who orders day and night, the lord of all that sees. The creator made sun and moon in turn, the sky and the earth and the air, and then the heaven.'

In another place the *Ri*bhus discuss among themselves whether water is best or fire, Rv. I. 161, 9, ấpa*h* bhū́yish*th*â*h* íti éka*h* abravît, agní*h* bhū́yish*th*a*h* íti anyá*h* abravît, which probably refers to the question as to what was the beginning of all things, whether water or fire. In one hymn, X. 121, 7, it is decidedly implied that the waters gave birth to fire or Agni (ấpa*h* ha yát b*ri*hatí*h* vísvam ấyan gárbham dádhânâ*h* *g*anáyantî*h* agním). One of the earliest commentators in the Taittirîya-âra*n*yaka I. 23, 9, explains what he thought the true meaning of this verse, by 'adbhyo vâ idam samabhût,' 'this world arose indeed from water.'

When we see with how much freedom these various cosmogonic theories or guesses are started, we begin to feel how little necessity there is for supposing that Herakleitos borrowed from India or Persia, simply because he looked upon fire as the moving principle of the world.

We saw that Herakleitos, like the Vedic poets, recognised the same power as dwelling in the fire, in the lightning, and, as it would seem, in the sun also. And this is again so natural a conception, that we can perfectly well understand how it arose independently both in India and in Greece. If we look further, we find a very similar conception of the identity of fire, sun, and lightning, even among Semitic nations, but who would say that therefore the Semitic nations borrowed from the Vedic poets, or the Vedic poets from Semitic sources?

Fire as worshipped in Babylon.

It is generally admitted, I believe, that the chief deity worshipped at Babylon was a solar deity [1]. He was called *Bilu*, the lord, and many of the Babylonian gods might claim that name. This *Bilu* appears in the Old Testament as *Baal*, in the plural *Baalim*, and in Greek as Βῆλος. Now the Bilu or Baal of Babylon was Merodach, the lord of Babylon, originally a representative of the sun. But we are told [2] that he represented not only the sun, but that he absorbed also the god of fire. 'Among most primitive people,' Professor Sayce remarks, 'fire is endowed with divine

[1] Sayce, *Hibbert Lectures*, p. 100. [2] Sayce, l. c., p. 179.

attributes. It moves and devours like a living thing; it purifies and burns all that is foul; and it is through the fire upon the altar—the representative of the fire upon the hearth—that the savour of the burnt sacrifice ascends to the gods in heaven. Fire is itself a messenger from above. It comes to us from the sky in the lightning flash, and we feel it in the rays of the noontide sun. The Fire-god tended therefore to become on the one side the messenger and intermediary between gods and men, and on the other side, the Sun-god himself.'

You see in this description of the Fire-god in Babylon the exact counterpart of Agni in the Veda. But there is in this case also this great difference, that while we see in Babylon the last results only, we can watch in India the whole course of development from the first perception of a burning log to the highest concept of a Supreme Being. We should never say that in the Veda fire had been endowed with divine attributes, because that would presuppose the very thing which we want to explain. What we learn from the Veda is the very evolution of these divine attributes arising from the ever-varying concepts of fire and of similar, both natural and supernatural, phenomena. When we once have arrived at a Fire-god, and a Lightning-god, and a Sun-god, our task is really done. Our first chapter ends with the Fire-god, the Lightning-god, and the Sun-god. It begins with fire, lightning, and sun.

The True Antiquity of the Veda.

This is what imparts to the Veda its unique character among the historical monuments of the old world. Tradition assigns to the Sacred Books of China an enormous antiquity, and the students of Babylonian and Egyptian antiquities claim without hesitation for the earliest written relics of these two countries a date far beyond that which we assign to the Veda. But though more modern, if we measure antiquity by the revolutions of the heavenly bodies, the Veda is far more ancient than anything in China, Babylon, or Egypt, when we measure antiquity by the evolution of ideas. If we found the Veda to have been the composition of the inhabitants of an unknown island, and to be not older than the last century, its value for our studies, the analysis of religious ideas, would be but little impaired. India was a kind of unknown island in the ancient history of the world, its ancient literature was thoroughly autochthonous, its earliest religion untouched by any foreign influence. All attempts at discovering Semitic or Egyptian influences in the ancient, that is, in the Vedic literature of India, have totally failed, and at the present moment to attempt to derive the ideas of the Veda from Babylon or Egypt would be as hopeless as former attempts to derive Sanskrit from Hebrew or from the language of the pyramids. The trunklines of ancient language, thought, and religion are sufficiently well known by this time to enable us to declare certain crossings as impossible, and there is no scholar now living who would venture to say that the ancient lines of Indian religion could have been crossed by trains of thought which started from China, from Babylon, or from Egypt.

LECTURE XI.

THE MYTHOLOGICAL DEVELOPMENT OF AGNI.

Tales about Agni.

AFTER having examined the religious and philosophical aspects which the concept of Fire assumed in India and elsewhere, we have now to consider what are called its purely mythological aspects. The line of demarcation between religion, philosophy, and mythology seems often very arbitrary, for the same statements about such a being as Agni may convey to one mind a religious, to another a philosophical lesson, while to the people at large they may be no more than a simple tale, a legend, or a myth. We may, of course, distinguish between a tale, a legend, and a myth, and many more or less artificial definitions have been given of each of these terms.

In a general way, however, these names are given to ancient traditions which have neither a religious nor a philosophical purpose, but simply relate more or less imaginary events. The number of such myths is very considerable, and they often vary, as you know, from the sublime to the ridiculous. There are but few actual tales to be found in the hymns of the Rig-veda, but we can discover here and there some of the elements out of which later tales were formed.

If we remember that Agni represented the light of the sun, we can easily understand why he should have been called the son of Dyaus, the sky (X. 45, 8); or of heaven and earth (III. 25, 1), or of the Dawn (VII. 78, 3), or of the clouds (X. 2, 7); while, if he was the flash of lightning, it might truly be said of him that Indra generated him from two clouds as from two flints (II. 12, 3). And when Agni was obtained by the friction of two fire-sticks, these were naturally called his parents. One of these fire-sticks, the lower one, was called his mother; the other, his father. It might now be said that Agni was the child of these two pieces of wood, the two ara*n*is, and thus we can understand why he was called dvimâtắ, having two mothers (Rv. I. 31, 2), or 'the son of the trees' (sûnú*h* vánaspátînâm, VIII. 23, 25). But when we are told that Agni, as soon as born, devoured his father and mother (Rv. X. 79, 4), we have really an incipient myth. Agni lent himself less to mythological treatment, because his name remained always intelligible. It is always the ancient names which are no longer understood that produce the richest mythological growth.

Euhemeristic explanations of Mythology.

Still, such a statement, as that a child eats his own father and mother, is startling enough to take its place among mythological stories. If such a story, instead of being told of Agni, were told of Angiras, another, but no longer an understood name of fire, we should have had at once one of those myths which have formed such stumbling-blocks for Mr. Herbert

Spencer and other students of ethnology. These philosophers wish to account for everything in the development of the human race rationalistically. They want to discover a reason for these unspeakable atrocities of which the gods and heroes, even of such progressive races as the Indians, the Greeks, Romans, and Teutons, are believed to have been guilty. Their way out of the difficulty is certainly very ingenious and very simple; but is it supported by any evidence? First of all, they tell us that they see no reason why such names as Fire, or Sun, or Dawn should not be accepted as names of real individuals who lived a long time ago. They show that among the Karens certain people were called Evening, Moon-rising, &c.; that a Tasmanian lady was called Sunshine; and that, among Australians, names like Hail, Thunder, and Wind are by no means uncommon[1]. They prove, from modern Post-Office Directories, that even now some people are called Fire, Dawn, and Sun. As to the atrocities ascribed to these individuals, they recognise in them what they call survivals (*Überbleibsel*) of an earlier savage and half-brutal state, when the ancestors of the Hindus, Greeks, Romans, and Teutons were really capable of eating their parents, like Agni, or Mr. Fire, or of eating their children, like Kronos, or Mr. Time. I am not exaggerating, I am only abbreviating, and therefore,

[1] H. Spencer, *Sociology*, pp. 391–2. 'The initial step in the genesis of such a myth would be the existence of human beings named Storm and Sunshine. From the confusion inevitably arising in tradition between them and the natural agents having the same names, would result the personalising of these natural agents, and the ascribing to them human origins and human adventures: the legend, once having thus germinated, being, in successive generations, elaborated and moulded into fitness with the phenomena.'

perhaps, representing the theories of Mr. Herbert Spencer and other Euhemerists in a too naked, and therefore in a less persuasive and attractive form.

Of course, when we are carried off into prehistoric times, it is very difficult for us to prove a negative. We cannot prove that there never lived a Mr. Sun and a Miss Dawn, that this Mr. Sun never embraced Miss Dawn, and that she never fainted away or died in his embraces. There may have been a Mr. Fire, and he may have eaten his father and mother, and, as the Egyptians say, he may actually have died of indigestion.

But, on the other hand, scholars and historians have a perfect right to say that it will be time to consider these theories when all other theories have failed, and that in the meantime the historical footprints of language ought not to be neglected, but should be interpreted as all other vestiges of creation have been interpreted. If we hear of Ushas expiring in the embraces of Sûrya, we cannot forget that Ushas meant the dawn, and Sûrya the sun, and that, as a matter of fact, the dawn does expire every morning in the fiery embraces of the sun. If we read of Agni devouring his two parents, we cannot forget that Agni means fire, that his two parents are the two Ara*n*îs or fire-sticks, and that, as a matter of fact, the fire, when produced by rubbing, and nursed into flames, is apt to consume the fire-sticks that have given him life. I cannot even make that small concession, which I am told I ought to make, namely, that the fact of the Greeks accepting such atrocities as possible, proves that once, in prehistoric times, they committed them themselves. The ancient Âryas may formerly have eaten their parents, if Mr. Herbert Spencer can prove it; but the fact that they believed Agni to have been guilty of this breach of filial piety does not prove it, to my mind, any more than the unnatural treatment of his divine children by Kronos could persuade me that the earliest Greeks were in the habit of swallowing their children, and, what would even then, on the theory of survivals, remain inexplicable, that they were able to bring them up again, apparently intact.

I quite feel the power of the objections so often raised by anthropologists against the historical and linguistic explanations of these terrible myths. It has been said again and again, and apparently with a great deal of justice, that it would seem passing strange that the ancient Âryas should have spent their time in relating these strange, sometimes absurd and impossible, sometimes sublime and significant stories, if there had been no foundation whatever for them in fact. But, after all, we must take man as we find him. Thus, it would have seemed at first sight very unlikely that betting and gambling, which have lately been held up as the vices of modern society, should have belonged to the earliest amusements of man in the most distant parts of the world. Yet there can be no doubt that it was so. You remember how so ancient a philosopher as Herakleitos explains the government of the world by Zeus throwing dice[1]; and it is curious that Herakleitos himself is reported to have been fond of that game. At all events, the game was known. Still stranger it is that, in the hymns of the Rig-veda, we should meet with a

[1] Zeller, *Die Philosophie der Griechen*, vol. i. p. 536.

hymn, which I read to you in one of my former lectures, containing the despairing utterances of a gambler (X. 34), who accuses the dice of having ruined the happiness of his home by their irresistible attraction. Many critics would appeal to such a hymn as showing how advanced and how modern a state of society is presupposed in the Veda. But to the true critic it only conveys the lesson that our ideas of what primitive life was like, must submit to be corrected by facts. The epic poetry of India may almost be said to be built up on the passion for gambling, and we know how strongly addicted uncivilised races are, even now, to this ingrained vice of poor humanity.

Ancient Riddles.

If we study the tastes of the people as we find them represented to us in the Veda, there is one peculiar feature which may help to explain the liking for wonderful mythological stories, such as we find among the Âryas in India and in other parts of the world. This is their fondness for riddles. I have never dwelt on this before, because it might seem that riddles also were the amusement of our modern drawing-rooms rather than of the primitive huts of the Aryan conquerors of the world. But, as one out of many elements contributing to the rank growth of mythology, and as a very important element, I think it ought to be more carefully considered than it has been hitherto.

After the Âryas in India had once arrived at the conception that fire was apt to consume the fire-sticks, or that Agni had eaten his father and mother, they seem to have amused themselves by asking such questions as, Who eats his own parents? The answers given would then enter upon many details, more or less far-fetched, and the question would continue to be asked between old and young people, just as we ask our children to guess such riddles as:

'A flock of white sheep
On a red hill,
Here they go, there they go,
Now they stand still[1].'

Or again:

'Old Mother Twitchett had but one eye,
And a long tail which she let fly;
And every time she went over a gap,
She left a bit of her tail in a trap.'

This may be matched by the Mexican riddle:

'What goes through a valley and drags its entrails behind?' (A needle.)

Fire lent itself particularly well to the formation of riddles. Thus we find among the Zulus the following riddle, published by Bishop Callaway at the end of his Zulu Nursery Tales[2]:

'Guess ye a man whom men do not like to laugh, for it is known that his laughter is a very great evil, and is followed by lamentation, and an end of rejoicing. Men weep, and trees, and grass; and everything is heard weeping in the tribe where he laughs; and they say the man has laughed who does not usually laugh.'

This is a very elaborate riddle, and the solution is even more elaborate. What is meant is fire, and the

[1] See M. Di Martino, *Enigmes Populaires Siciliennes*, 1878, p. 9.

[2] *Nursery Tales of the Zulus*, by the Rev. Canon Callaway. Natal, 1868, p. 366. Tylor, *Primitive Culture*, vol. i. p. 81.

laughing of fire is intended for its crackling, cackling sound, not without a certain admixture of a mischievous grin.

This is how the Zulu solves his riddle: 'Fire is called a man that what is said may not be at once evident, it being concealed by the word "man." A riddle is good when it is not discernible at once. It is not liked that the fire, even indoors where it is kindled, should cause its sparks (its laughter) to start out and fall on the flour clothes. The owner [of them] cries because it burns, and when he sees a hole in it, he cries again. Or if food is cooked, if the fire is large, the pot may be burned by the fire, and the pot burn the food. So the man, that is the fire, laughs, and the people cry. Again, if a spark is cast into the thatch of a hut, it is seen by the fire. All the men will come together when the flame of the fire appears, and burns the house with the things which are in it, and there is a great crying. The goats are burnt, and the calves, and the children. (Remark, the children come last.) The cows cry for their calves; men cry for their goats; the wife and husband cry for their children. The children cry for their father who has been burnt whilst fetching precious things from the burning house, and the house fell in on him. The husband cries for the wife who was burnt when fetching her child from the burning house. The trees cry, crying for their beauty which is destroyed by the fire, the trees being shrivelled and withered. And the cattle cry, crying for the grass, because they have no longer anything to eat, but are dying of famine. This is the laughing of fire.'

This taste for riddles was very widely spread, and

most of them are so simple that we should hardly call them riddles. You remember Samson's riddle—'Out of the eater came forth meat, and out of the strong came forth sweetness.' No one could possibly guess such a riddle, least of all the Philistines, unless they had indeed ploughed with Samson's heifer.

The riddle of the Sphinx has more of the character of an old riddle, being descriptive rather than in any way deceptive. 'What has a voice and walks on four legs in the morning, on two at noon, and on three in the evening?'

To the same class belongs the well-known Greek riddle about Day and Night:

Εἰσὶ κασίγνηται διτταί, ὧν ἡ μία τίκτει
Τὴν ἑτέραν, αὐτὴ δὲ τεκοῦσ' ὑπὸ τῆσδε τεκνοῦται.

'There are two sisters of whom the one bears the other; and she who bears the other is borne by her.'

That the taste for these riddles was old in India we see from such hymns as I. 164 in the Rig-veda, which consists entirely of riddles, some of them so obscure that even Dr. Haug[1], who wrote a learned essay on that hymn, could not solve them all.

Brahmodya.

This asking and answering of riddles formed in fact an essential part of the amusements connected with the performance of the early sacrifices. It is called Brahmodya, which may have meant either simply the discourse or conversation of the Brâhmans, the priests, or a discourse on Brahman, the supreme being.

[1] *Vedische Räthselfragen und Räthselsprüche*, in *Sitzungsberichte der Kön. bayr. Akademie der Wissenschaften*, Bd. ii. Heft 3, 1875.

We find descriptions of these priestly discussions in the Vâ*g*asaneyi-sa*m*hitâ XXIII. 9–12; 45–62, and elsewhere. I shall translate some portions in order to give you an idea of the simple intellectual food that satisfied the taste of these ancient sages [1].

The Brahman priest begins by asking the Hot*ri* priest:

'Who, you think, walks alone, and who is born again? What is the medicine for cold? What is the great vessel?'

The Hot*ri* priest answers: 'The sun walks alone; the moon is born again. Agni, fire, is the medicine for cold; the earth is the great vessel.'

Here the riddles were easy to answer. But the next are more difficult.

The Hot*ri* priest asks the Brahman priest:

'What was the first thought? What was the large bird? Who was Pilippilâ, and who was Pisangilâ?'

You see, these questions are perplexing. The Brahman priest, however, answers them as follows:

'The sky,' he says, 'Dyaus, was the first thought.'

Now there may be some very profound truth in this. It is conceivable that these Indian sages thought that the first human concept, as distinct from mere percepts, must have been the sky; that the sky excited the first wonderment, the first reflection, the first thought, and the first name. But, as if this were too profound an interpretation, the commentator adds that by Dyaus or sky may here be meant the rain, and that it was rain, as an essential condition of life itself, that constituted the first thought among men.

[1] Cf. Maitrâya*n*î-sa*m*hitâ III. 12, 19; Taitt.-sa*m*hitâ VII. 4, 18, 1; Kâ*th*aka V. 4.

As to the large bird, the priest answers that it was the horse. This may be so, but it seems more likely that in this place the large bird was meant originally as a name for the sun.

The next questions are more difficult still.

Pilippilâ is a word which occurs nowhere else, one of the, no doubt, very numerous class of words which existed in the spoken languages of India, but have found no place in their literature. The Brahman priest explains Pilippilâ as meaning the earth, but the name which he uses for earth is again quite unknown elsewhere in that sense. For avi, which is here supposed to mean earth, means otherwise sheep, and is the same word as Lat. *ovis*, Gr. *ὄϊς*, our *ewe*. It seems to me not unlikely that avis was meant originally for a name of the morning or the dawn, which would then form a better pair with the next answer, What is Pisangilâ[1]? This is answered, and probably rightly, by declaring that it was meant for the night. Pisanga in Sanskrit means dark red, and Pisangilâ would therefore be an appropriate name for the gloaming[2].

Other riddles follow, but I shall only add one more, because it shows that philosophical subjects also were comprehended in these riddles. Thus in verse 51 the Udgât*ri* priest asks the Brahman priest:

'Into what did man (or the soul) enter? What things are placed in man? On that, O Brahman, we challenge thee, what canst thou tell us here?'

[1] The Satapatha Brâhma*n*a XIII. 2, 6, 16 explains pilippilâ by srî, happiness.

[2] In XXIII. 56, pisangilâ is explained by a*g*â, and a*g*â again by Mâyâ, or night.

The Brahman priest answers: 'Man has entered into the five, these five are placed in man. Thus I answer thee here, thou art not above me in wisdom.'

'The five' are meant for the five senses, the outward senses being those into which man has entered, the inward senses those which are placed inside him. Simple as this conception is, you see that it involves a recognition of man, or the essential element in man, as independent of the five senses. Man had been conceived as something different from the seeing, hearing, tasting, smelling, and feeling animal, and that is a view which forms the firm foundation of all future idealistic philosophy.

I feel convinced that this ancient and widely-spread taste for riddles has been a powerful element in the production of mythology, and that many strange features in the phenomena of nature were dwelt on and elaborated in order to amuse and puzzle people. After all, what subjects were there for conversation and intellectual amusement in those early days? Bucolic subjects are soon exhausted, and even the weather, that never-failing topic, could not afford much more variety to conversation than it does now. Subjects for sensational novels would not abound in the simple idyllic life of the Aryan peasants, and even wars could hardly have been more than raids and plunderings. What wonder then that what we now call mythology, as unconnected with religion and philosophy, should have been so welcome an amusement, and that the very eccentricities of the ancient mythologies and the oddities of their early riddles should have served to impress them on the minds of successive generations, and thus have secured their perpetuity.

The Disappearance of Agni.

Let us now consider another peculiar feature of Agni or fire. Whether fire came from the sun, or from lightning, or from the friction of fire-sticks, there was always the same fatality about it. It came and it disappeared again. The fire in the sun disappeared at sunset, and no one knew what became of it in the water. Some people imagined they heard the sea hissing when the sun entered into it. Such is human imagination. The fire in the lightning disappeared even more suddenly. It came and went, as we say, like lightning. Lastly, even the fire produced by friction was difficult to catch, and unless constantly watched and kept alive by dry leaves, sticks of wood, or by fat and oil poured on it, it was very apt to disappear.

This disappearance of fire was a most serious matter, particularly when the art of rubbing it out of wood was not yet generally known, or practised in certain priestly families only. To be without fire meant not only to be unable to perform sacrifices, though that was serious enough in the eyes of the Brâhmans; in the northern regions of India it meant dying of cold and starvation. No wonder therefore that the disappearance of fire occupied the minds of the early myth-makers, or riddle-makers, or story-tellers, and that all possible reasons were invented to account for the flight of Agni.

Dialogue between Agni and Varu*n*a.

How old these stories must be, we may gather from the fact that in the hymns which are generally free as yet from very elaborate legends, we find already a dialogue between Agni and another god, Varu*n*a, who tries to persuade Agni to leave his hiding-place, and to return to men and gods. I shall give you a translation of the hymn, though it belongs to that class which most Vedic students would look upon as comparatively recent. (Rv. X. 51.)

Varu*n*a speaks:

'That covering was great and stout, covered by which thou hast entered the waters. O Agni, all-knowing one, there is one god who often perceived all thy bodies.'

Agni replies:

'Who saw me? What god was it who often espied my bodies? Where then, O Mitra and Varu*n*a, dwelt all the brands of Agni which ascend to the gods?'

Varu*n*a:

'We often longed for thee, all-knowing Agni, after thou hadst entered the waters and the herbs. It was Yama, O brilliant one, that discovered thee, sparkling forth from ten coverings.'

Agni:

'I went away from the sacrifice, O Varu*n*a, fearing lest the gods should employ me there. Often have my bodies been hidden there. I, Agni, did not like that work.'

Varu*n*a:

'Come hither, the god-loving man desires to sacrifice; thou dwellest in darkness long enough. Make the ways to the gods easy, and carry the offering willingly.'

Agni:

'The brothers of Agni have formerly accomplished that work, as a driver his journey. Therefore, O Varu*n*a, I went far away from fear, I trembled like a deer before the bowstring of the hunter.'

Varu*n*a:

'We give thee a life that is without decay, so that thou shouldest not suffer, when employed, O all-knowing Agni; then wilt thou willingly carry the share of the oblation to the gods, O noble one.'

Agni:

'Give then to me alone the first and the last offerings, and the vigorous portions of the oblation, the best of the waters, and the soul of the herbs, and let the life of Agni be long.'

Varu*n*a:

'Let the first and the last offerings belong to thee alone, and the vigorous portions of the oblation. May this whole sacrifice be thine, and may the four regions bow before thee.'

I look upon this hymn, as I said before, as a later production. The concluding verses, more particularly, are such as we might expect in the Brâhma*n*as rather than in the hymns. What I translated by 'the first and the last offerings,' are really technical sacrificial terms (prayâ*g*a and anuyâ*g*a), and probably put in, in order to explain why in certain sacrifices the first and last offerings are always dedicated to Agni.

Later Accounts of the Hiding of Agni.

The kernel of this and other stories about the hiding of Agni was always the same:—Agni was apt to go out, and had to be called back by some means or other. Everything else was added according to the fancies of individual story-tellers. Thus we read in the Taittirîya-sa*m*hitâ II. 6, 6, 1[1]: 'Agni had three elder brothers, who fainted while carrying oblations to the gods. Agni feared lest he should incur the same fate, and accordingly he disappeared and entered into the waters. The gods sought to discover him. A fish pointed him out. Agni cursed the fish, saying, "Since thou hast pointed me out, may men slay thee, whenever they like." Men, in consequence, slay a fish at their pleasure, because it was cursed. The gods found Agni, and said to him, "Come to us and bring us our oblations." He replied, "Let me ask a favour. Let whatever part of the oblation, after it is taken and before it is poured out, falls outside of the sacred enclosure, be the share of my brothers."'

You see how the myth goes on growing and growing. Agni has now three brothers, older than himself; possibly the three fires from the sun, from the lightning, and from the fire-sticks. Or possibly, as having gone out in former sacrifices, they may have been called his elder brothers. We can easily understand why what had been spilt at the sacrifice was supposed to have been offered to these three elder brothers; for, whatever had once been brought to the sacrifice, had to be assigned to some god or

[1] Muir, *O. S. Texts*, vol. iv. p. 203.

other. Hence recipients had to be found even for what had been spilt, and the three invalided brothers of Agni seemed the proper recipients for these wasted offerings[1].

All this is mere refinement, due to priestly influence. What is new in this account is that, instead of being discovered by Yama, or, as we find it stated elsewhere, by Indra, X. 32, 6, Agni is here betrayed by a fish, and again, in other places, by a frog. These animals may possibly have been meant for the first rays of the dawn, betraying the returning sun, but considering how much the further development of a myth was in the hands of any silly grandmother, and even of her grandchildren, we are hardly justified in our expectation that there must be some reason and some meaning in every particle of these stories.

The story of the disappearance of Agni has evidently been a very popular one, and we find it referred to again and again in the epic poetry, and even in the latest Purâ*n*as, though with ever so many modifications. It is through these modifications that the myth of the disappearance of Agni becomes so instructive to us. The original idea, as we saw, was simple enough. It was no more than the recording of the painful fact that fire was apt to go out. Everything else was simply an attempt to answer the very natural questions, Why does fire go out? Whither does it go, and how has it been recovered?

[1] That there was a superstitious feeling about the fragments of anything that had once formed part of a sacrifice we see again and again. Thus Vasish*th*a (XI. 22–23) quotes Manu that 'both what remains (in the vessels) and the fragments (of the meal) are the portions of those members of a family who died before receiving the sacraments.' They are not to be swept up before the sun has set.

We have already seen one answer, why Agni hid himself. It was because he was tired of having always to do duty at the sacrifices. Another reason is given in the Mahâbhârata III. 221. Here we read that Agni, having been used for burning corpses, felt contaminated and took refuge in the ocean. Atharvan was sent by the gods to persuade him to return, but he declined, saying that he felt too weak to carry the oblations to the gods, and that Atharvan might do it in his place. Agni then found another hiding-place, but was betrayed again by the fishes, whom he in consequence cursed and condemned to be eaten by other creatures[1]. When Atharvan urged him once more to return, he hid himself beneath the earth, and allowed his body to be dissolved. His liver, we are told, became iron, his bile emerald, his phlegm crystal, his bones the Devadâru tree, and so on. While in that state, he was roused by the efforts of Bh*ri*gu, Angiras, and others. He blazed forth again, but frightened at the sight of Atharvan, he went once more to hide in the ocean. Atharvan, however, succeeded at last in recovering Agni and persuading him to resume his sacrificial duties.

Another explanation of Agni's disappearance is that Bh*ri*gu, a saint, cursed him for having spoken the truth. The fact is that this saint had deprived the giant Puloman of his bride, Pulomâ. Puloman, on entering the house of the saint to recover his bride, asks Agni, the fire burning on the hearth, whether she is not the giant's legitimate bride. Agni, who cannot tell an untruth, speaks the truth, Puloman

[1] At Rome fishes were sacrificed to the god of fire at the Volcanalia. Varro, *L. L.* vi. 20; Plin. *Epist.* iii. 5, 8.

carries off his bride, and the saint curses Agni to become a sarvabhaksha, an indiscriminate eater, a devourer of unclean as well as clean things; though he adds that his flames shall always purify everything. Upon this, Agni fled and hid himself in a *S*amî-tree. The whole world then seemed in danger of perishing during the absence of Agni, but B*ri*haspati leads the suppliant gods to the *S*amî-tree in which Agni was hidden, and at last persuades him to return, even though he must remain a sarvabhaksha, or a promiscuous feeder [1].

There are several other legends about Agni and his vanishings, and it is easy to see that there is a certain purpose in all of them. For instance, the idea that fire consumed all things, whether clean or unclean, would naturally stagger the mind of the Hindus, who were so particular, at all events in later times, as to what might or might not be eaten. Hence the story of the curse of the saint pronounced against Agni, and his condemnation to consume everything, whether clean or unclean.

Agni's hiding in a *S*amî-tree is likewise intelligible. It was from that tree that one of the fire-sticks had to be taken, and as fire came out of it by mere rubbing, it was but a natural conclusion that Agni had been hiding in the tree.

Why Agni was supposed to have been hiding in the water is likewise intelligible. First of all he seemed to rise and to set in the clouds, so far as he was embodied in the sun. Secondly, in the shape of lightning, he burst forth from the clouds and seemed

[1] A similar story of Agni becoming leprous is told by Al-Birûnî (vol. ii. p. 140) from the Vish*n*u-dharma.

to be the cause of rain. Thirdly, it could not escape attention that the one element which was capable of overcoming fire was water, so that it might well be said in that sense also that Agni had been hidden or extinguished by water.

We see a similar idea expressed in a legend which tells us that Agni was once sent out to find Indra, who had been lost. When he returned from his voyage of discovery, he told the gods he had explored the whole world without finding Indra; only the waters he could not explore, because he would perish there, for fire, he says, is born from water, and the power of fire ceases where it had its origin.

Again, there is some sense in the story that Agni, when hidden in the earth, was changed into iron and other metals. It shows that the igneous origin of the metals had been guessed, and that traces of the action of volcanic fire had probably been discovered.

Lastly, as fire was conceived as heat, and heat as life, the idea that Agni was hidden in all living beings, and that even the growth and ripening of plants were dependent on his presence, was not unnatural.

The Meaning or Hyponoia of Mythology.

What I wished to put clearly before you in this collection of mythologic sayings about Agni is this, that there are grains of reason in all that heap of unreason which we call mythology. The constituent elements of mythology, when we can still discover them, are always perfectly natural. Their supernatural appearance is the result of growth and decay, of fancy and fun, of misunderstanding, sometimes, though rarely, of a wilful perversion. This is what

Comparative Mythology teaches us. It depends on us to draw from it those practical lessons which comparative studies will always convey, if only they are carried out in a truly philosophical and comprehensive spirit.

Lessons of Comparative Mythology.

There are two prejudices at all events which a comparative study of the religions of the world, and of the inevitable corruptions of those religions, may help to eradicate. The one is that the ancient dwellers on earth were so different from us that they can teach us nothing, that they cannot be judged by the same standards as we ourselves, and that even if they say the same thing, they do not mean the same thing.

The second prejudice, prevalent more particularly among a certain class of scholars, is that if poets and prophets, belonging to different countries, say the same thing, they must have borrowed it, one from the other.

With regard to this second prejudice, where is there any excuse for it? We can see how most of the thoughts in the Veda have grown up naturally and intelligibly. I tried to show this in the case of Agni, or fire, and its gradual development into a god of fire, and, at last, into a supreme god. If then we find the same development or the same final result elsewhere also, as, for instance, in Babylon, why should we say that Babylon has borrowed from India, or India from Babylon? Surely what was possible in one country was possible in another also; what was intelligible in India is intelligible in Babylon also. When there is a real historical intercourse between two nations in antiquity, that intercourse cannot easily be mistaken. For instance, the very name of *Alphabet* proves better than anything else that the Phenicians were at one time the schoolmasters of the Greeks. But when, as in the case of the Veda, there is no trace, so far as we know at present, of any foreign influence, whether Semitic or Egyptian, why should we look to Babylon, Nineveh, Egypt, or China for the antecedents of what shows to us its perfect natural development on Indian soil? On our maps the North of India may seem very near to Babylon, yet it is a far cry from Loch Awe, and the roads from India to Babylon are even now by no means easy or pleasant. I know there are coincidences, sometimes very startling coincidences, between the religion of the Vedas and those of other races. There are startling coincidences, as you have often heard of late, between Buddhism and Christianity. But to the scholar these coincidences are nothing as compared with the enormous dissimilarities between these religions. There are some stray coincidences even between Sanskrit and Hebrew, between English and Chinese, but what weight have these in the midst of a totally different body of words and grammar? This is a point that has strangely been neglected, though in the eyes of the scholar it is strong enough to make him unwilling to enter at all on such useless controversies.

If I have tried to show you how the human mind, unassisted by anything but the miraculous revelation of nature, arrived in India from the concept of fire at the highest concept of deity, my object was to show by one instance that could not be gainsayed, that such a process was not only possible, but was real. That is the only answer which the scholar can give to those who hold, for some reason which they have never explained, that it is impossible for unassisted human reason to arrive at the idea of God. But I hope that no one could have so far misunderstood me as to suppose that I wished to maintain that all other Aryan nations had borrowed their concept of deity from the hymns of the Veda, or from the concept of Agni. All I wished to prove was that what was real in the Veda was possible elsewhere also. There is a parallelism between the religions, as there is between the languages of the Aryan race, but the distant source from which these streams spring is not to be looked for in India. Yet there was such a source, and that source had a truly historical character.

When, on the contrary, we find similarities between any of the Aryan and any of the Semitic religions, there is no common historical source for these parallel streams. Their only common source, so far as we know at present, is our common inward nature, and that common outward nature by which we are surrounded. In all the lessons which the human mind learnt in that common school-room of the world, we share in the same truth, and we are exposed to the same errors, whether we are Aryan or Semitic or Egyptian in language and thought. Or, to put it in clearer language, in all the fundamentals of religion we are neither better nor worse than our neighbours, neither more wise nor more unwise than all the members of that great family who have been taught to know themselves as children of one and the same Father in Heaven.

This is the lesson which nothing can teach so

powerfully as a comparative study of the religions of the world. It teaches by facts, not by theories. I must often be satisfied with placing before you the dry facts: but I have no doubt that these facts will speak like texts, even without a sermon.

LECTURE XII.

RELIGION, MYTH, AND CUSTOM.

Difference between Religion and Mythology.

I WAS anxious to explain to you in my last lecture how the same source which supplied the ancient world with religious concepts, produced also a number of ideas which cannot claim to be called religious in any sense, least of all in that which *we* ourselves connect with the name of religion.

We saw how in the Veda the concept of Fire had been raised higher and higher, till at last it became synonymous with the Supreme Deity of the Vedic poets. But in the amorous vagaries of Agni, as related in the later poetry of India, or in Greece in the monstrous birth of Hephaestos, likewise a representative, or, as we sometimes say, likewise a god of fire, in his disgraceful ejection from the sky, in his marriage with Aphrodite, to say nothing of the painful *dénouement* of that ill-judged union, there is very little of religion, very little of 'the perception of the infinite under such manifestations as are able to influence the moral conduct of man.'

These mythological stories are, no doubt, chips and splinters from the same block out of which many a divine image has been chiselled by the human mind, but their character, their origin and purpose are totally different. This distinction, however, has not only been neglected, it seems often to have been wilfully neglected. Whenever it was necessary to criticise any of the non-Christian religions in a hostile spirit, these stories, the stories of Venus and Vulcan and Mars, have constantly been quoted as showing the degraded character of ancient gods and heroes, and of pagan religion in general.

This is most unfair. Neither does this mythological detritus, not to say rubbish, represent the essential elements of the religion of Greeks and Romans, nor did the ancients themselves believe that it did. We must remember that the ancient nations had really no word or concept as yet for religion in the comprehensive sense which we attach to it. It would hardly be possible to ask the question in any of the ancient languages, or even in classical Greek, whether a belief in Hephaestos and Aphrodite constituted an article of religious faith.

It is true that the ancients, as we call them rather promiscuously, had but one name for their gods, whether they meant Jupiter, the *Deus Optimus Maximus*, or Jupiter, the faithless husband of Juno. But when we speak of the ancients in general, we must not forget that we are speaking, not only of Homer and Hesiod, but likewise of men like Herakleitos, Aeschylos, and Plato. These ancient thinkers knew as well as we do that nothing unworthy of the gods could ever have been true of them, still less of the supreme God; and if they tolerated mythology and legends, those who thought at all about these matters looked upon them as belonging to quite a different sphere of human interests.

If we once understand how mythology and legends arose, how they represent an inevitable stage in the growth of ancient language and thought, we shall understand not only their outward connection with religious ideas, but likewise their very essential difference.

Secular Ideas become Religious.

While on the one hand it is perfectly true that the sources of religion and mythology are conterminous, nay, that certain concepts which in their origin might be called religious wither away into mere mythology and romance, we shall see that it likewise happens, and by no means unfrequently, that ideas, at first entirely unconnected with religion, are attracted into the sphere of religion, and assume a religious character in the course of time. This is an important subject, but beset with many difficulties.

Of course, the deification of an animal, such as an Egyptian Apis, or the apotheosis of a human being, such as Romulus or the Emperor Augustus, presupposes the previous existence in the human mind of the concept of divinity, a concept which, as we saw, required many generations for its elaboration. Again, the attribution of a divine sanction bestowed either on customs or laws, presupposes a belief in something superhuman or divine. But, after a time, all this is forgotten, and these later corruptions of religious thought are mixed up with the more primitive elements of religion in a hopeless confusion.

Let us consider to-day a few instances of secular

customs being afterwards invested with a religious authority.

Lighting and Keeping of Fire.

When we remember how difficult it must have been in early times to light a fire at a moment's notice, and what fearful consequences might follow if a whole community was left during the winter without a fire burning on the hearth, we require no far-fetched explanations for a number of time-hallowed customs connected with the lighting, and still more with the guarding of the fire. It was not necessary that every tribe which kept a sacred fire should have a belief in fire as a god, as was the case with the Vedic poets. Quite apart from any deeper religious convictions, mere common sense would have led men in a primitive state of society to value any new discovery for striking fire and to adopt measures for preserving it, whether for private or for public use. If the Romans appointed vestal virgins to keep a fire always burning, the Damaras [1] in Africa did exactly the same.

It is the custom, or it was till very lately, among German peasants, for a man when he married and left his father's house, to take a burning piece of wood from the paternal home and to light with it the fire on his own hearth. Exactly the same is told us of many uncivilised races. Among the Damaras, for instance, when a tribe migrated from one place to another, they took some burning logs from the old to the new home.

Nowhere, however, do we find this custom more fully described than in India. In the Vedic hymns

[1] Réville, *Religions des Peuples non-civilisés*, i. p. 144.

fire is the *gri*ha-pati, the lord of the house. A house was a fire, and 'so many fires' are mentioned even now in the census of half-nomadic tribes in Russia, nay even in Italy (*fuochi*), as meaning 'so many families, or houses.' In ancient India, as described to us in the G*ri*hya-sûtras, the most important act when a man married and founded his own household, was the kindling of the fire in his own house, with fire brought from the home of his bride, or with fire newly rubbed. In the fourth night after the wedding the husband has to establish the fire within his house. He assigns his seat to the south of it to the Brahman, places a pot of water to the north, cooks a mess of sacrificial food, sacrifices the two â*g*ya portions, and then makes five oblations to Agni, Vâyu, Sûrya, *K*andra, and Gandharva. Here Agni, Fire, holds the first place among the domestic gods. After him follow Wind, Sun, and Moon, and lastly the Gandharva, whoever he may be[1].

This domestic fire, when once lit, remained the friend and protector of the family in every sense of the word, and we see the most touching superstitions arising from this in India, and in every part of the world. Many years ago, in my article on 'Funeral Ceremonies' (1855)[2], I translated a passage from Âsvalâyana's G*ri*hya-sûtras (IV. 1), in which it is said that if a disease befall one who has set up sacred fires, he should leave his village (with his fires) and go in an eastern, northern, or north-eastern direction. And why? Because there is a saying, 'Fires love the village.' It is understood therefore that the

[1] Pâraskara, G*ri*hya-sûtras I. 11; and Sâṅkhâyana I. 18.

[2] *Zeitschrift der Deutschen Morgenländischen Gesellschaft*, ix. pp. 1 seq.

fires, longing to return to the village, will bless him and make him whole[1]. Here we see how a mere proverb, 'The fires love the village,' may lead without any effort to a metamorphosis of the fire into a friend, a friend with all the feelings of other friends, willing even to render a service and to restore a man to health, if thereby they may themselves be enabled to return to their beloved hearth.

Besides the fire in each house, the custom of keeping a public fire also is alluded to at an early date.

According to the Dharma-sûtras of Âpastamba, II. 10, 25, a king has to build a palace, a hall, and a house of assembly, and in every one of them a fire is to be kept, a kind of *ignis foci publici sempiternus*, and daily oblations to be offered in it, just the same as in every private house.

There are many sayings among civilised and uncivilised nations, implying a respect for fire and a recognition of its value for domestic purposes. The Ojibways[2], for instance, have a saying that one ought not to take liberties with fire, but we are never told that the Ojibways worshipped the fire as a god.

There is a very wide-spread feeling against spitting, or throwing anything unclean into the fire or into the water. We saw it mentioned by Herodotus and by Manu. It is a godless thing, they say in Bohemia, to spit into the fire. The Mongolians, as Schmidt tells us, consider it sinful to extinguish fire by water, to spit into the fire, or to defile it in any other way[3].

Such rules, though evidently intended at first for a

[1] See also Oldenberg, *S. B. E.*, xxix. p. 236.
[2] Réville, l. c., i. p. 221.
[3] Castrén, *Finnische Mythologie*, p. 57.

very definite and practical object, were soon invested with a kind of sacred authority. If the Bohemian says it is a godless thing to spit into the fire, he soon adds a reason: Because it is God's fire. This is, of course, a very modern idea; it may be called a Christian idea, based on a belief that all good and perfect gifts come from God—but it is nevertheless a very natural afterthought.

Religious Sanction for Customs.

What therefore we must try to find out in all these observances is, whether at first there was not an intelligible object in them, whether they did not serve some useful purpose, and whether the religious sanction did not come much later in the day. When there once existed a belief in divine beings, any custom or law, and particularly those which it was difficult to enforce by mere human authority, were naturally placed by the ancient lawgivers under the protection of the gods. Professor von Ihering, one of the highest German authorities on the history of law, has traced many of these sacred commandments back to their true origin, namely their *Zweck,* their practical object.

It is quite clear, for instance, that in early times it was necessary to guard the purity of rivers by some kind of religious protection. No sanitary police could have protected them in their long meandering courses. Pausanias (iii. 25, 4) tells a story of a spring on the promontory of Tainaron in Laconia (Cape Matapan) which possessed some miraculous qualities, but lost them because a woman had dared to wash dirty linen in it.

In a primitive household, where the central fire was, as it were, the property of all, a similar restriction against defilement was equally necessary. And when with the change of domestic arrangements the original object of such restrictions ceased to be understood, they became what we find them to be in many countries, mere unmeaning customs, and, for that very reason, often invested with a sacred authority. When the real purpose (*Zweck*) was forgotten, a new purpose had to be invented.

Baptism by Water and Fire.

For instance, people wonder why the inhabitants of Mexico, as well as of Peru [1], should have been acquainted with baptism by water and fire. Originally, however, these seem to have been very simple and useful acts of purification, which in later time only grew into sacramental acts. The nurse had to bathe the child immediately after birth, and to invoke the so-called goddess of water to cleanse the child from everything unclean, and to protect it against all evil. That is to say, every new-born child had to be washed. Afterwards there followed a more brilliant baptism. Friends and relations were invited to a feast, the child was carried about in the house, as if to present it to the domestic deities, and while the nurse placed it in water she recited the following words: 'My child, the gods, the lords of heaven, have sent thee into this miserable world; take this water which will give you life.' Then she sprinkled water on the mouth, the head, and the chest of the child, bathed the whole body, rubbed every limb, and said: 'Where art thou, ill luck? In which limb dost thou hide? Move away from this

[1] Müller, *Urreligionen*, p. 652.

child!' Prayers were then offered to the gods of the water, the earth, and the sky. The child had to be dressed, to be put in a cradle, and to be placed under the protection of the god of cradles and the god of sleep. At the same time a name was given to the infant.

All this is full of elements which remind us of similar practices among the Romans, the *Amphidromias* of the Greeks, and the name-giving ceremonies described in the Vedic Gr*i*hya-sûtras.

Next followed the baptism of fire. This also was originally nothing but an act of purification. Like water, fire also was conceived by many nations as purifying. 'Fire,' as Plutarch says in his *Quaestiones Romanae*, cap. i, 'purifies, water hallows [1].' Its very name in Sanskrit, pâvaka, means purifier. In India we were met by two trains of thought. Either fire was conceived as purifying everything, or it was represented as shrinking from contact with all that is impure. In Mexico the former idea prevailed. It had probably been observed that fire consumed deleterious substances, and that the fumes of fire served as a preservative against miasma and illness. Hence in the baptism of fire in Mexico the child was carried four times through a fire, and was then supposed to have been purified.

Purification by Fire.

Whether there is some truth in this belief in the purifying powers of fire, we must leave to medical men to determine. Anyhow it is a belief or a super-

[1] Τὸ πῦρ καθαίρει καὶ τὸ ὕδωρ ἁγνίζει. See also Vasish*th*a XII. 15, 16.

stition which has lasted for many centuries. When cholera rages in India, we still receive our letters well smoked. Menander tells us that Zemarchus, the ambassador of Justinian, was led by the Turks round a fire, so that he might be purified[1]. According to Plano Carpini, a foreign ambassador was actually led through two fires by the Mongolians. Castrén traces all these customs back to a religious reverence for the fire. It seems, however, much more plausible that the custom had a purely utilitarian foundation, that it was in fact the forerunner of our modern quarantine, which many medical authorities now look upon as equally superstitious.

Nor was the purificatory or disinfecting power of fire restricted to human beings. Cattle were often submitted to the same process of lustration. The object was originally purely practical, though superstitious ideas began soon to cluster around it.

Lustration of Animals.

The Romans had their annual lustrations. On the twenty-first of April, after a sacrifice had been offered, hay and straw were piled up in rows, and when they had been lighted, the flocks were driven through the burning fire. The shepherds often jumped through the flames, following their flocks[2].

This purely disinfecting character is still more clearly visible in the so-called *Need-fire* of the Teutonic nations.

[1] *Corpus Scriptorum Histor. Byzant.*, pars i. p. 381, ed. Bonn. Castrén, l. c., p. 57.

[2] Hartung, *Religion der Römer*, i. 46, 199; ii. 152.

Need-fire.

Joh. Reiskius, in a book published in 1696, tells us that whenever pestilence broke out among small or large cattle the peasants determined to have a *Notfeuer*. All other fires in the village had then to be put out, and by the usual method of rubbing pieces of wood, covered with pitch, a new fire was lighted. When it had grown large enough, horses and cattle were twice or thrice driven through it [1]. Afterwards the fire was extinguished, but each householder carried home a burning log to light his own fire, or dipped it afterwards in the wash-tub, and then let it lie in the manger.

This ceremony of the Need-fire might in fact have been witnessed in Scotland as late as the last century [2]. A Miss Austin relates that in the year 1767, in the isle of Mull, in consequence of a disease among the black cattle, the people agreed to perform an incantation, though they esteemed it a wicked thing. They carried to the top of Carnmoor a wheel and nine spindles of oak-wood. They extinguished every fire in every house within sight of the hill. The wheel was then turned from east to west over the nine spindles, long enough to produce fire by friction. If the fire were not produced by noon, the incantation lost its effect. If they failed for several days running, they attributed this failure to the obstinacy of one householder, who would not let his fires be put out for what he considered so wrong a purpose. How-

[1] On running through and jumping over the fire, see Grimm, *Deutsche Mythologie*, pp. 592–3; Ovid, *Fasti*, iv. 727 seq.; Müller, *Amerikanische Urreligionen*, p. 56.

[2] Grimm, *Deutsche Mythologie*, p. 574.

ever. by bribing his servants, they contrived to have them extinguished, and on that morning raised the fire. They then sacrificed a heifer, cutting in pieces and burning, while yet alive, the diseased part. They then lighted their own hearths from the pile, and ended by feasting on the remains. Words of incantation were repeated by an old man from Morven, who came over as master of the ceremonies, and who continued speaking all the time the fire was being raised. This man was living a beggar at Bellochrog. Asked to repeat the spell, he said the sin of repeating it once had brought him to beggary, and that he dared not say those words again. The whole country believed him accursed [1].

Tinegin in Ireland.

In Ireland also, according to Martin [2], the same heathenish custom might have been witnessed within the memory of men. The inhabitants made use of a fire called *tinegin*, i.e. a forced fire, or fire of necessity. This word is formed from the Irish *teine*, fire, and *eigin*, violence. It is either a simple translation of the English need-fire, or it expresses the same idea which is conveyed by the Vedic name for fire, sahasa*h* sûnu*h*, son of strength or effort. This Tinegin was used as an antidote against the plague or murrain in cattle, and it was performed thus: 'All the fires in the parish were extinguished, and then eighty-one (9 × 9) married men, being thought the necessary number for effecting this design, took two great planks of wood, and

[1] See Appendix XIV.

[2] *Description of the Western Islands*, p. 113; quoted by Borlase, *Antiquities of Cornwall*, p. 130.

nine of them were employed by turns, who by their repeated efforts rubbed one of the planks against the other until the heat thereof produced fire; and from this forced fire each family is supplied with new fire, which is no sooner kindled than a pot full of water is quickly set on it, and afterwards sprinkled upon the people infected with the plague, or upon the cattle that have the murrain. And this they all say they find successful by experience. It was practised on the mainland, opposite to the south of Skie, within these thirty years.'

Now suppose some Portuguese priests had visited Scotland and Ireland, as they visited the West Coast of Africa, and had described the religion of the natives from what they saw with their own eyes, as they described the fetish worship of the negroes. They might have described them, first of all, as fire-worshippers; secondly, as fetish-worshippers, for the fire, we are told, is a fetish when it is invoked for help; thirdly, as performing animal sacrifices, for they sacrificed a heifer and feasted on it; fourthly, as sorcerers, for they repeated unintelligible incantations; and lastly, as animists, for they believed that there was some kind of spirit in the fire. That these people were Christians, and that their religion was something quite different from these popular amusements, they could never have guessed. Yet it is on the strength of some stray observations made on the West Coast of Africa that we are asked to believe that the religion of the negroes is pure Fetishism, nay, that Fetishism was the primitive religion of all mankind.

It might be said that such heathenish customs existed in Scotland and Ireland only, and if, as careful travellers ought to do, our Portuguese missionaries had explored England also, they would have found there no traces of fetishism and sorcery. But no, in England also they might have witnessed similar heathenish ceremonies, for we are told by fair authorities that not long ago two ladies in Northamptonshire saw a fire in the field and a crowd round it. They said, 'What is the matter?'—'Killing a calf.' 'What for?'—'To stop the murrain.' The ladies went away as quickly as possible. On speaking to the clergyman he made inquiries. The people did not like to talk of the affair, but it appeared that when there is a disease among the cows, or the calves are born sickly, they sacrifice, that is, they kill and burn one for good luck.

We have still later testimony of the permanence of similar superstitious customs. They seem to have survived to the present day. At a meeting of the Society of Antiquarians of Scotland held at the Royal Institution, Edinburgh, and reported in the *Scotsman*, Tuesday, March 11, 1890, the Rev. Alexander Stewart, Nether Lochaber, gave an account of some examples which had recently come to his knowledge of the survival of certain superstitions relating to fire in the Highlands of Scotland and in Wigtownshire. The first case happened in March last, and was accidentally witnessed by Dr. Stewart's informant. Having gone to a small hamlet in a remote glen to leave a message for the shepherd, he was surprised to find there was no one in the houses, but seeing a slight smoke in a hollow at some distance, he concluded that he would find the women there washing. On reaching the bank above the hollow he was astonished to see five women engaged in the ceremony of passing a sick child through the fire. Two of the women standing opposite each other held a blazing hoop vertically between them, and two others standing on either side of the hoop were engaged in passing the child backwards and forwards through the opening of the hoop. The fifth woman, who was the mother of the child, stood at a little distance, earnestly looking on. After the child had been several times passed and repassed through the fiery circle, it was returned to its mother, and the burning hoop was thrown into a pool of water close by. The child, which was about eighteen months old, was a weakling, and was supposed to have come under the baleful influence of an evil eye. When taken home a bunch of bog-myrtle was suspended over its bed. The somewhat analogous superstition of putting a patient in the centre of a cart-wheel when the red-hot fire was put on it at the door of the smithy was practised in Wigtownshire half a century ago.

Purpose of Customs often Forgotten.

Now, I ask, is all this to be called religion? If Christians can perform these vagaries, why should not the negroes of Africa indulge in superstitious practices without therefore deserving to have their religion represented as nothing but fetish-worship? The negroes of Africa, and, in fact, most uncivilised races, are most unwilling to speak about what we mean by religion; they often have not even a name for it. They are proud, on the contrary, of their popular amusements, feastings, dances, and more or less solemn gatherings, and welcome strangers who come to see them. Some of these gatherings may in time have assumed a religious character. But the wide prevalence of many of the customs which we described, such as the ceremonial observed in the lighting and keeping of the fire, the purification of children, and the lustration of cattle, shows that in many of them there was originally a definite and practical object. Sometimes we can still discover it, but in other cases the real object has completely disappeared. We cannot tell, for instance, why, when the new fire was lighted, it should have been thought necessary to extinguish the fires in every house. Yet we find exactly the same custom which we met with in Germany in the island of Lemnos also, the very island on which Hephaestos was believed to have been precipitated by Zeus. Here all fires had to be extinguished during nine days, till a ship arrived from Delos, bringing the new sacred fire from the hearth of Apollo. This fire was afterwards distributed among all the families, and a new life was supposed to begin [1].

When, after the battle of Plataeae, the Greeks sent to Delphi to ask what sacrifices they ought to offer, they were told by the Pythian god to erect an altar to Zeus Eleutherios, but not to sacrifice till all the fires in the country had been extinguished, because they had been contaminated by the barbarians, and till new fire had been fetched from the common hearth at Delphi [2].

During the Middle Ages a similar custom prevailed in Germany. At Marburg and in Lower Saxony the fire was lighted once every year by rubbing two

[1] Philostrat. *Heroic.*, p. 740; Welcker, *Trilogie*, p. 247; Grimm, l. c., pp. 577, 580.

[2] Plutarch, *Aristides*, c. 20; L. v. Schroeder, in Kuhn's *Zeitschrift*, xxix. p. 198.

pieces of wood. This was the new fire which was to take the place of the old fires. These were supposed to have been contaminated by contact with impurities during the year[1].

Nor is it necessary that there should always have been a very deep motive for these customs. We can hardly imagine, for instance, a very stringent reason why the guardianship of the public fire should have been committed to Vestal virgins. It was so not only in Rome. In Ireland also the fire of Saint Brigida at Kildar was not allowed to be approached by men. The Damaras, an African tribe, entrusted their fire, as we saw, to young maidens. In Mexico, in Peru, in Yucatan, the sacred fire was likewise guarded by a company of virgins[2]. All we can say in this and similar cases is that in a primitive state of society the watching over the fire on the hearth would naturally fall to the unmarried daughters of a family who stayed at home, while other duties called their brothers into the field. The mere continuation of such an arrangement would in time impart to it something of a time-honoured and venerable character, and the less the original purpose of such ancient customs was understood, the more likely it was that a kind of religious sanction should be claimed for them.

Essential Difference between Religion, Mythology, and Ceremonial.

What I am anxious to place in the clearest light is that a great deal of what we class as religious, whether

[1] See M. Kovalevsky, *Tableau des origines et de l'évolution de la famille*, 1890, p. 80. He also quotes Geiger, *Ostiranische Kultur*.

[2] Müller, l. c., pp. 368, 387–8; Brinton, *Myths of the New World*, p. 147.

among ancient or modern peoples, had really in the beginning very little or nothing to do with what we ourselves mean by religion. Mythology affects ancient religion,—in one sense it may be said to affect all religion. But mythology by itself is never religion, as little as rust is iron. Ceremonial again affects religion; it may be, that in the world we live in, ceremonial has become inseparable from religion. But ceremonial by itself is never religion, as little as shade is light.

I wanted to show you how out of the same materials both religious and non-religious concepts may be formed. It was for that purpose that I chose Fire and tried to exhibit its threefold development, either as truly theogonic, or as mythological, or as ceremonial and sacrificial.

Theogonic Development of Agni.

In India we are able to prove by documentary evidence that the concept of Fire, embodying the concepts of warmth, light, and life, was raised gradually to that of a divine and supreme being, the maker and ruler of the world. And if in the Veda we have the facts of that development clearly before us, it seems to me that we have a right to say that in other religions also where Fire occupies the same supreme position, it may have passed through the same stages through which Agni passed in the Veda.

Mythological Development of Agni.

By the side of this theogonic process, however, we can likewise watch in the Veda the beginning at least of a mythological development which becomes wider and richer in the epic and paurâ*n*ic literature of India. This side is most prominent in Greece and Rome, where the legends told of Hephaestos retain but few grains of Agni, as the creator and ruler of the world.

Ceremonial Development of Agni.

Lastly, the ceremonial development of Fire is exhibited to us in what has sometimes been called fire-worship, but is in most cases merely a recognition of the usefulness of fire for domestic, sacrificial, and even medicinal purposes.

Definition of Religion Re-examined.

These three sides, though they have much in common, should nevertheless be kept carefully distinct in the study of religion. I know it may be said, in fact, it has been said, that the definition of religion which I laid down in my former course of lectures is too narrow and too arbitrary. In one sense, every definition may be said to be arbitrary, for it is meant to fix the limits which the definer, according to his own *arbitrium*, wishes to assign to a certain concept or name. Both in including and excluding the definer may differ from other definers, and those who differ from him will naturally call his definition arbitrary, and either too narrow or too wide.

I thought it right, for instance, to modify my first definition of religion as 'the perception of the Infinite,' by restricting that perception to such manifestations as are able to influence the moral conduct of man. My first definition was not wrong, but it was too wide. It cannot be denied that in the beginning the perception of the Infinite had often very little to do with moral ideas, and I am quite aware that many religions enjoin even what is either not moral at all, or even immoral. But if there are perceptions of the Infinite unconnected as yet with moral ideas, we have no right to call them religious till they assume a moral character, that is, till they begin to react on our moral nature. They may be called philosophical, metaphysical, even mathematical, but they form no part of what we call religion. The objection that some religions actually sanction what is immoral, is purely forensic.

If some religions sanction what is immoral, or what seems to us immoral, this would only serve to prove all the more strongly the influence of religion on the moral conduct of man. We are told [1], for instance, that 'the pre-historic Hebrews killed their first-born in sacrifice to their god. Abraham came very near doing the same thing. Jephtha killed his daughter, and David killed the murderers of the son of Saul, and kept them hanging in the air all summer long, to remind his God that Ishbosheth was avenged. If you catch a Yezidee in the act of stealing, he will tell you that theft is a part of his religion. If you catch a Thug in the act of assassination, he will tell you that murder is to him a religious rite. If you reprove the Todas of the Nilgheris Hills for living in polyandry, they will tell you that this is the very ground-work of their religion. If you reprove the Mormons for living in polygamy, they will remind you that this is the Biblical chart of their faith.'

Now suppose that all this were true, would it not prove the very opposite of what it is meant to prove?

[1] *The Open Court*, No. 112, p. 1883.

If religion can induce human beings to commit acts which they themselves, or which we at least, consider doubtful, or objectionable, or altogether criminal, surely it shows that religion, even in this extreme case, exercises an influence on the moral character of man such as probably nothing else could exercise.

From the moment, therefore, that the perception of something supernatural begins to exercise an influence on the moral actions of man, be it for good or for evil, from that moment, I maintain, and from that moment only, have we a right to call it religious.

We must be careful to keep within the limits of a definition which we have once accepted. The definition which I gave of religion, that it consists in a perception of the Infinite, under such manifestations as are able to influence the moral conduct of man, is not too narrow. It is wide enough, at all events, to tax the powers of any single student of the history of religion.

The Meaning of the Infinite.

When I said that religion is the perception of the Infinite, I took great pains to explain that this perception is to be taken as the true source of religion, as that without which religion would be impossible, or at least inconceivable. But as little as the source is the whole river, is the source of religion the full stream of religion. When Locke said, *Nihil est in intellectu quod non ante fuerit in sensu*, he did not mean that *sensus* was the whole of *intellectus*. He only meant that nothing could be in the intellect that had not come from sensuous perception. I meant the same when I said, *Nihil est in fide quod non ante fuerit in sensu.* I meant that nothing could be in our faith or in our religion that had not come from the perception of the infinite, but I did not mean that this perception of the infinite was the whole of religion. As our sensuous percepts grow into concepts and into all that belongs to conceptual thought, our perceptions of the infinite also are the living germs only which produce in time that marvellous harvest which we call the religions of the world. And if I limited the area of these perceptions of the infinite to that narrower field which is distinguished by its moral colouring, that field is still of an enormous extent, and will require better and stronger labourers to reap than it has hitherto found.

As to the name which I chose for what forms the real object of all religious perceptions, namely, the Infinite, I know quite well that it may be criticised. But has any one been able to suggest a better name? I wanted a name as wide as possible. I might have chosen Unknowable as equally wide. But to speak of a perception of the unknowable seemed to me a contradiction in terms. To know has many meanings, and in one of its meanings we may say, no doubt, that the Infinite is the Unknowable. We cannot know the Infinite as we know the Finite, but we can know it in the only way in which we can expect to know it, namely, behind the Finite. In perceiving anything limited, we also perceive what limits it, but to call this Unlimited or Infinite the Unknowable is to do violence to the verb to know.

I am quite aware that what other philosophers have called the Absolute was probably meant by them for what I call the Infinite. I likewise admit that what theologians mean by the Divine is in reality the same. Even the Transcendent might have answered the same purpose. But all those terms had a history. The Absolute reminds us of Hegelian ideas, the Divine is seldom free from a certain mythological colouring, and the Transcendent has its own peculiar meaning in the school of Kant. Infinite, therefore, seemed less objectionable than any of those terms, and submitted more readily to a new definition. It had likewise the advantage of having the term finite for its opposite. If some critics have proclaimed their inability to perceive any difference between infinite and indefinite, I can quite sympathise with them, for I see none whatever. The only distinction which usage would seem to sanction is that indefinite is generally applied to knowledge, infinite to the object of knowledge. We might then say that our knowledge of the infinite must always be indefinite, a proposition to which few critics would demur.

I did not wish, however, to monopolise the word religion in the sense which I assigned to it in my lectures. I simply wished to delimit the subject of these lectures, and to state once for all what segment of human thought would fall within our field of observation. If others define religion in a different sense, we shall know what to expect from them. All that I object to is an undefined use of that word. If Cicero[1], for instance, defines religion in one place as *cultus pius deorum*, he may be quite right from the Roman or from his own point of view, and we should be forewarned as to what to expect from him, if he

[1] Cic., *De Nat. Deorum*, i. 42: 'Superstitio in qua est timor inanis Deorum, religio quae Deorum cultu pio continetur.'

were to lecture on religion. Or, if Dr. Robertson Smith, in a recent course of excellent lectures on the ancient Semitic religions, assures us that with the Semites religion consisted primarily of institutions, such as sacrifices, ablutions, fastings, and all the rest, and not of what was believed about gods or God, we shall know in what sense he uses religion. In modern times also there are many people who hold that religion consists chiefly in ceremonial acts, such as going to church, kneeling, making the sign of the cross, and other ritual observances.

But though I quite admit the right of Cicero or anybody else to define religion in his own sense, and to treat of religion as mere cult, or as mere mythology, I hold as strongly as ever that neither cult nor mythology is possible without a previous elaboration of the concepts and names of the gods. Cult is one of the many manifestations of religion, but by no means the only one, nor a necessary one. The same applies to myths and legends. They are the parasites, not the marrow of religion. Besides, there are myths and legends altogether unconnected with religion, and there are solemn acts which have nothing to do with the gods. We saw how some ceremonies and myths connected with Agni, Fire, were religious in their origin, and ceased to be so, while others, purely secular in their origin, assumed in time a religious character. It is often difficult to draw a sharp line between what is no longer and what is not yet religious, but our definition of religion will generally help us in trying to discover whether there are any elements in a ceremonial act or in a mythological tradition which draw their origin, however distantly, from an original perception of the Infinite, and influence, directly or indirectly, the moral conduct of man.

The Religious Element.

Let me give you, in conclusion, one more illustration of the difficulties we have to contend with in trying to determine whether certain acts and certain sayings may be called religious or not.

We are told by an excellent Arabic scholar, Baron von Kremer, a member of the Imperial Academy at Vienna, that at Vienna, which is as advanced and refined a capital as any in Europe, you may still see people, when walking in the streets, picking up any bits of bread lying on the pavement and placing them carefully where poor people, or, at least, birds or dogs, may get at them.

Is that a religious act? It may be or it may not. It may be a mere inculcation of the old proverb, Waste not, want not. But as soon as the bread is called the gift of God, the reluctance to tread it under foot may become religious.

Manzoni, the Arabian traveller[1], tells us that the Kabili, the agricultural Arab, takes the greatest care not to scatter a crumb of bread. When he sees a piece of bread lying in the street, he lifts it, kisses it thrice, praises God, and puts it where no one can step on it, and where it may be eaten, if only by a dog.

Here we see religious elements entering in. Yet though the Kabili shows his reverence for bread, though he calls it 'aish, that is, life, as we call it the

[1] R. Manzoni, *El-Yemen, Tre Anni nell' Arabia felice*, Roma, 1884, p. 82.

staff of life, no one would say that bread had become a divine being in Arabia, still less, as some of our friends would say, that it had become a fetish, or a totem.

If, therefore, we find that similar reverence is shown to fire or water, we have not therefore to admit at once that they have thereby been raised to the rank of divine beings. If bread was called life, so was fire. The founder of a new sect among the Ojibways addressed his disciples in the following words: 'Henceforth the fire must never go out in thy hut. In summer and winter, by day and by night, in storm and in calm weather, remember that the life in thy body and the fire on thy hearth are the same thing, and date from the same time[1].'

Here fire and life are identified, but the fire within the body is no more than what we should call the warmth of the body, and to say that this warmth is the same as the fire on the hearth implies as yet no kind of divine worship for either the one or the other.

The same respect which is paid to bread, is also paid to other kinds of food. Thus Mohammed forbad to use even the stone of a date for killing a louse; and in another place he is reported to have said: 'Honour the palm, for she is your aunt[2].'

In the case of bread therefore, and also in the case of corn and dates and other kinds of food, we can well understand that they should have been treated with reverence as the gift of Allah, or of any other god, provided always that an acquaintance with such divine beings existed beforehand.

Without such previous knowledge, nothing, whether

[1] Müller, l. c., p. 55.

[2] Kremer, l. c., p. 4.

a ceremony or a myth, can be called religious. It seems to me, therefore, that we are perfectly justified in treating that previous knowledge by itself, and to reserve to it exclusively the name of religion. There was religion before sacrifice; there was religion before myth. There was neither sacrifice nor myth before religion, in the true sense of that word. Nothing is more interesting than to find out how sacrifice and myth sprang from the same field as religion. But they did not spring from that field until it had been touched by those rays of light which transform the finite into the infinite, and which called into life the unnumbered seeds that lay hidden in the ground, the seeds of tares as well as of wheat, both growing together until the harvest.

LECTURE XIII.

OTHER GODS OF NATURE.

The Development of Fire.

WE have seen thus far how the human mind by its natural, though at the same time most wonderful powers, can reach, and did reach, the highest conception of the godhead, though starting from the commonest impressions of the senses. I took my first illustration from fire, but all the other phenomena of nature would teach the same lesson, namely, that the human mind is capable of discovering the Supernatural in the Natural. Nothing seems to us more natural than that the various manifestations of fire should have been marked and named by the earliest inhabitants of the world. Yet if we restricted the meaning of natural to whatever animals, or beings endowed with sense only, are capable of performing, we should have to call even the simple naming of fire, achieved by man and by man alone, not a natural, but a supernatural, or, at all events, a *super-animal* act. Formerly, it would hardly have been necessary to insist on this distinction. But at present, when philosophy seems chiefly to consist in ignoring the frontier-lines that separate the animal kingdom from our own, it is necessary to show that there are certain limits to the mental faculties of mere animals. Some animals are scared by fire and run away from it, others are attracted by it, but they will never name and conceive it. When we see our fire burning, and hear it crackling in the grate, nothing seems to us more homely, more natural. Every child feels attracted by the fire, enjoys its genial warmth, and wonders what kind of thing it is. But try to think, once more, what the first appearance of fire must have been when it came down from the sky as lightning, killing a man and setting his hut ablaze,—surely there was a miracle, if ever there was a miracle; a theophany, if ever there was a theophany. There was nothing to compare it to in the whole experience of man, and if it was called a wild beast[1], or a bird of prey, or a poisonous serpent, these were all but poor similes, which could hardly satisfy an observing and inquiring mind.

And when after a time the beneficial aspects also of fire had been discovered, when certain families had found out how to elicit fire from flints, or how to produce it by friction, the mystery remained as great as ever. It was a weird power, a strange apparition, a something totally inexplicable at first to the human understanding. Thus there remained in the fire from the first, even after it had been named, something unknown, something different from all the ordinary and finite perceptions, something not natural, some-

[1] Herodotus, iii. 16, says that the Egyptians took fire to be a live beast, devouring everything, and dying with what it had eaten. See also *S*atap. Brâhma*n*a II. 3, 3, 1.

thing unnatural, or, as it was also called, something supernatural.

If we once see this clearly and understand how the supernatural element was there from the beginning, though not yet disentangled from its natural surroundings, we shall be better able to understand how the same supernatural element was never completely lost sight of by the poets of the Veda, and how in the end Agni, fire, after being stripped of all that was purely phenomenal, natural, and physical, stands before us, endowed with all those qualities which we reserve for the Supreme Being. He was adored as the creator and ruler of the world, as omnipotent, omniscient, just, kind, and compassionate. In that state all his physical antecedents were forgotten. It was no longer the fire crackling on the hearth that was believed in as the creator of the world. It was the unknown agent, recognised from the first in that motion which we call fire, who had been raised to a divine dignity, though the old name of Agni remained, as if to remind the people of their first acquaintance with him whom they called from the first, 'the friend of man, the immortal among mortals.'

The Agents behind other Phenomena of Nature.

This one road which we have hitherto explored, that led our ancestors from nature to nature's God, is, no doubt, an important road, but we must remember that it is but one out of many. Whether we examine the religions of civilised or of uncivilised races, we shall always find that they started not only from fire, but from many of the other of the great phenomena of nature, such as the storm-wind, the sun, the moon, the stars, the sky, the sea, the earth, the rivers, and the mountains, in their gropings after what lies beyond, after the invisible agent, the father, the author, after the God revealed to the senses in the countless miracles of nature. If the storm-wind was from the first called the crusher or shouter, people soon asked, who is it that shouts and crushes? If the sun was called the shining and warming, the question could not long be suppressed, who it was that shines and warms. The sky, as participating in the work of the sun and the moon and the stars, of the storm, the lightning and the rain, was also asked who he was, or who was behind and above the sky, who was the real agent of all the acts performed on the stage of heaven. The very earth, though so near and palpable and familiar, became nevertheless mysterious when it was asked, what life there was in her, and when it was felt how much she did in her quiet and much suffering way, for all who dwelt in her fields and forests.

The Theogonic Process.

If we like, we may call this primitive wonderment at what seems to us at present so very natural, and the religious and mythological phraseology that sprang from that wonderment, by such names as *Animism* (Beseelung), *Personification*, and *Anthropomorphism*. These names are all right, and they may be useful for the purpose of classification. Only we must remember that the historical student of religion cannot rest satisfied with mere names, with mere classification, but that his chief object is to account for facts, thus named and classified, and thus to learn to understand something, however little it may be, of the inevitable growth and development of religious and mythological concepts.

If we have once clearly understood the inseparable connection between thought and language, and if, more particularly, we have mastered the fact that the roots of our words and the roots of our concepts were expressions of acts, our task becomes much easier. But I know but too well how great a mental effort is required in order to apprehend that fact and all its far-reaching consequences. Important as these consequences are for a right understanding of all that we call thought, nowhere are they more surprising than in the study of what is called mythological and religious thought. All other keys that have been tried to unlock those ancient chests have lifted one bolt or another. The key handed to us by Noiré has turned and lifted them all, and the ancient chests now stand open and their treasures may be examined. When human beings were once in possession of the name and concept of *anima*, or soul, of *persona*, person, of *manhood*, and *godhead*, we can well understand that they should have predicated soul of the sun, personality of the moon, manhood of the storm, and godhead of the sky. But the real question is, how were these name-concepts of *anima*, *persona*, *homo*, and *deus* elaborated, and what organic connection was there between them and such concepts as the sun, the moon, and the sky? To imagine that mythology and religion could have arisen by ancient poets calling sun, moon, and sky animated, or personal, or manlike, or divine, would be, to use a homely metaphor, to put the cart before the horse. There is such a phrase in the later periods of the growth of the human mind. We ourselves are still living in it, our poetry draws most of its inspiration from it. We hear our poets express their 'faith that every flower enjoys the air it breathes.' They speak of 'the morn, in russet mantle clad, walking o'er the dew of yon high eastern hill.' We have read of 'a brotherhood of venerable trees,' and of the 'sable goddess, Night,' and we know perfectly well what is meant by all this, because we are in possession of a large dictionary of language and thought.

But if we want really to understand this phraseology, we have first to find our way into more distant prehistoric periods, into the dark subterranean caves where those weapons were forged with which man from the earliest days fought his battles and made his conquests.

Students of these prehistoric periods of thought and language are often blamed for taking unnecessary trouble, for trying to explain things which, we are told, require no explanation at all, for spreading darkness where all before seemed light. It is asked, what is there to puzzle us, when we see that the ancients spoke of the sun as a living thing, nay, as a person, as a man, as a god? Is it not simply a case of Animism, of Personification, of Anthropomorphism, and of Deification? Words, words, words! We first call what has to be explained by a name, and in this case by a very imperfect name. And then, after we have named this process, we turn round and say, O, it is all very simple, it is nothing but Animism, Personification, and Anthropomorphism! We imagine that our work is done, while it really is only beginning.

Even Mr. Herbert Spencer has risen in revolt against such perfunctory theories. The very dogs are able to sniff out the difference between what has life and what has not, between the animate and the inanimate; was man less sagacious than the dogs?

I thought it right in one case at least, in that of fire, to give a full description of the slow process by which that natural appearance was named. Having once been called 'he who moves,' Agni, or having been conceived as the agent of any other of his more striking acts, his further growth became easy to understand. We saw how almost by necessity he came after that to grow into a breathing and living agent (Animism), for fire breathes, lives, and dies; came to grow into a man-like being (Anthropomorphism), for fire, though not a man, is a man-like agent; came to grow into an individual person (Personification), for one fire differs from another; and came at last to grow into a Deva or a god (Deification). We looked for all the links in that chain of thought, and though we did not find them all, yet we found enough to allow us an insight into the true nature of that psychological process which led gradually and naturally from the mere percept of fire as an agent to the concept of an unseen power, revealed to us in the various manifestations of fire and light.

Wordsworth.

We shall now try to catch a glance of the same instructive process in other realms of nature, in order to see from how many points that irresistible impulse toward religion, towards true and natural religion, proceeded, which in the end made man feel that, however wide the horizon of his knowledge, there was always a Beyond, and that in spite of every effort of thought and language, there always remained something that could not be named and could not be comprehended except as an agent, invisible, yet omnipresent. This psychological process began with the senses—for how else could it begin?—but it did not end with them, but called forth:

> 'That sense sublime
> Of something far more deeply interfused,
> Whose dwelling is the light of setting suns,
> And the round ocean, and the living air,
> And the blue sky, and in the mind of man
> A motion and a spirit, that impels
> All thinking things, all objects of all thought,
> And rolls through all things.'

I doubt whether we could give a better definition of Physical Religion than what Wordsworth has given us in these few lines.

The Storm-wind.

Next to fire, the most important phenomenon in nature which led to the conception of a divine being was the wind, more particularly the storm-wind. In the most distant parts of the world, and among people unrelated in language and thought, the storm-wind appears not only as one among many gods, but often as the supreme and only god. The agent, or, as we say, the agency or the force of the wind, was so palpable, and often so overpowering, that we find traces of this god in almost every pantheon.

The Storm-wind in America.

Let us begin with America[1]. Here we find that with the Choctaws the general word for deity is *Hushtoli*, which means the storm-wind. In the Creek language also *ishtali* means the storm-wind, and *hustolah* the windy season. The Quichés call the mysterious creative power *Hurakan*. This word has no meaning in their language, but it finds its explanation in the ancient tongue of Haity, from which the Quichés must have borrowed it. Dr. Brinton, in his *Essays of an Americanist*, 1890, p. 121, doubts the derivation of Huracan from Haytian, and derives it from Maya. In the dialects of the Maya group *rakan* is said by him to express greatness, and *hun* one or first. In Cakchiquel *hurakan* means a giant. The Spaniards and other European nations made us familiar with the word as the name of the terrible tornado of the Caribean Sea[2]. It lives on in French as *ouragan*, in German as *Orkan*, in English as *hurricane*. Neglectful of its biography, German etymologists derived *Orkan* from *Orcus*, English etymologists discovered in *hurricane* something of the *hurry* of the storm, or, like Webster, something of its *fury;* but Oviedo, in his description of Hispaniola[3], leaves no doubt that the name was borrowed from the ancient language of Haity, and had been carried there by the Quichés from the Antilles.

[1] Brinton, *Myths of the New World*, p. 51.

[2] In the *Dictionnaire Galibi* (Paris, 1743) diable is translated by *iroucan, jeroucan, hyorokan*, and Coto's *Vocabulario* (MS.) gives *hurakan* as the equivalent of *diablo* in Cakchiquel. See Brinton, *Essays of an Americanist*, p. 123.

[3] *Historia dell' Indie*, lib. vi. cap. 3.

This Hurakan has been identified by some American scholars with Cuculcan, Gucumatz, and Votan, all names of the god of the storm-wind in Central America.

The chief divinity of several tribes in ancient Mexico was called *Mixcohuatl*, and this is to this day the name of the tropical whirlwind. The natives of Panama worshipped the same phenomenon under the name of *Tuyra*.

It is curious that Mr. Brinton, from whose interesting work on *The Myths of the New World* these facts are quoted, is convinced that man never did and never could draw the idea of God from nature. He thinks that the deeper and far truer reason for the divinity ascribed to the wind is to be found in the identity of wind with breath, of breath with life, of life with soul, and of soul with God. Mr. Brinton may be quite right that the transition of meaning from wind to breath and life and soul has acted as a powerful ingredient in 'the evolution of ancient deities.' But even then, the starting-point of that evolution would have been in nature, namely, in the real wind, which by a perfectly intelligible process became sublimised into breath, spirit, life, soul, and God. It may be granted to Mr. Brinton (l. c., p. 75) that the motions of the air are often associated in thought and language with the operations of the soul and the idea of God. We are told that in Peru the commonest and simplest adoration of the collective deities consists in kissing the air—a very significant mode of prayer. But surely the various manifestations of the wind, so well described by Mr. Brinton himself, are quite sufficient by themselves to evoke in the human mind and in human language the concept and name of a powerful, superhuman agent. He describes very eloquently, 'the power of the winds on the weather, bringing as they do the lightning and the storm, the zephyr that cools the brow, and the tornado that levels the forest. They summon the rain to fertilize the seed and refresh the shrivelled leaves. They aid the hunter to stalk the game, and usher in the varying seasons. In a hundred ways they intimately concern his comfort and his life, and it will not seem strange, he adds himself, that they almost occupied the place of all other gods in the mind of the child of nature.'

The Aztec prayer addressed to the Tlalocs, the gods of the showers, began with the following invocation: 'Ye who dwell at the four corners of the earth,—at the north, at the south, at the east, and at the west.'

The Eskimo also prayed to *Sillam Innua*, the owner of the winds, as their highest god, and the abode of the Dead was called by them *Sillam Aipane,* the house of the winds.

As the rain-bringers and life-givers the winds were naturally called the fathers of the human race, and Mr. Brinton has recognised in the four brothers, who appear in so many traditions of America as the ancestors and leaders of ancient tribes, coming from the four corners of the earth, the later representatives of the four winds, the North, the South, the East, and the West winds.

What he says of these traditions applies in so many words to the traditions of Aryan races. 'Sometimes,' he writes, 'the myth defines clearly these fabled characters as the spirits of the winds; sometimes it clothes them in uncouth, grotesque metaphors; sometimes again it so weaves them into actual history that we are at a loss where to draw the line that divides fiction from truth' (p. 77).

In the mythology of Yukatan the four gods Bacab were supposed to stand one at each corner of the world, supporting, like gigantic caryatides, the overhanging firmament. When at the general deluge the other gods and men were swallowed by the waters, they alone escaped to people the earth anew. These four, known by the names of Kan, Muluc, Ix, and Cauac, represented respectively the East, North, West, and South. The East was distinguished by yellow, the South by red, the West by black, the North by white, and these colours appear again in different parts of the world with the same meaning, as representing the four quarters of the world. According to the Quichés, these four beings were first created by *Hurakan*, the Heart of Heaven. If we translate the Heart of Heaven into the Sanskrit Dyaus, the subjective or active Heaven, or Heaven as an agent, we see how near he, as the father of the Maruts or storm-winds, comes to Hurakan, the father of the four winds. The description of these winds also is sometimes almost identical with that given of the Maruts by the Vedic poets. It is said that they measured and saw all that exists at the four corners and the four angles of the sky and the earth; that they did not bring forth and produce when the season of harvest was near, until he blew into their eyes a cloud, until their faces were obscured, as when one breathes on a mirror. Then he gave them four wives whose names were Falling Water, Beautiful Water, Water of Serpents, and Water of Birds.

In Aztec legends these four beings are said to have emerged from a cave called *Pacavitampu*, and this is said to mean, either 'the house of existence,' or 'the lodging of the Dawn.' There in the distant East the Aztecs placed Tula, the birthplace of their race. This again reminds us of Vedic mythology, and the description of the four beings that came from the cave of the Dawn leaves little doubt as to their similarity with the Vedic storm-gods, the Maruts. 'Their voices,' we are told, 'could shake the earth, and their hands heap up mountains. Like the thunder-god, they stood on the hills and hurled their sling-stone to the four corners of the earth. When one was overpowered, he fled upward to the heaven or was turned into stone. It was by their aid and counsel that the savages who possessed the land renounced their barbarous habits and commenced to till the soil' (l. c., p. 83).

Truly indeed might Mr. Brinton say that 'the winds producing the thunder and the changes that take place in the ever-shifting panorama of the sky, the rain-bringers, the lords of the seasons,—and not this only, but the primary type of the soul, the life, the breath of man and the world,—are second to nothing in their *rôle* in mythology.' The road from the naming of the different winds to the naming of the Storm-wind, as the father of the winds, or, again, to the naming of the Sky, as the father of the winds as well as of the other heavenly powers, is as clearly traced in America as anywhere else. The surroundings of nature have, no doubt, a considerable influence on the formation of storm-myths. We find them most fully developed in mountainous countries, and the more the very existence of man was felt to depend on the beneficial or hurtful influences of the winds and thunderstorms, the more readily did the human mind arrive at the conception of a supreme beneficent or malignant power behind the storm-wind, controlling the fates of man.

This will explain the fact, to which I alluded in my first course of Gifford Lectures (p. 453), that in many of the American languages the same word is used for storm and god[1]. In Africa also Dr. Nachtigall was struck by the same fact, and he instances the Baghirmi as having but one name for storm and God. We shall see that in India also the old name of the storm-gods, Marut, was used in the language of the Buddhists as a general name of gods (Maru).

The Storm-wind in Babylon.

Let us now turn our eyes from America to Babylon. The primitive inhabitants of Babylon beheld in the winds powers of good and evil[2]. The good wind cooled the heat of summer and brought moisture to the parched earth. The evil wind was the tempest, the freezing blast of winter, and the burning sirocco of the desert. Their number is sometimes given as four, sometimes as seven, the seven sons or messengers of Anu. In the battle against the dragon of chaos, they were the allies of Merodach, as the Maruts were the allies of Indra. Matu occurs fre-

[1] Bancroft, *History of the Native Races of North America*, vol. iii. p. 117.

[2] Sayce, *Hibbert Lectures*, p. 199.

quently as the name of the destructive storm-wind, whose favour had to be conciliated. He is called the lord of the mountain, and his wife the lady of the mountain (cf. Sk. Pârvatî). But we also hear of many Matus, the children of the sea.

The Storm-wind in India.

We now return to India, where the storms meet us under the name of the Maruts. In their purely physical aspect the storms or Maruts are represented in the Veda as powerful and destructive, but at the same time as beneficent also, as clearing the air, as bringing rain, as fertilising the soil, and reinvigorating the body. I shall quote a few passages from the Rig-veda.

They are said to shake heaven and earth like the hem of a garment. They cause a long and broad unceasing rain to fall (I. 37, 11), so that the cows have to walk knee-deep. Mountains shake, men tremble (I. 38, 10), the kings of the forest, the trees, are rent asunder (I. 39, 5). The Maruts bring winds and lightning (I. 64, 5), and they pour down rain (I. 64, 6). But after the storm is over, they are praised for bringing back the light and, like the dawn (II. 34, 12), driving away the hideous darkness (I. 86, 10). They are also celebrated for restoring fertility to the soil, and for making the autumn plentiful through their invigorating rain (I. 171, 6; II. 34, 4). Thus they bring, not only food to men, but water, medicine, and health (V. 53, 14; VI. 74, 3), being in this respect like their father Rudra, who is often implored to bring medicine and to bestow health (VII. 46; II. 33, 13).

In most of the hymns of the Veda, however, the

Maruts, as the representatives of the storm, the thunderstorm and all its concomitant features, have assumed a very definite dramatic character. They appear brilliant on their chariots (I. 37, 1), with spears, daggers, rings, axes, and with whips which they crack in the air (I. 37, 2; 3). They shoot arrows (I. 64, 10), and fling stones (I. 172, 2). They have golden headbands round their heads (V. 54, 11). Often they are represented as musicians, as singers, pipers (I. 85, 10), and dancers (VIII. 20, 22), sometimes as birds (I. 87, 2), and as wild boars with iron tusks (I. 88, 5). They are called the manly sons of Rudra (I. 64, 2), and they are likewise called the youthful Rudras themselves who never grow old (I. 64, 3). In some places their mother is called P*ris*ni (I. 85, 2), their father or lord Dyaus (X. 77, 2; VIII. 20, 17), or Svar, sky (V. 54, 10). They are the constant companions of Indra in his fight against his enemies, such as V*ri*tra, Ahi, and other demons. They are even represented as themselves the conquerors of V*ri*tra (VIII. 7, 23), and as the protectors of Indra (VII. 7, 24). But occasionally they seem slighted by Indra, who claims all glory for himself (I. 165). Dyaus also is invoked as their companion, as when we read, V. 58, 6, 'Let Dyaus roar down, the bull of the Dawn.' (See also V. 59, 8.) As Agni represents both light and lightning, it is but natural that he too should appear in their company (V. 60, 7). Rodasî, who is often mentioned as the friend or wife of all of them, seems to be intended for the lightning (V. 61, 12). At times they become so completely personified that the poets, forgetful of their physical origin, actually compare them to the wind, and call them blazing with wind (vâta-tvish, V. 57, 4). It is more difficult to discuss in what sense Vish*n*u is sometimes mentioned as their friend and helper (V. 87, 4), while Soma, when joined with them, can only be meant as the rain of the thunderstorm (VIII, 20, 3).

Though the Maruts are almost always invoked as a company, sometimes of twenty-one, sometimes of a hundred and eighty, being all alike in strength, yet in one place the poet speaks also of one son of Rudra, and calls him Mâruta, belonging to the Maruts (VI. 66, 11).

After a time these Maruts, like Agni and other gods of nature, assume a strongly marked moral character, and in the end they take their place among the highest gods. Thus one poet (I. 38, 6) addresses them in the following words: 'Let not one sin after another, difficult to be conquered, overcome us; may it depart together with greed.' 'Whatever fiend attacks us, deprive him of power and strength' (I. 39, 8). 'The mortal whom ye, O Maruts, protected, he surpasses all people in strength through your protection. He carries off booty; he acquires honourable wisdom, and prospers' (I. 64, 13). The Maruts themselves are called, not only heroes, but wise poets also (V. 52, 13). They impart not only strength to their worshippers, but even immortality (V. 55, 4). Some of the qualities which seem to us peculiar to the highest deities only, such as the punishing of sin, and likewise the forgiving of sin, where there is hearty repentance, are in the end ascribed to the Maruts also. Their peculiar physical nature disappears more and more, and they are implored almost in the same words as Varu*n*a and the Âdityas (X. 77, 8). Thus one poet says: 'May your bright thunderbolt be far from us, O Maruts, whatever sin we may have committed against you, men as we are, O worshipful, let us not fall under its power, let your best favour rest on us' (VII. 57, 4).

The Marus of the Buddhists.

In Pali, Maru is used in the general sense of deva, though deva-hood is no longer a very exalted position in the eyes of the Buddhists.

Rudra, the Father of the Maruts.

But though we can watch this gradual transition from the Maruts as the storms, to the Maruts as sub-natural agents, as dramatic heroes, and lastly as supreme gods, the fact of their being a company or a host could not but lead to the supposition of a lord or father of the Maruts, generally called Rudra. We saw the same in America, where the four winds were represented by Hurakan, the most powerful wind. And as in the Veda Dyaus, the bright sky, is sometimes conceived as the father of the winds, we find in America also that the lord of the winds, the prince of the powers of the air, whose voice is the thunder, and whose weapon the lightning, is *Michabo*, the Great Light, the Spirit of Light, of the Dawn, or the East, literally, as Brinton has shown[1], the Great White One.

The Storm-wind in Germany.

Another country where the god of the storm-wind was raised in the end to the rank of a supreme deity

[1] Brinton, *Myths of the New World*, p. 166.

was Germany, or whatever may have been the last home of the united German family. It has been shown that the Teutonic tribes possessed originally a deity corresponding very nearly in name and character to the Vedic Dyaus, the Greek *Zeus*, and the Latin *Ju-piter*. This was *Tiu*, a name preserved in Anglo-Saxon, *tîwes-dæg*, our Tuesday, the *dies Jovis*. The same name occurs in the Edda as *Tŷr*, in Old High-German as *Zio*. But in the same way as in the Veda the ancient god Dyaus was driven back, and at last superseded by Indra, the god of the thunderstorm, we find that in Germany also the common Aryan god of the sky had to make room for *Odin* or *Wodan*, originally a representative of storm and thunder. The gods of storm and thunder were generally represented as fighting gods, as brave warriors, and, in the end, as conquerors; and with warlike nations, like the Germans, such gods would naturally become very popular, more popular even than the god of light, who was supposed to live enthroned in silent majesty above the dome of heaven, the one-eyed seer, the husband of the earth, the All-father, as he was called in Germany also.

Odin, Wuotan.

According to a view which was very prevalent in former days, and which even now counts some very distinguished scholars amongst its adherents, *Odin* was originally a man, the founder of the ancient Northern and Teutonic religion, who was afterwards worshipped as the supreme god, the fountain-head of wisdom, the founder of culture, the inventor of writing and poetry, the progenitor of kings, the lord of battle and victory, so that his name and that of *Alföðr*, All-father, were blended together[1].

Those who take this view derive *Odin's* name not unnaturally from an old word, akin to the Latin *vâtes*[2], a prophetic singer or bard, and compare with it the O. N. *óðr*, inspiration. But they have never shown how *vâtes* in Latin could become *Óðinn* in Old Norse, and *Wuotan* in Old High-German[3].

Grimm, in his *Deutsche Mythologie*, did not look upon this view of *Odin* as any longer requiring even a refutation. He treated the name of *Wuotan* and *Odin* as from the beginning a name of a superhuman being. He derived the O. H. G. *Wuotan*, the Lombardian *Wôdan* or *Guôdan*, the Old Saxon *Wuodan* and *Wôdan* (Westphalian *Guôdan* and *Gudan*), the A. S. *Wôden*, Frisian *Wêda*, the Old Norse *Óðinn*, from the O. H. G. verb *watan*, *wuot*, O. N. *vaða*, *óð*, meaning to move along quickly, then to be furious, a transition of meaning which is likewise found in Lat. *vehi* and *vehemens*, *peto* and *impetus*. This root

[1] Cleasby and Vigfusson, *Icelandic Dictionary*, s.v.

[2] *Corpus Poeticum Boreale*, Vigfusson and Powell, vol. i. p. civ. The etymology of Latin *vâtes* is as yet unknown. The root *vat* in *api-vat* is very obscure. It occurs four times only in the Veda, and seems to me to mean no more than to go near, to obtain, in the causative to invite or to welcome. How from *vâtes* we could possibly arrive at *Óðinn* and *Wuotan* has never been explained. Wilhelm, *De verbis denominativis*, p. 14. See note to Rv. I. 165, 13.

[3] Verner's Law is extremely useful to account for exceptions to Grimm's Law, and in the true sense of the old saying, *exceptio probat regulam*. But Verner's Law must not be used as a mere excuse. If we could prove that the accent in *vâtés* was originally on the last syllable, we might accept Low German d, though hardly the High German t. But to invert this reasoning, and to postulate the accent on the final syllable of *vâtés*, because we wish that it should correspond to *Óðinn* and *Wuotan*, is a very dangerous proceeding. It is equally dangerous to speak of a root *vat* in the sense of to know. It is not used in that meaning either in the Veda or in the Avesta.

watan, however, cannot be connected with Latin *vâdere*, unless we take the Latin d as the representative of an original media aspirata. From this *watan* Grimm derives the substantive *wuot*, wrath, fury, *θυμός*, and the O. N. *óðr*, mind, poetry, song; A. S. *wôð*, voice, song.

As the supreme god of the Teutonic nations, Wuotan's character is summed up by Grimm in the following words[1]: 'He is the all-pervading creative and formative power, who bestows shape and beauty on man and all things, from whom proceeds the gift of song and the management of war and victory, on whom at the same time depends the fertility of the soil, nay wishing, and all the highest gifts and blessings.'

In the popular legends, however, what may be called his etymological character is still far more clearly perceptible. *Wuotan* is there the furious god, the god of war and victory, armed with his spear (*Gûngnir*), and followed by two wolves (*Geri* and *Fleki*), two ravens (*Huginn* and *Muninn*). He also sends the storm, rides on the gale, has his waggon or wain, and his horse. In the Old Norse legends he is an old man with a broad hat and a wide mantle, *heklu-maðr*, a hooded man, and as such he appears in the German *Hakolberend*, the leader of the wild host, whose memory lives on even now in *John Hacklebirnie's* house, though he is no doubt quite unconnected with *Hakleberg*, i. e. Mount Hecla[2].

This root, in High German *watan*, would presuppose

[1] Translation of Grimm's *German Mythology*, by Stallybrass, vol. i. p. 132.

[2] Why *Mercury* was identified with *Wuotan*, see M. M., *Selected Essays*, i. 406; ii. 210; Grimm's *Deutsche Mythologie*, pp. 137–148.

a Low German d, and a classical dh. As h in Sanskrit is a neutral exponent of gh, dh, bh, we should have to postulate an original vadh, for vah (part. vo*dh*a, for vah-ta). In *vehemens* also we see traces of the same transition of meaning as in *wuot*, fury.

Grohmann proposed to identify *Wuotan* with the Vedic Vâta, wind, and at first sight that etymology is very tempting. But vâta is known to have the accent on the first syllable, and ought therefore to show th in Low, d in High German.

Still, Grohmann was right in making *Wuotan* the god of wind and weather, only that his etymon seems to me to lie not so much in the wind, as in the weather. *Weather*, before it took its general meaning, meant stormy weather. This is still very clear in the German, *Wetter-leuchten* (*wëter-leich*, cf. *rik*-van), *Donner-wetter, Wind und Wetter, Unwetter, Wetterschlag*, &c., and even in the English *weather-beaten*. It is the O. H. G. *wetar*, A. S. *weder*, O. N. *veðr*. The th in Modern English *weather* is dialectic. The same word exists in the Veda, namely, as vádhas and vádhar (Delbrück, in *K. Z.* xvi. 266); but it there means the actual thunderbolt of Indra and of his enemies, and also weapon in general. From the same root we have vadhá, striker and weapon; vádhatra, weapon; vadhasná, Indra's thunderbolt. In Greek this root has been preserved in ὠθέω, in ἐν-οσί-χθων, earth-striker, &c. (see Curtius, s. v.). From this root, and from no other, is derived *Wuotan*, literally the striker with the thunderbolt, the weather-god, the storm-god[1].

[1] There is another word in Old Norse, *óðr*; and as Freyja is called *óds mey* (Od's maid), this can only be another name for *óðinn* (Volusp. 87, *Corp. Poet. Bor.*, vol. ii. p. 624; Hyndla's Lay, ibid., vol. ii. p. 517).

If then the name of *Wuotan* meant originally the weather-god, the wielder of the thunderbolt, we must begin with that concept, and slowly trace the transition from the furious huntsman to Odin, the All-father, the solemn and majestic deity, just as we saw[1] *Hurakan*, the lord of the winds, assume the supremacy over all other gods among certain American tribes, and as in India we could watch the Maruts becoming changed into purely moral divinities, presided over by Rudra or Dyaus, as sovereign gods.

The Mixed Character of Ancient Gods.

Besides the lesson which we have thus learnt from a comparative study of American, Babylonian, Indian, and Teutonic mythologies, as to the possible development of the highest concept of divinity out of the simplest phenomena of nature, there is another lesson which was impressed upon us when studying the history of Agni, and which is even more strongly inculcated by the history of the storm-gods. The ancient gods were not restricted to one character. Agni, for instance, was, no doubt, the fire on the hearth, but any poet might speak of him as born in the sky, as lightning, as rising, as the sun in the morning, and setting in the evening, as generated by

'Odhin, welcher mit dem Blitzdorn die Sonnenjungfrau verzaubert, ist nicht bloss typisch der in Wolkenmantel und Nebelkappe verhüllt auftretende Gewittergeist, der als solcher auch den Beinamen *Drepsvarpr*, d. h. *lethaliter jaciens*, "der mit dem Blitzspeer Tödtende" führt, und so auch geradezu zum Todesgott wird, sondern speciell auch noch in analogem Sinn der *dominus larvarum et spectrorum*, als welchen ihn der nordische Beiname *Draugadrottin* vor allem kennzeichnet, welcher ihn so recht eigentlich in der Gewitternacht an der Spitze alles Spukes auftreten lässt.' Schwartz, *Indogermanischer Volksglaube*, 1885, p. 163.

[1] *Gifford Lectures*, vol. i. p. 453.

the fire-sticks, nay, as identical with the warmth and life of the vegetable and animal world. In like manner, the father of the Maruts is not only a meteoric deity, sending his arrows from the clouds, he is also a celestial deity, he is, in fact, one side of that power of light and life which is recognised in the sky, and called Dyaus, and recognised in the sun, and called Svar. We distinguish between the sky, and the sun, and the morning, and the thunderstorm, and so, no doubt, did the ancient poets of the Veda. But they also recognised a common element, or, if you like, a common agent behind all these phenomena of nature, and they had no difficulty in ascribing the same deeds to Agni, Dyaus, Svar or Sûrya, the Maruts, and the Rudras. Thus it happens that in later phases of mythology one god who has assumed a definite personality may nevertheless display some solar or celestial or meteoric characteristics which cling to him from an earlier stage of his existence. Apollo, as we know him in Homer, is not the sun, but he has retained some solar qualities. Athene is not the dawn, but she has not lost all matutinal features. Zeus certainly is not simply the sky, and yet his character would be unintelligible unless we could trace him back to the Vedic Dyaus, the sky.

The Theogonic Development.

I hope it will not be supposed that, because in this course of lectures I have given such prominence to the fire and the storm-wind as powerful stimulants in the religious life of mankind, my conviction has been changed that it was the sky and the sun who gave from the first the most powerful impulse to the growth of mythological and religious ideas. My only reason for passing these two theogonic processes over at present was that they have been most fully analysed before by myself and by others, and that I thought I might without presumption refer my hearers here to what I have written on this subject in my Lectures on the Science of Language, and in my Hibbert Lectures on the Origin and Growth of Religion with special reference to India. What has been called the Religion of Dyaus and the Solar Myth may be reckoned among the best secured gains of modern scholarship. Μωμήσεταί τις μᾶλλον ἢ μιμήσεται. The only new light which has been thrown on these theogonic processes is that we understand now how what were considered hitherto as mere facts are in reality the necessary results of our mental constitution. We know now that, like the fire and the storm-wind, the sky and the sun also could only be named by names expressive of agency. Whether we call this a necessity of language or thought, it is, as we saw, a necessity from which we cannot escape. At first these celestial, solar, igneous or meteoric agents, having become the objects of early thought, were described according to their manifold manifestations, particularly such as influenced the life and the acts of man. After a time, however, these various manifestations were recognised as external only, and the agent, being more and more divested of these external veils, was slowly recognised as something else, something by itself, something beyond the finite knowledge of man, and in the end as something sub-natural, supernatural, and infinite. This led naturally to the two phases of

Henotheism and Polytheism, and by a still more powerful abstraction, to Monotheism, that is, the recognition of one agent, one author, one father, one God, hidden behind the magic veil of nature, but revealed by an irresistible necessity which postulates something infinite and divine in the agents of the objective world, because it has discovered something infinite and divine in the subjective world, in the agent within, or in the self.

We may thus discover in all the errors of mythology, and in what we call the false or pagan religions of the world, a progress towards truth, a yearning after something more than finite, a growing recognition of the Infinite, throwing off some of its veils before our eyes, and from century to century revealing itself to us more and more in its own purity and holiness. And thus the two concepts, that of evolution and that of revelation, which seem at first so different, become one in the end. If there is a purpose running through the ages, if nature is not blind, if there are agents, recognised at last as the agents of one Will, behind the whole phenomenal world, then the evolution of man's belief in that Supreme Will is itself the truest revelation of that Supreme Will, and must remain the adamantine foundation on which all religion rests, whether we call it natural or supernatural.

LECTURE XIV.

WHAT DOES IT LEAD TO?

Value of Historical Studies.

I HAVE finished my survey of Physical Religion, and I feel that I ought not to shrink in my last lecture to-day from answering a question that has often been asked, namely, What does it all lead to?

You know that Lord Gifford's idea of founding lectureships on Natural Religion in the four Universities of Scotland has been criticised from different quarters, and that the lecturers also, who have endeavoured to the best of their powers to carry out the noble plan of the founder, have not escaped the strictures of unfriendly critics.

What can it all lead to? What can be the use of lectures on the origin and the history of the ancient or so-called natural religions of mankind? has been the outcry of many writers, both in religious and anti-religious papers, and proposals have not been wanting as to how this munificent benefaction might be employed for other and more useful purposes.

Our schools and universities have long been told that much of what they are teaching is useless in the battle of life. Greek and Latin are called dead languages. Ancient history is condemned as a medley of legendary traditions and of one-sided partisan views, while our newspapers are said to contain more wisdom than the whole of Thucydides; nay, as has lately been calculated, more words also—which is quite possible. As to philosophy, it is looked upon as obsolete, nay, even as mischievous, and the athletics of the cricket-field are praised as far more efficacious in forming manly and practical characters than the intellectual gymnastics of Logic and Metaphysics.

While every effort is being made to sweep away all ancient lumber and classical rubbish, we can hardly be surprised that an attempt to introduce into our universities a new study, the study of dead religions, should have met with anything but a friendly welcome on the part of educational reformers.

So far as these attacks are directed against all scientific studies which cannot at once show what they lead to, or produce useful and marketable results, no defence seems to me necessary. We surely know by this time how often in the history of the world the labours of the patient student, jeered at by his contemporaries as mere waste of time and money and brains, have in the end given to the world some of its most valued possessions. Faraday died a poor man, but the world has grown richer and brighter by his labours. Copernicus, while he was quietly observing, measuring, and calculating,—looked upon as a strange and even as a dangerous man by his fellow-canons at Frauenburg,—never asked what all his work would lead to. Like every true student, he was simply in love with truth. And yet there has scarcely ever been a greater revolution achieved in the world of thought, or a more important advance made in our knowledge of the universe, nay, in our knowledge of ourselves, than by that solitary philosopher in the North of Germany, when he proved that we and our globe did not form, as was fondly supposed, the centre of the universe, but had to take the place assigned to us by the side of other planets, all moving at a greater or smaller distance around one central sun.

The only question which deserves to be considered is, whether a study of Natural Religion is ever likely to produce a similar revolution in our world of thought, is ever likely to lead to a similar advance in our knowledge of the universe, nay, in our knowledge of ourselves, is ever likely to teach us that our own religion also, however perfect, is but one out of many religions, all moving, at a greater or smaller distance, around one central truth.

We are asked, What can a study of the old and dead religions of the world teach us who are in possession of a new and living religion? What can we learn from Natural Religion, who pride ourselves on the possession of a Supernatural Religion?

Lessons of Natural Religion.

What can a study of Natural Religion teach us? Why, it teaches us that religion is natural, is real, is inevitable, is universal. Is that nothing? Is it nothing to know that there is a solid rock on which all religion, call it natural or supernatural, is founded? Is it nothing to learn from the annals of history that 'God has not left Himself without witness, in that He did good, and gave us rain from heaven, and fruitful seasons, filling our hearts, and the hearts of the whole human race, with food and gladness?'

If you examine the attacks that have been made on religion, which have proved the more dangerous—those on Natural or those on Supernatural Religion?

Christianity, to which alone, at least among ourselves, the name of a Supernatural Religion would be conceded, has been surrounded during the nineteen centuries of its existence with many ecclesiastical outworks. Some of these outworks ought probably never to have been erected. But when they were attacked and had to be surrendered, Christianity itself has remained unaffected, nay, it has been strengthened rather than weakened by their surrender. The Reformation swept away a good many of these ecclesiastical fences and intrenchments, and the spirit of the Reformation, dangerous as it was supposed to be at the time to the most vital interests of Christianity, has never been at rest again, and will never be at rest. Under the name of Biblical Criticism the same reforming spirit is at work in our own days, and whatever may be thought of it in other countries, in the country of Knox, in the ancient home of free thought and free speech, that reforming spirit will never be stifled, however dangerous it may seem at times even in the eyes of old and honest reformers. There can be no doubt that free inquiry has swept away, and will sweep away, many things which have been highly valued, nay, which were considered essential by many honest and pious minds. And yet who will say that true Christianity, Christianity which is known by its fruits, is less vigorous now than it has ever been before? There have been dissensions in the

Christian Church from the time of the Apostles to our own times. We have passed through them ourselves, we are passing through them even now. But in spite of all the hard and harsh and unchristian language that has been used in these controversies, who would doubt now, after their lives and their deepest convictions have been laid open before the world, that Kingsley was as deeply religious a man as Newman, that Stanley served his Church as faithfully as Pusey, and that Dr. Martineau, the Unitarian, deserves the name of a Christian as much as Dr. Liddon?

But now let us look at the attacks which have of late been directed against Natural Religion—against a belief in anything beyond what is supplied by the senses, against a conception of anything infinite or divine, against a trust in any government of the world, against the admission of any distinction between good and evil, against the very possibility of an eternal life—what would remain, I do not say of Christianity, or even of Judaism, Mohammedanism, Buddhism, or Brahmanism, but of anything worth the name of religion, if these attacks could not be repelled?

And yet we are asked, What can a study of Natural Religion teach us?

And when we have shown that Natural Religion is the only impregnable safeguard against atheism, we are told that unaided reason cannot lead to a belief in God. This is an orthodoxy which may become the most dangerous of all heresies. Cardinal Newman was not a man who trusted in reason rather than in authority. And yet what does he say of Natural Religion? 'I have no intention at all,' he writes in his *Apologia*, p. 243, 'of denying, that truth is the real object of our reason, and that, if it does not attain to truth, either the premiss or the process is at fault; but I am not speaking here of right reason, but of reason as it acts in fact and concretely in fallen man. I know that even unaided reason, when correctly exercised, leads to a belief in God, in the immortality of the soul, and in future retribution; but I am considering the faculty of reason actually and historically; and in this point of view, I do not think I am wrong in saying that its tendency is towards a simple unbelief in matters of religion.'

I give the Cardinal's words with all his restrictions. I am not concerned with the question whether historically the tendency of reason has been everywhere towards unbelief, except in the Roman Catholic Church. I only lay stress on his admission, an admission in which he felt himself supported by the highest authorities of the early Church, that 'unaided reason, when correctly exercised, can lead to a belief in God, in the immortality of the soul, and in future retribution.'

In my present course of Lectures I have had to confine myself to *one* branch of Natural Religion only, to what I call Physical, as distinguished from Anthropological and Psychological Religion. Leaving out of consideration, therefore, the two great problems, that of the immortality of the soul, and that of man's true relation to God, which form the subject of Anthropological and Psychological Religion, I may now sum up in a few words what a study of Physical Religion can teach us, and, I may hope, has taught us.

The Agents in Nature.

A study of the ancient religions of the world, and more particularly of the earliest religion of India, teaches us, first of all, that many things in nature which we are now inclined to treat as quite natural, as a matter of course, appeared to the minds of the earliest observers in a much truer light, as by no means natural, as by no means a matter of course, but on the contrary, as terrific, as astounding, as truly miraculous, as supernatural. It was in these very phenomena of nature, the sky, the sun, the fire, and the storm-wind, which to us seem so natural, so ordinary, so hackneyed, that man perceived for the first time something that startled him out of his animal torpor, that made him ask, What is it? What does it all mean? Whence does it all come?—that forced him, whether he liked it or not, to look behind the drama of nature for actors or agents, different from merely human agents, agents whom in his language and thought he called superhuman, and, in the end, divine.

We must not imagine that these early observers and namers of nature did not distinguish between these phenomena, as mere phenomena, and the agents postulated by their very language. The names given to these phenomena, were in reality the names of *noumena*, of unseen powers. Zeus, and Jupiter, and Dyaush pitâ in Sanskrit, were not meant for the dead sky; they were names, at all events in the beginning, of an agent within or behind or beyond the sky. They were masculine names, not neuters. They represent, as I tried to show, the first attempt at grasping that Infinite which underlies all our finite perceptions, and at naming the Supernatural, as manifested in the Natural. They are the first steps which led in the end to a faith in God, as revealed in Nature.

What I chiefly wished to establish by means of the evidence so unexpectedly supplied to us in the hymns of the Rig-veda was the simplicity and almost necessity of Physical Religion, or of the discovery of God in nature. Given man, such as he is, not, of course, as a *tabula rasa*, but as endowed with reason and language, and armed with the so-called categories of the understanding; and given nature, such as it is, not as a chaos, but as a text that can be construed, what we call Physical Religion, a naming of and believing in Agents behind the great drama of nature, was inevitable, and, being inevitable, was, for the time being, true.

One Agent in Nature.

But it was true as a first step only in an unbroken chain of intellectual evolution, for it was soon recognised that these various agents were really doing one and the same work, whether their presence was perceived in the sky, or in the sun, or in the fire, or in the storm-wind. Hence the various names of these agents, the Devas or the Bright ones, as they were called, were recognised after a time by the more thoughtful poets, as names of one all-powerful Agent, no longer a mere Deva by the side of other Devas, but the Lord, the Lord of all created things, hence called Pra*g*âpati, the universal Will, hence called Brahma, and, in the end, the eternal Self of the objective world, as recognised by the Self of the subjective world, the Âtman of the Vedânta philosophy.

We also examined the different epithets that were assigned to the Devas, and to Him who was recognised in the end as above all Devas, and we found that they closely corresponded to the attributes of God in our own religion. If there are any other divine attributes, supposed to be beyond the reach of natural religion, all we can say is that they should be pointed out, so that we may determine, once for all, whether they can or whether they cannot be matched even in so primitive a religion as that of the Veda.

If then so much of our religious knowledge, and more particularly our concept of God as the all-powerful Agent in nature, which was believed to be beyond the reach of the unassisted human intellect, or supernatural in its origin, has been proved to be perfectly natural, nay inevitable, have we lost anything?

Craving for the Supernatural.

I see nothing that has been lost, and I see much that has been gained. Like the Copernican discovery, this discovery also will teach us both humility and gratitude, humility on learning that other people also were not left in utter darkness as to what lies beyond this finite world, gratitude for that we have been spared many of the struggles through which other people had to pass in their search after God.

Unfortunately, it is still with many of us, as it was with the Jews of old. They were always hankering for something exclusive and exceptional, for something supernatural and miraculous. They alone, they thought, were the chosen people of God. They would not believe, unless they saw signs and wonders, designed for their special benefit, while they remained blind to the true signs and wonders that appealed to them on every side.

And yet the founders of the three greatest religions of the world, however much they may differ on other points, are unanimous on *one* point, namely in their condemnation of this hankering after the miraculous, and after the supernatural, falsely so called.

Miracles condemned by Mohammed.

Orthodox Mohammedans delight in relating the miracles wrought by Mohammed. But what does Mohammed say himself in the Korân? He expresses the strongest contempt of miracles, in the usual sense of that word, and he appeals to the true miracles, the great works of Allah in nature. And what are these great works of Allah, these true miracles of nature? 'The rising and setting of the sun,' he says, 'the rain that fructifies the earth, and the plants that grow, we know not how.' You see, the very phenomena of nature in which the Vedic poets discovered the presence of divine agents are what Mohammed calls the great works of Allah. After that, Mohammed continues: '*I* cannot show you signs and miracles, except what you see every day and every night. Signs are with God [1].' Here you see the true religious view of the world, which perceives the Supernatural in all things natural, and does not bargain for special miracles before it will believe.

[1] See Lane Poole, *The Speeches of Mohammed*, p. 64: 'Nothing hindered our sending thee with signs but that the people of yore called them lies.' 'Verily in the alternations of the night and the day, and in all that God created in the heavens and the earth, are signs to a God-fearing folk,' p. 88.

Miracles condemned by Buddha.

No religion, as handed down to us, is so full of miracles as Buddhism. The Brâhmans also, the predecessors of the Buddhists, were staunch believers in every kind of miracle. When Buddhism became a rival faith in India, the Brâhmans twitted the Buddhists with not being able to perform such miracles as they performed, and still profess to perform. But what did Buddha say to his disciples, when they asked his permission to perform such miracles, as making seeds to sprout, healing diseases, sitting in the air, or ascending to the clouds? At one time he does not seem to question the possibility of acquiring supernatural powers (iddhi), but he says that the only way to them lies through the eightfold noble path, as it were, through much prayer and fasting. At other times he forbids his disciples to do anything of the kind, but he allows them instead to perform one miracle, which may be called the greatest moral miracle. 'Hide your good deeds,' he says, 'and confess before the world the sins you have committed.' That was in Buddha's eyes the only miracle which his disciples might safely be allowed to perform; everything else he left to the Brâhmans, who might perform signs and wonders to please and to deceive the multitude.

Miracles condemned by Christ.

And what did the founder of Christianity say, when asked to perform miracles, in the sense ascribed to that word by the multitude? 'An evil and adulterous generation,' he said, 'seeketh after a sign.' And again, 'Except ye see signs and wonders ye will not believe.'

Such utterances from the founders of the three great religions should at all events make us pause and reflect what the true meaning of a miracle was in the beginning. It was not the supernatural forced and foisted into the natural; it was the natural perceived as the supernatural; it was the reading of a new and deeper meaning both in the workings of nature and in the acts of inspired men; it was the recognition of the Divine, reflected in the light of common day.

A French philosopher and poet, Amiel, has truly said: 'A miracle depends for its existence far more on the subject who sees, than on the object that is seen. A miracle is a perception of the soul, the vision of the divine behind nature. There is no miracle for the indifferent. Religious souls only are capable of recognising the finger of God in certain events.'

And even Cardinal Newman admits that we might be satisfied with the popular view of a miracle, 'as an event which impresses upon the mind the immediate presence of the Moral Governor of the world' (*Apologia*, p. 305). Is it not clear then that in the eyes of those who believe in the omnipresence of the Moral Governor of the world, miracles, in the ordinary sense of the word, have become impossible, and that to them either every event is miraculous or no event can claim that name. Before the great miracle of the manifestation of God in nature, all other miracles vanish. There is but one eternal miracle, the revelation of the Infinite in the finite.

The Supernatural as Natural.

But while on one side a study of Natural Religion teaches us that much of what we are inclined to class as natural, to accept as a matter of course, nay to pass by as unmeaning, is in reality full of meaning, is full of God, is, in fact, truly miraculous, it also opens our eyes to another fact, namely that many things which we are inclined to class as supernatural, are in reality perfectly natural, perfectly intelligible, nay inevitable, in the growth of every religion.

Thus it has been the chief object of my lectures to show that the concept of God arises by necessity in the human mind, and is not, as so many theologians will have it, the result of one special disclosure, granted to Jews and Christians only. It seems to me impossible to resist this conviction, when a comparative study of the great religions of the world shows us that the highest attributes which we claim for the Deity are likewise ascribed to it by the Sacred Books of other religions.

This is either a fact or no fact, and, if it is a fact, no conscientious scholar would in our days try to explain it away by saying that the poets of the Veda, for instance, had borrowed their concept of God and His essential attributes from the Jews.

I have never been able to understand the object of these futile endeavours. Do we lose anything, if we find that what we hold to be the most valuable truth is shared in and supported by millions of human beings? Ancient philosophers were most anxious to support their own belief in God by the unanimous testimony of mankind. They made the greatest efforts to prove that there was no race so degraded and barbarous as to be without a belief in something Divine. Some modern theologians, on the contrary, seem to grudge to all religions but their own the credit of having a pure and true, nay any concept of God at all, quite forgetful of the fact that a truth does not cease to be a truth because it is accepted universally. I know no heresy more dangerous to true religion than this denial that a true concept of God is within the reach of every human being, is, in fact, the common inheritance of mankind, however fearfully it may have been misused and profaned by Christian and non-Christian nations.

Common elements of all Religions. The Ten Commandments.

And this universal consensus is not restricted to the concept of God only. Many of the moral commandments, which we are accustomed to consider as communicated to mankind by a special revelation, such as the *Ten Commandments*, for instance, occur, sometimes in almost the same words, in the Sacred Books of other religions also. Instead of being surprised, or, what is still worse, being disappointed by that discovery, would it not be perfectly awful if it were otherwise? Or can anybody really persuade himself that what we call the heathen-world had to wait and borrow from the Jews such commandments as 'Thou shalt not steal,' 'Thou shalt not kill,' 'Thou shalt not bear false witness'?

When people are told that the Buddhists have their Ten Commandments, the Dasasîla, they are startled at once by the number ten. But we shall see that this number ten is a mere accident. The next step is to suppose that these Ten Commandments must have been borrowed from the Jews by some unknown subterraneous channel, or, as some will have it, that they constitute a fragment of that primeval revelation which, we are assured, was given once and once only to the human race, but preserved in its entirety and purity by the Jews alone. All these are utterly futile defences, thrown up to guard against purely imaginary dangers.

We have only to look at the so-called Ten Commandments of the Buddhists to see that they could not possibly have been borrowed from the Bible. They are divided into three classes; five for the laity at large, three more for what we should call religious people, and two more for the priests. Every man who calls himself a follower of Buddha must vow—

1. Not to destroy life.
2. Not to steal.
3. To abstain from all unchastity.
4. Not to lie, deceive, or bear false witness.
5. To abstain from intoxicating drinks.

A layman of higher aspirations must promise in addition—

6. Not to eat food at unseasonable times, that is, after the mid-day meal.

7. Not to dance, not to sing light songs; in fact, to avoid worldly dissipation.

8. Not to wear any kind of ornament, not to use any scents or perfumes; in short, to avoid whatever tends to vanity.

The priest, or as it would be more correct to render

Bhikshu, the friar or mendicant, has to obey two more commandments, viz.—

9. To sleep on a hard and low couch.

10. To live in voluntary poverty.

You see at once how impossible it would be to suppose that the Buddhists had borrowed these ten commandments from the Ten Commandments of the Old Testament. The most essential commandments, no doubt, are there: 'Thou shalt do no murder,' 'Thou shalt not commit adultery,' 'Thou shalt not steal,' 'Thou shalt not bear false witness against thy neighbour,' and possibly, 'Thou shalt not covet.' But does any student of the history of civilised or uncivilised nations really suppose that these commandments required what is called a special revelation, and that they were not engraved on the tablets of the human heart, before they had been engraved on the tablets of stone on Mount Horeb?

And how could we account for the absence of the other commandments, some of them the most characteristic of the Decalogue? The fifth commandment, 'Honour thy father and mother,' is one that is often inculcated by Buddha in his numerous sermons, yet it finds no place in the Dasasîla of the Buddhists; while another religion, that of Confucius in China, may be said to be mainly founded on that commandment, on what he calls filial piety, the honour paid by children to their fathers and mothers.

In the Vedic literature we find nothing corresponding to the ten commandments. Nevertheless, all the essential commandments were known to the ancient Hindus quite as much as to the Jews and the Buddhists. Five of them are often comprehended under the name of 'the summary of Manu's laws for the four castes.' These are (Manu X. 63)—

1. Abstention from injuring.
2. Veracity.
3. Abstention from unlawfully appropriating.
4. Purity.
5. Control of the organs of sense.

Here the first commandment corresponds to the sixth in the Decalogue, and to the general commandment of ahi*m*sâ, not injuring, among the Buddhists. The second corresponds to the ninth of the Decalogue, the third to the eighth, the fifth to the seventh, while the fourth, which enjoins purity, cannot be matched in the Decalogue. But besides these five commandments, there are four or five others which, in the Vedic literature, appear in the shape of the great sacred acts incumbent upon every member of society. These so-called Mahâya*gñ*as, as described in the Brâhma*n*as (*S*at. Br. XI. 5, 6), consist of—

1. Daily offering of Bali to the seven classes of beings (Bhûta-ya*gñ*a).
2. Daily gift of food to men (Manushya-ya*gñ*a).
3. Daily offering to the Manes, accompanied by the exclamation Svadhâ, which may consist even of a vessel with water only (Pit*ri*-ya*gñ*a).
4. Daily oblation to the gods, accompanied by the exclamation Svâhâ, which may consist of a piece of wood only (Deva-ya*gñ*a).
5. Daily recitation for the *Ri*shis (Brahma-ya*gñ*a).

Here we see that the worship of the gods, though not enjoined in the form of a command, is clearly implied, because the neglect of the five daily sacrifices entails sin. The daily offerings to the Manes are in reality a continuation of the honour due to father and mother during life, while the daily giving of food to men and even to other beings implies, to a certain extent, the absence of covetousness which is enjoined in the last commandment of the Decalogue.

There is, therefore, in the commandments of the Brâhmans both more and less than in the Ten Commandments. As the Brâhmans had not arrived at the exclusive worship of one national God, and had never excelled in making images, the first commandment not to worship other gods, and not to make graven images, is naturally absent in India. The danger of using the name of God in vain, seems likewise to have been unknown in Vedic times. The duty to honour father and mother is almost taken for granted, and when it is mentioned, it is generally joined with the command to honour the teachers also. On the other hand, the duty of kindness towards all men, and even towards animals, and lastly the duty of honouring the dead, are passed over in the Decalogue [1].

If Comparative Theology has taught us anything, it has taught that there is a common fund of truth in all religions, derived from a revelation that was neither confined to one nation, nor miraculous in the usual sense of that word, and that even minute coincidences between the doctrines, nay, between the external accessories of various religions, need not be accounted for at once by disguised borrowings, but can be explained by other and more natural causes.

Very often we find that what at first sight seems

[1] See on all this Professor Leist in his excellent work, *Jus Gentium*, pp. 247–384.

identical in two religions, is in reality not identical, when we succeed in tracing it back to its original source. Many of the similarities between the lives of Christ and Buddha, for instance, of which we have heard so much of late, belong to that class. They are at first sight puzzling, nay startling, but they generally become quite natural, if subjected to the examination of a scholarlike criticism.

Similarities between Christianity and Buddhism.

I shall try to give you one specimen at least of what I mean by scholarlike criticism, for it is really high time that an end should be put to the uncritical mixing up of Buddhism and Christianity, which, if true, would upset nearly all we know of the real history of the ancient religions of the world. As Buddhism is about five centuries older than Christianity, it is Christianity only that could have been the borrower, if borrowing had taken place at all; and I ask, by what historical channel could Buddhism have reached Palestine in the first century before our era? Buddhism is an historical religion, and so is Christianity. No one, I suppose, would write about Christianity who has not read the New Testament. Why then should so many people write about Buddhism, without reading the Sacred Canon of the Buddhists, or, at least, those large portions of it which have been translated into English and published in my series of the 'Sacred Books of the East'? Why should they instead read fanciful novels, or worse than imaginary accounts of Mahâtmas and Theosophists which, if they contain a few grains of Buddhism, contain tons of rubbish and trash? It is a shame to see so beautiful a religion as Buddhism certainly is in many of its parts, misrepresented, caricatured, nay, degraded by many of those who call themselves Neo-buddhists or Theosophists, and who by their own ignorance try to impose on the ignorance and credulity of the public.

Let us take one instance. Mr. Oswald Felix writes, 'that according to the Lalita-Vistara, which is one of the Sacred Books of Buddhism, or, more correctly of Northern Buddhism or Bodhism, Buddha converted his first disciples, half of them formerly followers of his precursor, Rudraka, while sitting under a fig-tree. The first disciples of Christ were seceders from the followers of John the Baptist, the precursor of the world-renouncing Messiah. "I have seen you under the fig-tree," says Jesus, when his converts introduce Nathanael. Nathanael then at once recants his doubts. Sitting under the sacred fig-tree is one of the mystic tokens of Buddhist Messiahship.'

So far Mr. Oswald Felix, who is, I must say, one of the more conscientious and fair-minded students of Buddhism. But let us now examine the case more closely. That the founders of the Christian and Buddhist religions should both have had precursors, can hardly be called a very startling coincidence, particularly when we consider how different was the relation of John the Baptist to Christ from that of Rudraka to Buddha. But that the Buddhist and the Christian Messiah should both have converted their disciples under a fig-tree, does sound strange, and, being without any apparent motive, would seem to require some explanation. If there was borrowing on this point between the two religions, it could only have been on the Christian side, for Buddha died

477 B.C., and the Buddhist Canon was settled, as we saw, in the third century B.C. under king Asoka.

But let us look more carefully into this matter. That Buddha should be represented as sitting under a fig-tree is most natural in India. He was for a time a hermit. Hermits in India lived under the shelter of trees, and no tree in India gave better shelter than what we call the Indian fig-tree. Different Buddhas were supposed to have been sitting under different trees, and were distinguished afterwards by the trees which they had chosen as their own.

There would seem to be no similar explanation for Christ sitting and teaching under a fig-tree, and hence the conclusion that this account must have been borrowed from the Buddhist scriptures seems not altogether unreasonable. The fig-tree in Palestine has little in common with the fig-tree in India, nor do we ever hear of Jewish Rabbis sitting under trees while teaching.

But are we really told that Christ sat under a fig-tree? Certainly not. The words are, 'Jesus answered and said unto him, "Before that Philip called thee, when thou wert under the fig-tree, I saw thee."' Where is then the coincidence, and where the necessity of admitting that the Christian story was borrowed from the Buddhists? People who compare the gospels of Buddha and Christ ought at all events to be acquainted with the New Testament. Nathanael happened to be under a fig-tree when he was first seen by Christ. That fig-tree was not an Indian fig-tree, nor was it the shelter under which Christ sat when choosing His disciples.

Much as has been made of this, there seems to me

nothing left that requires explanation, nothing to support the theory that two religions, so diametrically opposed to each other on the most essential points, could have borrowed such accounts one from the other, whether Buddhism from Christianity, or Christianity from Buddhism.

I do not mean to say that all similarities between Buddhism and Christianity have been fully accounted for as yet. It would not be honest to say so. All I say is that most of them have been, and that the rest are not such as to justify us in admitting an historical intercourse between India and Palestine before the rise of Christianity[1].

The real coincidences, not only between Christianity and Buddhism, but between all the religions of the world, teach us a very different lesson. They teach us that all religions spring from the same soil—the human heart, that they all look to the same ideals, and that they are all surrounded by the same dangers and difficulties. Much that is represented to us as supernatural in the annals of the ancient religions of the world becomes perfectly natural from this point of view.

Divine character ascribed to the Founders of Religions.

For instance, the founders of most, if not of all religions were after a time believed in as superior beings, as superhuman or divine, in the old-world sense of the word. An ordinary birth, therefore, was not considered sufficient, nor, in many instances, an ordinary death. All this is perfectly natural, it is almost inevitable.

If I say that it is almost inevitable, this might be

[1] See Appendix XV.

called a mere assertion or a theory, and the Science of Religion, as I have often said in my lectures, deals not in theories, but in facts only. These facts, which speak with a louder voice than any theories, are collected from historical documents, and it is in them that we must learn to study the origin and growth of religions, and all the accidents that befall them, when entrusted to the keeping of weak mortals, call them laymen or priests.

Buddha's Birth.

Let us begin with the birth of Buddha. At first it is no more than the birth of a prince, the son of the Rajah of Kapilavastu. He is certainly the first-born child of his mother, and it was in that sense that first-born children were often called the children of virgin mothers. Thus even Moses is called in the Talmud the son of a virgin. When Mahâ-mâyâ, the wife of king *S*uddhodana, was near her confinement, we are told [1] that she expressed a wish to go to Devadaha, the city of her own people. The king, saying, 'It is good,' consented, and had the road from Kapilavastu to Devadaha made plain and decked with arches of plain-trees, and well-filled waterpots, and flags, and banners. And seating the queen in a golden palanquin, carried by a thousand attendants, he sent her away with a great retinue. When approaching the Lumbinî grove, the queen was carried in, and when she came to the monarch Sal-tree of the glade, she wanted to take hold of a branch of it, and the branch bending down approached within reach of her hand. Stretching out her hand, she took hold of the branch,

[1] See *Buddhist Birth-Stories*, p. 65.

and then standing, and holding the branch of the Sal-tree, she was delivered.

This is as yet a very sober account of Buddha's birth, and even what follows is not more than we should expect from an Oriental narrator. 'Four pure-minded Mahâ-Brahma angels came there, bringing a golden net, and receiving the future Buddha on that net, they placed him before his mother, saying, "Be joyful, O lady! a mighty son is born to thee." Of course Buddha is born pure and fair, and shining like a gem placed on fine muslin of Benares. Two showers of water came down from heaven to refresh mother and child[1].'

But the plot thickens as we go on. We are told (p. 62) that the queen had had a dream in which the four archangels, the guardians of the world, lifted her up in a couch, carried her to the Himâlaya mountains, and placed her under the Great *S*âlâ-tree. Then their queens took her to the lake Anotatta, bathed, dressed, and anointed her, and laid her on a couch in the

[1] It seems a curious coincidence that according to the Korân the mother of Jesus, like the mother of Buddha, was delivered while standing under a tree, and that water should have streamed forth for the benefit of mother and child. See the Qurân, translated by Palmer, *S. B. E.*, vol. ix. p. 28: 'And the labour pains came upon her at the trunk of a palm-tree, and she said, "O that I had died before this, and been forgotten out of mind!" and he called to her from beneath her, "Grieve not, for thy Lord has placed a stream beneath thy feet; and shake towards thee the trunk of the palm-tree, it will drop upon thee fresh dates fit to gather; so eat, and drink, and cheer thine eye; and if thou shouldst see any mortal, say, 'Verily, I have vowed to the Merciful One a fast, and I will not speak to-day with a human being.'"' See also G. Rösch, *Die Jesusmythen des Islam*, in *Theologische Studien und Kritiken*, 1876, pp. 437 seq. He points out that in the *Evang. infantiae* the child Jesus, on the third day of the Flight into Egypt, caused a palm-tree to bend down its fruit-laden branches into the hands of Mary, and a spring of water to issue from its roots.

golden mansion of the Silver Hill. There she saw the future Buddha, who had become a superb white elephant, ascending the Silver Hill, entering the golden mansion, and after thrice doing obeisance, gently striking her right side and seeming to enter her womb.

This was at first a dream only, but it was soon changed into a reality. In later accounts we are told that Buddha really entered his mother's right side as a white elephant, and this incarnation has become one of the favourite scenes in Buddhist sculptures.

At the time of this wonderful incarnation, we are further told that the worlds shook, and that an immeasurable light appeared in the ten thousand worlds! The blind received their sight, as if from very longing to behold his glory. The deaf heard the noise. The dumb spake one with another. The crooked became straight. The lame walked [1].

These miraculous stories connected with the birth of Buddha are all the more surprising in Buddhism, because they seem so objectless. They are never used as a proof of Buddha's divine character, for Buddha's was high above all gods, nor are they quoted in support of the truth of the doctrines which he preached later in life. When we think of the exalted character of Buddha's teaching, we wonder what he would have said if he could have seen the fabulous stories of his birth and childhood.

Birth of Mahâvîra.

Still more extraordinary is the birth of Buddha's contemporary, Mahâvîra, the reputed founder of

[1] For the rest of this quotation see Appendix XV, p. 392.

*G*ainism[1]. After his first incarnation, he is actually transferred from one mother, who belonged to the caste of the Brâhmans, to another who belonged to the caste of the Kshatriyas, because—and this is very significant—the Kshatriyas were then considered as more noble than the Brâhmans. And when at last he is born, there is a divine lustre originated by many descending and ascending gods and goddesses, and in the universe, resplendent with one light, the conflux of gods occasioned great confusion and noise. In that night in which the venerable ascetic Mahâvîra was born, many demons in Vaisrama*n*a's service, belonging to the animal world, rained down on the palace of king Siddhârtha one great shower of silver, gold, diamonds, clothes, ornaments, leaves, flowers, fruits, seeds, garlands, perfumes, sandal, powder, and riches.

It is the story of Buddha, only carried to greater extremes.

Mohammed's Birth.

We saw before how opposed Mohammed was to all miracles, falsely so called. But in the later accounts of his life we read of many miraculous events which accompanied his birth. We are told[2] that a Jew in Jathrib (Medîna) called his friends together on the morrow after Mohammed's birth, and said to them: 'This night the star has risen under which Ahmed will be born.' Before his birth a spirit appeared to his mother, Âmina, saying: 'Thy child will be the lord of this people. Say at his birth, "I place him under the protection of the Only One against the

[1] *G*aina-sûtras, in *S. B. E.*, vol. xxii. pp. 191, 251.

[2] See Krehl, *Das Leben des Mohammed*, p. 1.

wickedness of all enviers, and I call him Mohammed."' While she was with child, she is said to have seen a light which spread its rays from her, so that one could see by its lustre the castles of Busra in Syria.

Some Mohammedans now go so far as to believe that 'when the prophet was born, the gods and goddesses and saints of heaven descended upon the earth, praised and saluted him, and thanked his mother Âmina.' Again, one feels tempted to ask what Mohammed himself would have said to such gods and goddesses descending from heaven, he whose chief doctrine was that there is but one God, and Mohammed His prophet.

Other Prophets.

But these superstitions are not confined to Buddha and Mahâvîra, both born in the sixth century B.C., or to Mohammed, who was born in the sixth century A.D. In much more modern times, and in the broad daylight of history, the same stories spring up and are believed. Nânak, for instance, was the founder of the Sikh religion; he lived in the sixteenth century, and was a contemporary of our reformers. Yet we read of him that when he was born (A.D. 1469, April–May), in a moonlight night at an early hour, while yet about a watch of the night was remaining, unbeaten sounds were produced at the gate of the Lord, thirty-three crores of gods paid homage, the sixty-four Yoginîs, the fifty-two heroes, the six ascetics, the eighty-four Siddhas, the nine Nâthas, all paid homage, because a great devotee has come to save the world[1].

[1] See Trumpp, *Âdi-Granth*, pp. ii, vii, IL.

*K*aitanya, the founder of one of the most popular modern systems of religion in India, is a still later and perfectly historical character. He was born in 1485. Yet his birth also could not escape the miraculous halo which is considered essential to every founder of a new religion or of a new sect. At his birth also, as his followers assure us, 'men from all sides began to send presents. Sa*k*î, his mother, saw in the heavens beings with spiritual bodies making adoration. There was an eclipse when the child was born, and the men of the world shouted aloud. The women also cried the name of Hari, and made sounds of Hooloos. The saints of heaven danced and played music with joy [1].'

These are facts,—I do not mean the miracles themselves, but the poetical tendency of man which, without any thought of fraud, is led on irresistibly to these imaginary representations of the birth of great heroes and prophets [2], even of those who were themselves most opposed to the idea of appealing to signs and wonders in support of the truth of their doctrines.

The Birth of Christ.

Should we hesitate then to assign the same origin to the accounts of the birth of Christ which were preserved in some of the Apocryphal Gospels, while some of them have actually found their way, we do not know through what channels, into two of our Synoptical Gospels?

When we think of the exalted character of Christ's

[1] *Asiatic Researches*, xvi. p. 111.

[2] Similar cases are mentioned by E. Carpenter in *The Synoptic Gospels*, pp. 252 seq.

teaching, may we not ask ourselves once more, What would He have said if He had seen the fabulous stories of His birth and childhood, or if He had thought that His divine character would ever be made to depend on the historical truth of the *Evangelia Infantiae?*

Signs changed to Miracles.

It is due to the same psychological necessities of human nature, under the inspiring influence of religious enthusiasm, that so many of the true signs and wonders performed by the founders of religion have so often been exaggerated, and, in spite of the strongest protests of these founders themselves, degraded into mere jugglery. It is true that all this does not form an essential element of religion, as we now understand religion. Miracles are no longer used as arguments in support of the truth of religious doctrines. Miracles have often been called helps to faith, but they have as often proved stumbling-blocks to faith, and no one would in our days venture to say that the truth as taught by any religion must stand or fall with certain prodigious events which may or may not have happened, which may or may not have been rightly apprehended by the followers of Buddha, Christ, or Mohammed.

Dr. Robert Lee.

Let me quote here the words of an eminent Scotch divine, whose memory is still widely loved and revered, I believe, the late Dr. Robert Lee. His Life, written by Dr. Story, is probably known to most of you. On one occasion, a gentleman undertook a long journey to gain his advice on a point that troubled him. He could not bring himself to a belief in the Christian miracles. 'I asked him,' Dr. Lee said, 'if he believed the doctrines which the miracles were designed to recommend and illustrate.' On receiving a reply in the affirmative, the wise spiritual guide added: 'Then for you, belief in the miracles themselves is unnecessary. To lead to such belief was their purpose; it is sufficient, if that is attained.'

Far more important, however, than the discovery of a number of outward coincidences between the miracles of various religions, is another lesson which a comparative study of the religions of the world has taught us, namely, that there is a common fund of truth in the most essential doctrines which they teach.

The Highest Commandments.

We saw before how the most important of the Ten Commandments could be traced in Buddhism and other religions of the world, while the idea that they must have been borrowed from the Jews was shown to be utterly untenable.

But what has been proved with regard to the Ten Commandments of the Old Testament, is equally true with regard to the fundamental commandment of Christianity. 'Love thy neighbour as thyself,' has long been proved to form an integral part of that eternal religion which has never been quite extinct in the human heart, and has found utterance, more or less perfect, by the mouths of many prophets, poets, and philosophers.

I shall here quote one instance only. We read in the

Confucian Analects, XV. 23[1], 'Tsze-kung asked, saying, "Is there one word which may serve as a rule of practice for all one's life?" The Master said: "Is not reciprocity such a word? What you do not want done to yourself, do not do to others."'

How difficult Confucius considered this rule of life, is shown in the same Analects, V. 11. Here Tsze-kung is introduced as saying, 'What I do not wish men to do to me, I also wish not to do to men.' But the Master replied: 'Tsze, you have not attained to that.'

The Talmud says that when a man once asked Shamai to teach him the Law in one lesson, Shamai drove him away in anger. He then went to Hillel with the same request. Hillel said, 'Do unto others as you would have others do unto you. This is the whole Law; the rest, merely commentaries upon it[2].'

But we may go one step further still. The commandment, not only to love our neighbour, but to love our enemy, and to return good for evil, the most sublime doctrine of Christianity, so sublime, indeed, that Christians themselves have declared it to be too high for this world, can be shown to belong to that universal code of faith and morality from which the greatest religions have drawn their strength and life.

Let me first quote the words of Christ[3]: 'You have heard that it hath been said, Thou shalt love thy neighbour, and hate thine enemy.

'But I say unto you, Love your enemies, bless them that curse you, do good to them that hate you, and

[1] Legge, *The Life and Teachings of Confucius*, p. 111.
[2] See Sir John Lubbock, *The Pleasures of Life*, vol. ii. pp. 226.
[3] St. Matthew v. 43.

pray for them which despitefully use you and persecute you.

'That you may be the children of your Father which is in heaven: for he maketh his sun to rise on the evil and on the good, and sendeth rain on the just and the unjust.'

Let us now consult a religion which cannot possibly be suspected of having borrowed anything from Christianity. Let us take Taoism, one of the three great religions of China, such as we know it from the writings of Lao-tze, who lived about 600 B.C. His birth also, you may remember, was represented as very miraculous, more miraculous perhaps than that of any other religious teacher. As I explained in my first course of Gifford Lectures, Lao-tze was believed to have been seventy years old when he was born, and to have actually come into the world with a head of grey hair [1]. Yet all this was probably not meant to convey more than that Lao-tze was a wise child, as wise as a man of seventy.

In chapter sixty-three of the Tao-te-king, Lao-tze says in so many words: 'Recompense injury with kindness;' or, as Julien translates, 'Il venge ses injures par des bienfaits [2].'

How widely spread and how old this doctrine must have been in China, we may gather from some curious remarks made by Confucius, the contemporary of Lao-tze, and the founder or reformer of the national religion of China. In the Analects [3] (bk. xiv. c. 36), we read:

[1] It was believed that Moses addressed his mother soon after his birth. See Thilo, *Codex Apocryphus Novi Testamenti*, p. 146; Rösch, l. c., p. 439.

[2] See Balfour, *The Divine Classic of Nan-Hua*, p. xix.

[3] Legge, l. c., p. 113.

'Some one said, "What do you say concerning the principle that injury should be recompensed with kindness?" The Master said: "With what then will you recompense kindness?" Recompense injury with justice, and kindness with kindness.'

This is evidently the language of a philosopher rather than of a religious teacher. Confucius seems to have perceived that to love our enemies is almost beyond human nature, and he declares himself satisfied therefore with demanding justice to our enemies—and who does not know how difficult it is to fulfil even that commandment?

However, the true prophets who thought not so much of what men are as what men ought to be, insisted on love, or, at all events, on pity for our enemies, as the highest virtue. Thus Buddha said: 'Let a man overcome evil by good; let him overcome the greedy by liberality, the liar by truth. . . For hatred does not cease by hatred at any time; hatred ceases by love; *this is an old rule*[1].'

Remark here again the same expression, that the commandment to overcome hatred by love is an old rule in the eyes of Buddha, as it was in the eyes of Confucius. What then becomes of the attempts to show that the doctrine of love towards our enemies must have been borrowed, wherever we find it, from the New Testament, as if that doctrine would become less true, because other religions also teach it, or because it had been revealed, in the truest sense of that word, to all who had eyes to see and hearts to love. It is truth that makes revelation, not revelation that makes truth.

[1] Dhammapada XVII. 223, in *S. B. E.*, vol. x. p. 58; *Jâtaka Tales*, by Morris, p. 7.

So far from trying by more or less specious arguments to claim this doctrine as the exclusive property of Christianity, we should rather welcome it, wherever we meet it.

The Hitopadesa, a Sanskrit collection of fables, is, in the form in which we possess it, certainly far more modern than the New Testament. But if we read there:

> 'Bar thy door not to the stranger, be he friend or be he foe,
> For the tree will shade the woodman, while his axe does lay it low,'

is there any reason why we should say that it must have been borrowed from Christian sources? The same idea meets us again and again with varying metaphors taken from nature, such as it was in India, and nowhere else. The sandal-wood tree was a tree peculiar to India, and thus the Indian poet tells us to love our enemies as the sandal tree sheds perfume on the axe that fells it.

Hafiz, one of the greatest poets of Persia, might, no doubt, have taken his thoughts from the New Testament. But, as Sir William Jones remarks, there is not the shadow of reason for supposing that the poet of Shiraz had borrowed his doctrine from the Christians[1]. This is a translation of some of his verses:

> 'Learn from yon orient shell to love thy foe,
> And store with pearls the hand that brings thee woe:
> Free, like yon rock, from base vindictive pride,
> Imblaze with gems the wrist that rends thy side:
> Mark, where yon tree rewards the stony shower
> With fruit nectareous, or the balmy flower;
> All nature calls aloud. Shall man do less
> Than heal the smiter and the railer bless?'

[1] *The Works of Sir William Jones*, 1807, vol. iii. p. 243.

I have no time left to quote other instances, all showing that this, the highest truth of Christianity, had been reached independently by what we call the pagan religions of the world. When I call it the highest truth of Christianity, I am but quoting the language of well-known theologians who declare that this is the most sublime piece of morality ever given to man, and that this one precept is a sufficient proof of the holiness of the Gospel and of the truth of the Christian religion.

So, no doubt, it is. But what shall we say then of the pagan religions which teach exactly the same doctrine?

Shall we say they borrowed it from Christianity?

That would be doing violence to history.

Shall we say that, though they use the same words, they did not mean the same thing?

That would be doing violence to our sense of truth.

Conclusion.

Why not accept the facts such as they are? At first, I quite admit, some of the facts which I have quoted in my lectures are startling and disturbing. But, like most facts which startle us from a distance, they lose their terror when we look them in the face, nay, they often prove a very Godsend to those who are honestly grappling with the difficulties of which religion is full. Anyhow, they are facts that must be met, that cannot be ignored. And why should they be ignored? To those who see no difficulties in their own religion, the study of other religions will create no new difficulties. It will only help them to appreciate more fully what they already possess. For with all that I have said in order to show that other religions also contain all that is necessary for salvation, it would be simply dishonest on my part were I to hide my conviction that the religion taught by Christ, and free as yet from all ecclesiastical fences and intrenchments, is the best, the purest, the truest religion the world has ever seen. When I look at the world as it is, I often say that we seem to be living two thousand years before, not after Christ.

To others again, whose very faith is founded on honest doubt, the study of other religions will prove of immense service. If, in my present course of lectures, I have proved no more than that the concept of God, in its progress from the imperfect to the more and more perfect, constitutes the inalienable birthright of man; that, without any special revelation, it was revealed to every human being, endowed with sense, with reason, and language, by the manifestation of God in Nature; and that the admission of, and the belief in a real Agent in all the works of nature is found under various and sometimes strange disguises in all the religions of the world; if, I say, I have succeeded in proving this by facts, by facts taken from the Sacred Books of all nations, then my labour has not been in vain. We can now repeat the words which have been settled for us centuries ago, and which we have learnt by heart in our childhood—'I believe in God the Father, Maker of heaven and earth,' with a new feeling, with the conviction that they express, not only the faith of the apostles, or of œcumenical councils, but that they contain the Confession of Faith of the whole world, expressed in different ways, conveyed in thousands of languages, but always embodying the same fundamental truth. I call it fundamental, because it is founded in the very nature of our mind, our reason, and our language, on a simple and ineradicable conviction that where there are acts there must be agents, and in the end, one Prime Agent, whom man may know, not indeed in his own inscrutable essence, yet in his acts, as revealed in nature.

You may have wondered why in these lectures on Physical Religion I should have so often appealed to the Veda, the sacred book of the Brâhmans. It was because nowhere else can we watch the natural evolution of the concept of God, as the Prime Agent of the world, better than in these ancient hymns. I have quoted many passages from them, showing how the simple observers of nature in India discovered the presence of supernatural agents in the fire, the storm-wind, the sky, the dawn, and the sun; how they called them by many names, but most frequently by that of deva, and how this name deva, meaning originally bright, after being applied to the brightness of the dawn, the sun, the sky, and the fire, became in the end to mean divine, is, in fact, the same word which we still use, as *Deus*, God.

Let me finish by one more quotation from the same Veda, showing how these early observers of nature in India were not satisfied with a belief in many Devas, in many bright and beneficent agents, but were led on irresistibly to a belief in one Prime Agent, in one God. It is a precious line, and I shall quote it first in the original Sanskrit, as it may have been recited, three thousand years ago, in the silent groves watered by the waves of the sacred river Sarasvatî:—

Yá*h* devéshu ádhi devá*h* éka*h* ắsît.

'He who above the gods, was the one God[1].'

Unless the whole chronology of Sanskrit literature is wrong, that line was composed in the north of India at least 1000 B.C. It was not the result of what historians mean by a special or supernatural revelation. It was the natural outcome of man's thoughts such as they had been fashioned in response to the impressions of nature. There was nothing artificial in it: it was simply what man could not help saying, being what he was, and seeing what he saw. If, as some philosophers tell us, man was wrong in this belief in God, then all we can say is that the whole world is a fraud, but a fraud beyond the ingenuity of any human detective.

I say once more, in conclusion, what I have often said in the course of these lectures,—the Science of Religion has to deal with facts, not with theories. The line from the Veda with which I close these lectures is a fact. It proves as a fact what I wished to establish, that the human mind, such as it is, and unassisted by any miracles except the eternal miracles of nature, did arrive at the concept of God in its highest and purest form, did arrive at some of the fundamental doctrines of our own religion. Whatever 'the impregnable rock of scripture truth' may be, here we have 'the impregnable rock of eternal and universal truth.' 'There is a God above all the gods,' whatever their names, whatever their concepts may have been in the progress of the ages and in the growth of the human mind. Whoever will ponder on

[1] Rig-veda X. 121, 8.

that fact in all its bearings, will discover in time that a comparative study of the religions of the world has lessons to teach us which the study of no single religion by itself can possibly teach, and that Lord Gifford's idea of founding Chairs of Natural Religion in the Universities of Scotland showed greater wisdom and a truer appreciation of the signs of the times than some of his critics have given him credit for.

APPENDIX I.

P. 23.

ARE PARTHIANS, PERSIANS, AND BACTRIANS MENTIONED IN THE VEDA?

The Parthians.

We hear of a Vedic poet (VI. 27, 8) praising the liberality of the Pârthavas. But what proof is there that these were the ancestors of the Parthians, and what evidence that the Parthians had reached the frontiers of India at that early time? P*ri*thu is a familiar name of royal personages in Indian literature, and so is Pârtha. P*ri*thu and P*ri*thî occur as names of Vedic Rishis. Why then may not the Pârthavas be simply the people of P*ri*thu? See Taitt. Br. I. 7, 7, 4; *S*atap. Br. V. 3, 5, 4.

The Persians.

The Persians have been suspected behind the name of Par*s*u and Pâra*s*avya. We read in Rv. VIII. 6, 46:

*S*atám ahám Tiríndire sahásram Pár*s*au ấ dade rấdhâ*m*si Yấdvânâm.

The poet, after praising the greatness of Indra, records a gift which he has received for his services, and says:

'I have taken a hundred with Tirindira, a thousand with the Par*s*u, presents of the Yâdvas.'

Whether Tirindira and Par*s*u were the same person seems doubtful, though the Indian tradition has evidently taken them in that sense[1]. But what evidence is here for taking Tirindira Parsu for Tirindira, the Persian? A similarity of sound exists, no doubt, between Tirindira and either Tirabazos (Ludwig) or Tiridates (Weber), but Parsu never occurs elsewhere in the sense of a Persian, and in the old names for Persia we never meet with a final u[2]. It seems difficult on such evidence to bring Persians near the Pan*g*âb about 1000 B. C.[3]

Another name, Balhika, which occurs in the Atharva-veda, V. 22, 9, has been pointed out as possibly showing an acquaintance of the author of that verse with the Bactrians. This name occurs frequently in later Sanskrit works as Bâlhîka. Now the original name of Bactria is *Bâkhtri* in the cuneiform inscriptions, *Bâkhdhi* in the Avesta, *Baktra* in Herodotus. It is said that the change to *Bâhr* and *Bahl*, the latter occurring in Moses of Chorene, could not have taken place till about the beginning of the Christian era. This would bring the date of this verse in the Atharva-veda down to a very late date, provided always that Balhika is meant for the people of Bactria, provided also that the phonetic change can really be fixed chronologically, as Professor Nöldeke maintains. *Balkh* is the form used by Arabic writers for Bactria.

[1] In the *S*ânkhâyana *S*rauta Sûtra XVI. 11, 20 we read—
Vatsa*h* Kâ*n*vas Tirindire
Pâra*s*avye sani*m* sasâna.

[2] Ludwig quotes Parsua from the obelisk of Salmaneser (855 B.C.).

[3] In Rv. X. 86, 23, pár*s*u*h* ha nâma mânaví, Parsu is used as a proper name. In I. 105, 8, X. 33, 2, pár*s*ava*h* may mean the ribs. A curious compound occurs in VII. 83, 1, p*ri*thu-pár*s*ava*h*, but this has nothing to do with either Parthians or Persians, but seems to mean either with broad ribs or with broad weapons. Pár*s*u, meaning a rib, then a bent knife, a sickle, probably originally of bone, exists in a fuller form as para*s*ú, the Greek πέλεκυς. If this word, as has been supposed by Dr. Hommel, is the same as the Sumerian *balag*, the Babylon-Assyrian *pilakku*, which seems doubtful, we should have to admit that the Sumerians borrowed the word and the weapon from India. For *balag*, as far as we know, has no etymology in Sumerian, while para*s*ú has a history in Sanskrit.

APPENDIX II.

P. 26.

SKYLAX AND THE PAKTYES, THE PASHTU OR AFGHANS.

There were several writers of the name of Skylax, which, considering its meaning, is rather strange. The Periplus or Circumnavigation of Europe, Asia, and Libya, ascribed to Skylax, is a modern work[1], and does not contain anything about India. Amidst all the confusion, however, that has gathered round the name of Skylax, two facts stand out, one recorded by Herodotus, the other by Aristotle. Aristotle[2] knew of a Skylax, and that he had stated that among the Indians the kings are taller than the rest of the people. And Herodotus[3] tells us that when Darius Hystaspes (521–486) wished to know where the river Indus fell into the sea, he sent a naval expedition, and also Skylax, a man of Karyanda. 'The ships,' he continues, 'started from Kaspatyros and the land of Paktyika down the river toward the east and the rising of the sun to the sea; then sailing on the sea westward, they arrived in the thirtieth month at the place where the king of Egypt despatched the Phenicians, whom I before mentioned, to sail round Libya. After these persons had sailed round, Darius subdued the Indians, and frequented this sea.'

There are some facts in this statement of Herodotus which deserve more attention than they have hitherto received. First of all, there is no reason to doubt what he says about Skylax, and though Herodotus does not refer to an actual

[1] *Geograph. Græci Minores* (Didot), vol. i. p. 15.

[2] Polit. vii. 13, 1, *ὥσπερ ἐν Ἰνδοῖς φησὶ Σκύλαξ εἶναι τοὺς βασιλέας τοσοῦτον διαφέροντας τῶν ἀρχομένων*. . . . It is curious that in the Periplus it is said of the Ethiopians, *καὶ βασιλεύει αὐτῶν οὗτος, ὃς ἂν ᾖ μέγιστος*.

[3] Herod. iv. 44.

book written by him—he seldom refers to books—we know at all events that Herodotus knew the name of Ἰνδοί or Indians, the name of *Kaspatyros*, and the name of *Paktyika*. These are facts and names full of meaning. The name of Ἰνδοί was mentioned first by Hekataeos, a century before Herodotus. The name *Paktyika*, however, is new, and seems to be the old name of the Afghans. The Afghans call themselves even now *Pashtûn* in the West, *Pachtûn* in the East, and this, by a regular Prâkritic assimilation, would, as Trumpp [1] remarks, have become *Pathân* in Indian dialects. Whether the Pakthas mentioned in the Rig-veda (VII. 18, 7) are the same race must remain doubtful [2]. The persistence of some of these ancient national and local names, however, is quite marvellous, and shows a continuity of tradition even in places where we should least expect it. The old seats of the Paktyes seem to have extended westward into Arachosia [3], and there they would really have been part of the Persian Empire [4]. Herodotus also tells us that Paktyes served in the Persian army.

Still more curious, however, is the name of the town *Kaspatyros*, if known to Skylax. Everybody seems agreed that Herodotus wrote *Kaspatyros* by mistake for *Kaspapyros*, which is the name, used by Hekataeos, for what he calls *Γανδαρική πόλις, Σκυθῶν ἀκτή*, i. e. a town of the *Gandari*, the limit of the Scythians. In *pyros* of *Kaspa-pyros*, the Sanskrit word pura, town, has been discovered.

Lassen (I². p. 515) and others after him have attempted to identify these Paktyes (Pakhtu) with *Pahlava*, a name of the ancient Persians, and to trace that name back to Pers. *pahlû*, side, Sk. parsu. But Quatremère seems to me to

[1] Trumpp, *Grammar of the Pasto* (1873), p. xv.
[2] See Zimmer, *Indisches Leben*, p. 430.
[3] Trumpp, l. c., p. xiii.
[4] Lassen, I². p. 509.

have proved that *Pahlava* was really the old name of the Parthians. The name of Parthia occurs in the inscriptions of Darius and in Herodotus as the name of the province of Chorasan, so far as it belongs to Persia. Ardawân, the last king of Parthia, is called the Pahlavî, by Tabari, and Olshausen considered the Pehlevi language and alphabet as Parthian. Rh and lh, hr and hl, in Persian often represent an original rth and rt, e. g. *puhl*, bridge=*pĕrĭtu*; *puhlum*= Sk. prathama, first, and Nöldeke, as we saw, tried to prove that this phonetic change took place in the first century A. D. In that case no Sanskrit text in which Pahlava occurs—it does not occur in the Rig-veda—could be earlier than that date. Pahlava occurs in the Girnâr inscription of Rudradâman, which, as Bühler and Fleet have shown, is dated 21–22 A. D.[1]

APPENDIX III.

P. 31.

BUDDHIST PILGRIMS ACQUAINTED WITH THE VEDA.

Hiouen-thsang's Life and Travels were first made known through Stanislas Julien, in his great work, *Voyages des Pèlerins Bouddhistes.* The first volume (1853) contained *Histoire de la vie de Hiouen-thsang et de ses voyages dans l'Inde depuis l'an* 629 *jusqu'en* 645, par Hoeï-li et Yen-thsong. The second and third volumes (1857, 1858) contained Hiouen-thsang's *Mémoires sur les Contrées occidentales.* The same work was afterwards translated into English by the Rev. Samuel Beal, under the title of *Si-yu-ki*, Buddhist Records of the Western World. See M. M., Buddhist Pilgrims (1857), in *Selected Essays*, vol. ii. p. 234.

[1] See Bühler's Translation of Manu, in *S. B. E.*, vol. xxv. p. cxiv.

When speaking of the study of the Vedas, Hiouen-thsang says:—

'The Brâhmans study the four Vêda *S*âstras. The first is called Shau (*longevity*); it relates to the preservation of life and the regulation of the natural condition. The second is called Sse (*sacrifice*); it relates to the (*rules of*) sacrifice and prayer. The third is called Ping (*peace* or *regulation*); it relates to decorum, casting of lots, military affairs, and army regulations. The fourth is called Shu (*secret mysteries*); it relates to various branches of science, incantations, medicine[1].

'The teachers (of these works) must themselves have closely studied the deep and secret principles they contain, and penetrated to their remotest meaning. They then explain their general sense, and guide their pupils in understanding the words which are difficult. They urge them on and skilfully conduct them. They add lustre to their poor knowledge, and stimulate the desponding. If they find that their pupils are satisfied with their acquirements, and so wish to escape to attend to their worldly duties, then they use means to keep them in their power. When they have finished their education, and have attained thirty years of age, then their character is formed and their knowledge ripe. When they have secured an occupation, they first of all thank their master for his attention. There are some, deeply versed in antiquity, who devote themselves to elegant studies, and live apart from the world, and retain the simplicity of their character. These rise above mundane presents, and are as insensible to renown as to contempt of the

[1] This account is full of mistakes, owing, no doubt, to the fact that Hiouen-thsang devoted his time in India chiefly to the study of Buddhist literature. It is very doubtful whether the four Vedas here mentioned were intended for the Âyur-veda, the Ya*g*urveda, the Sâma-veda, and the Atharva-veda, as Stanislas Julien suggested.

world. Their name having spread afar, the rulers appreciate them highly, but are unable to draw them to the court. The chief of the country honours them on account of their (mental) gifts, and the people exalt their fame and render them universal homage. This is the reason of their devoting themselves to their studies with ardour and resolution, without any sense of fatigue. They search for wisdom, relying on their own resources. Although they are possessed of large wealth, yet they will wander here and there to seek their subsistence. There are others who, whilst attaching value to letters, will yet without shame consume their fortunes in wandering about for pleasure, neglecting their duties. They squander their substance in costly food and clothing. Having no virtuous principle, and no desire to study, they are brought to disgrace, and their infamy is widely circulated.' (Beal, i. pp. 79 seq.)

'To the north of the great mountain 3 or 4 li, is a solitary hill. Formerly the *Ri*shi Vyâsa (Kwang-po) lived here in solitude. By excavating the side of the mountain he formed a house. Some portions of the foundations are still visible. His disciples still hand down his teaching, and the celebrity of his bequeathed doctrine still remains.' (Beal, ii. p. 148.)

A very important passage, showing that Hiouen-thsang came in contact with Brâhmans who knew the Veda, occurs in Julien's translation, vol. i. p. 168. He there gives a short account of Sanskrit grammar, and in repeating the paradigm of bhavâmi, I am, he remarks that in the four Vedas, instead of the regular form po-po-me, bhavâmas, we are, there occurs the form p'o-po-mo-sse. This can only be meant, not for bhavâmas, as Julien supposes, but for bhavâmasi, which is really the ancient Vedic form for the 1st pers. plur.

I-tsing, another Buddhist pilgrim, who visited India in the seventh century, likewise refers to the Vedas, and states that they were handed down by oral tradition. 'The Brâhmans,' he writes, 'revere the scriptures, namely the four Vedas, containing about 100,000 verses. These Vedas are handed down from mouth to mouth, not written on paper. There are in every generation some intelligent Brâhmans who can recite these 100,000 verses.'

APPENDIX IV.

P. 51.

SANSKRIT MSS. BOUGHT BY GUIZOT.

'PARIS, 10 RUE BILLAULT,
'1er *Mars*, 1869.

'J'ai été heureux, Monsieur, de concourir à votre nomination comme associé étranger de l'Institut. Précisément l'été dernier, j'avais lu vos *Lectures* à la *Royal Institution,* sur la science et la formation du langage, et j'avais été extrêmement frappé de l'élévation, de la profondeur et de l'abondance des idées que vous y avez exposées. Je ne suis pas un juge compétent de vos travaux sur les *Védas,* mais je me félicite d'avoir un peu contribué à vous en fournir les matériaux, et je vous remercie d'en avoir gardé le souvenir. Mon seul regret est de ne vous avoir pas acquis vous-même à la France. C'est une fortune que j'envie un peu à l'Angleterre, tout en lui en faisant mon compliment.

'Recevez, Monsieur et savant confrère, l'assurance de ma considération la plus distinguée.

'GUIZOT.'

APPENDIX V.

P. 64.

DATE OF THE PRÂTISÂKHYA.

I have tried to settle the date of the Rig-veda-prâtisâkhya in the Introduction to my edition and translation of this work (1869). Nothing that has been discovered since has necessitated any change. If we accept the date of about

400 B.C., assigned hypothetically to Pâṇini, we are safe in placing our Prâtiśâkhya before Pâṇini, because he quotes it. (Introduction, p. 11; *History of Ancient Sanskrit Literature*, p. 140.) Śaunaka is the editor rather than the author of our Prâtiśâkhya. The authority for his doctrines, and the author of the Pada-text is Śâkalya. Yâska, the author of the Nirukta, who is admitted by all scholars to be anterior to Pâṇini, quotes our Śâkalya as padakâra, the maker of the text in which the words (pada) are divided. He is fully acquainted with the work done by the padakâra, he declares that the Saṃhitâ-text is based on the Pada-text, and he adds (I. 17) that the Pârshada books of all schools, i.e. the Prâtiśâkhyas, are based on that Pada-text. The Pârshada literature or the Prâtiśâkhyas are therefore presupposed by Yâska, and though Yâska may have been not much older than or even a contemporary only of the author of the Pârshadas, they must both have preceded the work of Pâṇini. We may therefore assign the period from about 400 to 500 B.C. to the production of the Prâtiśâkhyas and other Pârshada works.

APPENDIX VI.

P. 65.

MINUTIAE OF THE PRÂTIŚÂKHYA.

The observations of the Prâtiśâkhya are most minute. For instance, in Sûtra 465, certain words are enumerated which, if they stand at the beginning of a line, must always lengthen their final vowel. One of them is arka, which must become arkâ. This applies to the whole of the Rigveda. But the author of the Prâtiśâkhya adds, 'there is an exception in the case of Bharadvâga, that is, in the hymns of Bharadvâga in the sixth Maṇḍala. And so it is. In the sixth Maṇḍala (VI. 68, 9) all our MSS. have arka unchanged before devâya.

The author of the Prâtisâkhya must therefore have known the names of the Vedic poets, as they are given in the Anukramanîs. He quotes (313, 895, 909) the hymns of Agastya, Rv. I. 166–191; those of the Atris (170); of Kutsa (509); of Gotama (167); of Parukkhepa (169); of Medhâtithi (309); of Lusa (166); of Vimada (509, 993); of Vâmadeva (486).

APPENDIX VII.

P. 66.

NUMBER OF VERSES IN THE RIG-VEDA.

The total number of verses is given as 10,402 in the *Kh*anda*h*-sankhyâ, an appendix to one of the Anukramanîs, viz. the *Kh*andonukramanî. This number seemed formerly not to agree with the total of the different classes of verses given in the same place. But, with some corrections of the text and with the help of better MSS., the two are now found to agree. There are—

1.	Gâyatrî-verses	2,451
2.	Ushnih-verses	341
3.	Anushtubh-verses	855
4.	Brihatî-verses	181
5.	Pankti-verses	312
6.	Trishtubh-verses	4,253
7.	Gagatî-verses	1,348
8.	Atigagatî-verses	17
9.	Sakvarî-verses	19
10.	Atisakvarî-verses	9
11.	Ashti-verses	6
12.	Atyashti-verses	84
13.	Dhriti-verses	2
14.	Atidhriti-verse	1
15.	Ekapadâ-verses	6
16.	Dvipadâ-verses	17
17.	Pragâtha Bârhata-verses	388
18.	Pragâtha Kâkubha-verses	110
19.	Mahâbârhata-verses	2
		10,402

According to the Anuvâkânukrama*n*î, vv. 32–35, the number of Anuvâkas in the ten Ma*nd*alas and the number of hymns is as follows:—

Ma*nd*ala	Anuvâkas	Sûktas
I	24	191
II	4	43
III	5	62
IV	5	58
V	6	87
VI	6	75
VII	6	104
VIII	10	92 + 11
IX	7	114
X	12	191
	85	1017 + 11 = 1028

According to v. 36 the Bhâshkala recension contained eight additional hymns, that is, 1017 + 8 = 1025. It is curious that the Aitareya-brâhma*n*a (VI. 24) speaks of eight Vâlakhilya hymns. This, however, does not prove that there were not more than these eight which were required for certain sacrifices, still less, that these eight were the same as the eight additional hymns of the Bâshkalas.

*S*aunaka knows the division into Ma*nd*alas, Anuvâkas, hymns and verses, but he does not in his genuine works seem to have been acquainted with the division of the Rig-veda into eight Ash*t*akas and sixty-four Adhyâyas, each Adhyâya being subdivided into Vargas. In the Prâti*s*âkhya (S. 848–860) the term adhyâya occurs, but it there means the daily lesson of the pupil, consisting of sixty pra*s*nas or questions, each question containing on an average three verses. The verses 38 to 45 in the Anuvâkânukrama*n*î are therefore probably not *S*aunaka's, and they had been suspected for different reasons by Meyer, in his Rigvidhâna, p. xxvii. They give the following list of Vargas:—

Vargas		Containing verses.	Total of verses.	
1	(1)	1	1	
2	(2)	2	4	
97	(93)	3	291	(279)
174	(176)	4	696	(704)
1207	(1228)	5	6035	(6140)
346	(357)	6	2076	(2142)
119	(129)	7	833	(903)
59	(55)	8	472	(440)
1	(1)	9	9	
2006	(2042)		10,417	(10,622)

Immediately afterwards (v. 43) the total number of verses is given as 10,580, and one pâda (Rv. X. 20, 1); the number of half-verses as 21,232, and one pâda (therefore 10,614 verses, and one pâda); the number of words as 153,826; the number of *k*ar*k*âs as 110,704; the number of syllables as 432,000.

The *K*ara*n*avyûha gives a list of Vargas and verses differing from that of the Anuvâkânukrama*n*î. The numbers have been added in brackets. See on all this Dr. Macdonell's careful edition of the Sarvânukrama*n*î, in the *Anecdota Oxoniensia.*

The Rig-veda-prâti*s*âkhya presupposes the Pada-text, and teaches the changes which the padas or words undergo when joined together in the Sa*m*hitâ-text. But its author knows the far more artificial Krama-text also, which presupposes both the Pada and Sa*m*hitâ-texts (Sûtra 590 seq.). This Kramapâ*th*a must have been practised considerably in the Parishads, and have given rise to many different opinions, which are discussed in the Krama-hetu-pa*t*ala. Thus Bâbhravya, a teacher of the Krama, declares (S. 676) that the doctrine of the Krama is good as taught at first, not as taught differently by different teachers. But others attacked it as useless and as not based on *S*ruti or sacred authority, and the author of the Prâti*s*âkhya has therefore to defend it against various attacks, and to show that it can claim the highest authority. On these various modifications of the text of the hymns, the three Prak*ri*tis and the eight Vik*ri*tis, there is a treatise by Madhusûdana, Ash*t*avik*ri*ti-viv*ri*ti, edited by Satyavrata Sâma*s*rami, in the Ushâ, vol. i. The original is ascribed to Vyâ*d*i.

APPENDIX VIII.

P. 72.

BRÂHMA*N*AS OF THE SÂMA-VEDA.

According to Satyavrata Sâma*s*rami (Ushâ, vol. i) the real Brâhma*n*a of the Sâma-veda is the Tâ*nd*ya or Prau*dh*a-brâhma*n*a. It belongs to the *S*âkhâ of the Kauthumas, and consists of forty adhyâyas. The first thirty adhyâyas describe the *S*rauta ceremonies. What is sometimes called the Sha*d*vi*ms*a-brâhma*n*a, adhyâyas 26–30, is part of the same Brâhma*n*a. Then follow what are called 'Mantras and the Upanishad,' forming together 2 + 8 adhyâyas, so as to bring the total number of the adhyâyas in the Brâhma*n*a of the *Kh*andogas to the required number of forty. Adhyâyas 31–32 give the Mantras of the G*ri*hya ceremonies, as described in the Gobhila-G*ri*hya-sûtras; adhyâyas 33–40 cont. in the Upanishad.

The other Sâma-veda-brâhma*n*as are treated by Satyavrata as Anu-brâhma*n*as, viz. the Sâma-vidhâna, the Ârsheya, the Devatâdhyâya, the Sa*m*hitopanishad, and the Va*ms*a-brâhma*n*a. See *Academy*, June 7, 1890.

APPENDIX IX.

P. 88.

SANSKRIT WORDS IN SUMERIAN.

Two other words might here be mentioned which, as Professor Hommel maintains, are shared in common by Sumerian and Sanskrit namely, Sumerian *urud*, copper,

Lat. *raudus*, Old Slav. *ruda*, metal, O. N. *rauði*, red iron ore, Pehlevi *rôd*, Persian *roi*, Sk. lohá, copper; and Sumerian *balag*, Babyl.-Assyrian *pilakku*, axe, Sk. parasú, Gr. πέλεκυς. Both words could have their origin in an Aryan language only, and would prove that the borrowing must have been on the Sumerian side. Parasú is the same word as pársu, and meant originally a rib-bone. As such bones were used for knives, parsu came to mean a bent knife, and then any kind of weapon[1]. The word had therefore a history of its own among the Âryas, before it could have been adopted by the Sumerians. As to loha, its etymology is more doubtful. It has been traced back to an original *raudho and compared with ἐ-ρυθ-ρός. If the similarity to Sumerian *urud* is more than accidental, the borrowing again must have been on the Sumerian side. The Bask word for copper is *urraida*[2].

APPENDIX X.

P. 94.

TECHNICAL TERMS BORROWED BY THE BUDDHISTS.

Other technical terms which the Buddhists borrowed from the Brâhmans, and the gradual growth of which we can watch in the Brâhma*n*as and Upanishads, are Arahâ, the Sk. Arhat (the worshipful), Sama*n*a, ascetic, the Sk. *S*rama*n*a (the performer of penance), and even Buddha (pratibuddha sarvavid[3], the awakened and omniscient)—all titles of honour given to the Buddha himself[4]. Other terms of the same kind which presuppose the existence of the Brahmanic literature in which they were first created,

[1] *Biographies of Words*, p. 178.
[2] See Schmidt, *Die Urheimath der Indogermanen*, p. 9; Schrader, *Prehistoric Antiquities*, p. 191.
[3] Brahmopanishad, *Bibl. Ind.*, No. 271, p. 251.
[4] Schröder, pp. 190, 255.

matured, and defined, are Attâ, life, self, the Sk. âtmâ, breath, life, soul, person; Nibbâna, annihilation of human passion, Sk. nirvâ*n*a. It has long been known that this word occurs in the Mahâbhârata, as, for instance, XIV. 543, Vihâya sarvasankalpân buddhyâ *s*ârîramânasân, *s*anair nirvâ*n*am âpnoti nirindhana ivânala*h*, 'Leaving behind in thought all bodily and mental desires, he slowly obtains Nirvâ*n*a, like a fire without wood.' But it was thought possible that the technical term Nirvâ*n*a might here and elsewhere have been borrowed from the Buddhists. That this was not the case we see, first of all, from passages in the Upanishads, where the origin of the metaphor is quite clear, as when a lamp gone out is called nirvâ*n*a. Secondly, the word actually occurs in the Maitreyopanishad, probably the simplest text of the Maitrâya*n*a-brâhma*n*a-upanishad, and there it means the absorption in the highest being, beyond which there is neither being nor not-being (*S. B. E.*, vol. xv. p. xlvi. l. 19). As this Upanishad is an old one, it follows that the term Nirvâ*n*a, like nirv*ri*ti, was borrowed by the Bauddhas from the Brâhma*n*as. Nirutti, grammar, is the Sk. nirukti, etymology, the Vedânga, the Nirukta. In the sense of etymology it occurs *Kh*ând. Up. VIII. 3, 3. Pabba*g*ita, a Buddhist monk; the Sk. pravra*g*ita, gone away from home.

Another class of words, occurring in the Northern Buddhist texts, shows still more clearly the posteriority of Buddhism to Brahmanism. It was Childers who pointed out first that when the Northern Buddhists tried to render certain Buddhist terms in their own Sanskrit, they had so completely forgotten the true original Sanskrit form, that they invented a new and mistaken Sanskrit rendering. Thus the Pâli uposatho, the Buddhist fast-day, is clearly the Sanskrit upavasatha, the day preceding certain sacrifices. Childers says that upavasatha does not belong to classical Sanskrit. We know

now that it occurs frequently in the Brâhma*n*as (*S*atap. Br. I. 1, 1, 7). But Northern Buddhists, not knowing the etymology of the word (though they constantly use upavâsa, fasting), and having forgotten its true form upavasatha, rendered the Pâli uposatha by uposhadha, a word without any authority or etymology. Other words belonging to this class are iddhipâdo, pâtimokkho, upâdiseso, pa*t*isambhida, phâsu, opapâtiko; see Childers, s.v. opapâtiko.

That marut, the name of the storm-gods in the Veda, should in Pâli have become maru, a general name of devas or gods, is likewise an indication both of the continuity between Buddhism and Brahmanism, and of the distance which divides the two.

APPENDIX XI.

P. 97.

PISCHEL AND GELDNER'S 'VEDISCHE STUDIEN.'

From what extraordinary quarters the arguments in support of a more modern date of the Vedic hymns are sometimes fetched, has been shown lately in a book, otherwise full of learning, the *Vedische Studien* by Pischel and Geldner (1889). I agree with these two scholars on many points, and with regard to the right system of interpretation which they think ought to be applied to the hymns of the Rig-veda, there is nothing which they will not find fully confirmed by what I have written on the subject during the last forty years. But with regard to the general character of the civilization reflected in these hymns, I differ from them considerably. That the Aryan settlers in India, as represented to us in the Vedic hymns, were neither mere savages, mere sons of nature, as they are called, nor even mere hunters or nomads, I tried to show in my first essay on Aryan Civilization[1],

[1] *Selected Essays*, vol. i. pp. 299 seq.

published in 1856. Nor do I think that anybody has questioned the fact that they lived in villages or hamlets. Whether we should translate the word pur by town seemed doubtful, because in the Veda pur is always spoken of as a stronghold rather than as an inhabited camp. How easily, however, a camp may grow into a town, we see from the many names of towns ending in *castra*. But in the absence of any allusions to streets and market-places inside the pur, it certainly seemed safer not to translate that word by town in Vedic poetry. Besides, even at present, nine-tenths of the population of India live in villages, and yet we should not hesitate to call them civilized.

That the Vedic poets knew the sea I have been myself the first to maintain, and, I hope, to prove. That they knew salt is more difficult to establish, but that, as Pischel and Geldner maintain, they knew the art of writing, has never been proved, and would run counter to all we know of the historical progress of alphabetic writing in India and in Asia in general. There is not one atom of evidence in support of such an assertion;—at all events, neither Professor Pischel nor Professor Geldner has brought forward a single fact in support of their opinion.

It is perfectly true, as they allege, that some of the Vedic poets are very greedy. But is gold-hunger peculiar to an advanced civilization only? Gold had been named before the Aryan family broke up[1], and so long as we know anything of ancient people, we find them searching for gold. ornamenting themselves with gold, and defending their *meum* against all intruders.

Professors Pischel and Geldner seem still to be under the influence of Rousseau's ideas as to the simplicity and purity and innocence of primitive man. Because the Vedic poets barter with their gods, because they curse the rich who will

[1] *Biographies of Words*, p. 180.

not give them their proper reward, because they hate their rivals, they are represented as modern.

It used to be said that because the people of the Veda recognised the sanctity of marriage, and because they had elaborated names for several degrees of relationship, therefore they could not be considered as representing a very primitive stage of civilization. Now we are told on the contrary that because we find in the Veda traces of a freer and unlawful intercourse between men and women, because we hear of female slaves, and of Aspasias, therefore the Vedic Indians must have reached the very summit of civilization, and could no longer be looked upon as representing a very early stage in the history of our own, the Aryan, race.

I think we have every right to say that the recognition of marriage as a solemn and sacred and binding act marks everywhere an epoch in the progress of humanity; but that epoch lies far beyond the beginning of what we call history, in the ordinary sense of that word. What has somewhat euphemistically been called by Sir John Lubbock Communal Marriage, is a mere postulate of the anthropologist, and unknown to the student of historical records, except under very different names. To say that bigamy, trigamy, and polygamy are peculiar to an advanced civilization is a libel on history. It certainly does not help the scholar to fix the chronology of the Vedic age. We find in the Veda a full list of all the vices to which poor humanity is liable, murder, plunder, theft, gambling, drinking, running into debt, fraud, and perjury; but to say that these vices are of modern date is, I am afraid, a view too charitable to the past, and not quite fair to the present.

APPENDIX XII.

P. 128.

EGYPTIAN ZOOLATRY.

Mr. Le Page Renouf, in his interesting Preface to the Book of the Dead, p. 8, goes so far as to maintain that Egyptian zoolatry is entirely symbolical. 'The animal forms,' he writes, 'in which the gods are often represented are symbolical throughout. The origin of the symbol is not always apparent, but it is so in certain cases. *Thoth* (*Teḥu-ta*), the Moon, appears most frequently as an ibis, or as a man with the head of an ibis. This is because the moon was the measurer (*techu-ta*) in the oldest Egyptian, as in the oldest Indo-European system. It is mere folly to say that the Egyptians believed the moon to be an ibis. Thoth, as the Moon, was just as often symbolised by a cynocephalus.

'It is not less disgraceful to assert that the Egyptians believed the human soul to be a bird with a human head. The kings who put their names on lions and sphinxes, and gloried in being called bulls, jackals, and crocodiles, did not expect people to consider them as quadrupeds.

'*Seb*, the Earth, had a goose for its symbol, but this was the result of homonymy. *Sêbu*, the Whistler or Piper, is the name given to a species of goose. And if we knew the original meanings of all the divine names, the symbolism would be intelligible enough.'

It is possible that the ancient Egyptian system of writing may likewise have influenced the popular mind. It is well known that if there was a hieroglyphic sign for a bird, called *Sebu*, the same sign would be used to express the sound of *sebu*, though its meaning might be quite different.

APPENDIX XIII.

P. 219.

WRITING MENTIONED IN THE OLD TESTAMENT.

It is true, no doubt, that in several books of the Old Testament, writing, writers, and written books are spoken of, as well known in very ancient times. But a scribe who was himself familiar with writing, might easily forget himself, and transfer his ideas about writing to earlier ages. Thus Mr. Butler, when discussing the question whether written books existed before the time of Hilkiah, forgets himself so far as to say (p. 74), 'that there were laws or traditions of law in the courts, and memories of oral decisions, and that some of the laws may have been *printed*, we cannot doubt.' Scholars cannot help speaking of Vedic literature, though they know quite well that *literae*, written letters, had nothing to do with it. In the same way we can well understand that the Jews spoke of Moses as writing the laws, though he only composed them. We read of scribes and chroniclers for the first time at the courts of David and Solomon, but there is nothing to prove that these scribes were acquainted with alphabetic writing. It has been supposed that, like his masons and carpenters, these scribes might have been sent by king Hiram from Phenicia, but it has never been proved that alphabetic writing for literary purposes was known, even in Phenicia, at that early time. David's letter to Joab about Uriah (2 Sam. xi. 15) seems the first authentic specimen of epistolary writing, but even here mere *σήματα λυγρά*, as in the case of Proetos and Bellerophon[1], would have answered every purpose. We never hear of Elijah writing anything.

[1] Od. vi. 168.

APPENDIX XIV.

P. 287.

NEED-FIRE.

Jamieson, in his Scottish Dictionary, s. v. *neid-fire*, gives a very similar account of what took place, it would seem, as late as 1788:

'In those days [1788], when the stock of any considerable farmer was seized with the murrain, he would send for one of the charm-doctors to superintend the raising of a *need-fire*. It was done by friction, thus: Upon any small island, where the stream of a river or burn ran on each side, a circular booth was erected, of stone and turf (barhis), as it could be had, in which a semicircular or highland couple of birch, or other hard wood, was set; and, in short, a roof closed on it. A straight pole was set up in the centre of this building, the upper end fixed by a wooden pin to the top of the couple, and the lower end in an oblong trink in the earth or floor; and lastly, another pole was set across horizontally, having both ends tapered, one end of which was supported in a hole in the side of the perpendicular pole, and the other end in a similar hole in the couple leg. The horizontal stick was called the auger, having four short arms or levers fixed in its centre, to work it by; the building having been thus finished, as many men as could be collected in the vicinity (being divested of all kinds of metal in their clothes, &c.) would set to work with the said auger, two after two, constantly turning it round by the arms or levers, and others occasionally driving wedges of wood or stone behind the lower end of the upright pole, so as to press it the more on the end of the auger: by this constant friction and pressure, the ends of the auger would take fire, from which a fire would be instantly kindled, and thus the *need-fire* would be accomplished. The fire in the farmer's house, &c., was immediately quenched with water, a fire kindled from this *need-fire*, both in the farmhouse and offices, and the cattle brought to feel the smoke of this new and sacred fire, which preserved them from the murrain. So much for superstition.'

APPENDIX XV.

P. 350.

SIMILARITIES BETWEEN CHRISTIANITY AND BUDDHISM.

Dr. Seydel, in his 'Das Evangelium von Jesu in seinen Verhältnissen zu Buddha-sage und Buddha-lehre' (1882), tells us that Abubekr recognised Mohammed as sent by God, because he sat under a tree, and because no one could sit under that tree *after Jesus*. This, he maintains, proves that Jesus also sat under a tree, and that this was a sign of his Messiahship. But the tree thus mentioned in a Mohammedan legend is not a fig-tree, but, as we are told distinctly, a Sizyphus tree. Nor is it said that Mohammed was recognised as sent by God because he sat under a tree under which no one could sit after Jesus had sat under it. The words are simply: 'The prophet sat under the shadow of a tree, where he and Abubekr had before been sitting together. Abubekr then went to a hermit, and asked him for the true religion. The hermit asked: "Who is the man under the shadow of the tree?" He answered: "Mohammed, the son of Abd Allah." The hermit said: "By Allah, this is a prophet; no one but Mohammed, the messenger of God, sits after Jesus under that tree."' Nothing is said that the hermit recognised Mohammed because he sat under a tree. Sitting under a tree never was a sign of prophethood with the Mohammedans. It simply means he recognised him while sitting in the shadow of a tree, as the prophet who should come after Jesus.

When I say that some of the similarities between Christianity and Buddhism have not yet been accounted for, I do not mean such outward similarities as that a star stood over the palace in which Buddha was born, or that his conception was supposed to be miraculous, or that his advent was expected, or that he was tempted by Mâra, before he began the preaching of his doctrine.

With regard to the star, we know that no auspicious event could happen in India without an auspicious star. At the birth of former Buddhas also certain constellations were inevitable [1].

As to the advent of a Buddha being expected or foretold, it seems doubtful whether this was an historical fact in India. The hope for the coming of a deliverer or a Messiah was an historical fact among the Jews, but it cannot be proved to have existed in India before the rise of historical Buddhism. We find it, indeed, as part of the Buddhist system in the canonical books of the Buddhists, but an independent trace of it, before the birth of Buddha, has not yet been discovered.

Nor can we be surprised that Buddha should be represented as having been tempted by an evil spirit, called Mâra, for such temptations form again an inevitable element in the lives of saints and founders of religions.

Far more perplexing are such coincidences as that, for instance, at the birth of Buddha the wise people should have been in doubt whether he would found a great kingdom on earth or become the preacher of a new doctrine, just as the Jews were in doubt whether the Messiah would found a great earthly kingdom, or the true kingdom of God. For here we seem to deal with historical facts. Buddha was of princely birth, and his adopting the humble life of a preacher

[1] See *Buddhist Birth-Stories*, p. 17.

and teacher was always considered by the Brâhmans as an unpardonable breach of caste[1].

Again, the visit of the old sage Asita, his desire to see the royal babe, his clear prophecy of his coming greatness, and his lament that he himself was born out of time (akshana) to profit by his teaching—all these together are startling.

I must confess that I was startled also when I read for the first time that at the incarnation of Buddha, 'a great light appeared, the blind received their sight, the deaf heard a noise, the dumb spake one with another, the crooked became straight, the lame walked,' &c. But, on more careful consideration, I soon found that this phrase, as it occurs in Buddhism and Christianity, had its independent antecedents in the tradition both of Judæa and of India.

Of course, Oriental fancy, if once roused, is not satisfied with such simple miracles. The author of the Nidâna-kathâ[2] goes on: 'All prisoners were freed from their bonds and chains. In each hell the fire was extinguished. The hungry ghosts received food and drink. The wild animals ceased to be afraid. The illness of all who were sick was allayed. All men began to speak kindly. Horses neighed, and elephants trumpeted gently. All musical instruments gave forth each its note, though none played upon them. Bracelets and other ornaments jingled of themselves. All the heavens became clear. A cool soft breeze wafted pleasantly for all. Rain fell out of due season. Water, welling up from the very earth, overflowed. The birds forsook their flight on high. The rivers stayed their waters' flow. The waters of the mighty ocean became fresh. Everywhere the earth was covered with lotuses of every colour. All flowers blossomed on land and in water. The trunks, and branches, and twigs of trees were covered with bloom appropriate to

[1] *History of Ancient Sanskrit Literature*, p. 79, note.
[2] Rhys Davids, *Buddhist Birth-Stories*, p. 64.

each. On earth tree-lotuses sprang up by sevens together, breaking even through the rocks; and hanging-lotuses descended from the skies. The ten thousand world-systems revolved, and rushed as close together as a bunch of gathered flowers; and became, as it were, a woven wreath of worlds, as sweet-smelling and resplendent as a mass of garlands, or as a sacred altar decked with flowers.'

Such is the rush of Eastern fancy, if the sluices are once opened. The fundamental idea, however, is simple enough. When a new teacher arises and a new life begins, men hope that all evils will be cured, all injuries will be redressed. The first evils that suggest themselves are naturally blindness, deafness, and lameness. It was hoped, therefore, that these and many other evils would cease, when Buddha appeared and a new order of things began.

But here is the difference between Buddhism and Christianity. There is no trace of Messianic prophecies in India. The expectation of a Buddha has never been traced in pre-Buddhistic writings. All we can say is that the idiomatic phrase of 'the blind will see, and the lame will walk,' existed in the ancient language of India, and was adopted by the Buddhists like many others.

Thus we read, Rv. II. 15, 7:

> Práti *sronáh* sthât ví anák a*k*ash*t*a
> sómasya tắ máde Índra*h* *k*akâra.

'The lame stood, the blind saw, Indra did this in the joy of Soma.'

This may really refer to parâv*ri*g or the sun, as in II. 13, 12, but in IV. 30, 19 the same expression occurs without reference to any special hero. In VIII. 79, 2 the same miracle is ascribed to Soma himself:

> Abhí ûr*n*oti yát nagnám bhishákti vísvam yát turám
> prá îm andhá*h* khyat ní*h* *s*roná*h* bhût.

'Soma covers what is naked, he heals all that is weak, the blind saw, the lame came forth.'

See also in X. 25, 11. In I. 112, 8 the Âsvins are said to have helped the blind and lame Parâv*rig* to see and to walk.

If the ancient Vedic gods could do this, it was but natural that the same miracle in almost the same words should be ascribed to Buddha.

It was very different with the Jews. The Jews had for centuries expected a Messiah, a deliverer from all the evils which they endured in their captivity and political servitude. Thus Isaiah prophesied (xxix. 18): 'And in that day shall the deaf hear the words of the book, and the eyes of the blind shall see out of obscurity, and out of darkness.' And again (xxxv. 5): 'Then the eyes of the blind shall be opened, and the ears of the deaf shall be unstopped. Then shall the lame man leap as an hart, and the tongue of the dumb sing: for in the wilderness shall waters break out, and streams in the desert,' &c.

When therefore John wishes to convince himself, whether the Christ has really appeared, he is informed that 'the blind receive their sight, and the lame walk, the lepers are cleansed, and the deaf hear, the dead are raised up, and the poor have the gospel preached to them' (Matt. xi. 5; Luke vii. 22). And the people at large also, when they were beyond measure astonished at the works done by Jesus, exclaimed: 'He hath done all things well: he maketh both the deaf to hear, and the dumb to speak' (Mark vii. 37).

We thus see that though the coincidence is startling at first sight, there is nothing in it that would require the admission of an historical borrowing either on the Christian or on the Buddhist side.

One more coincidence deserves to be pointed out. Kumârila, when attacking Buddha's doctrine, says: 'And this very transgression of Buddha and his followers is represented as if it did him honour. For he is praised because he said: "'Let all the sins that have been committed in this world fall on me, that the world may be delivered[1].''"

I have not found this saying of Buddha anywhere in the Buddhist Canon itself, but its genuineness can hardly be doubted considering by whom it is mentioned.

[1] *History of Ancient Sanskrit Literature*, p. 80.

INDEX.

ABRAHAM and Nimrod, 183.
— his belief in one God, 220, 221.
Absolute, the, 297, 298.
Adhvara, sacrifice, 108.
— unhurt, 171.
Adhvaryus, or labouring priests, 69, 70.
— the officiating priests, 108.
Afghans, their names, 372.
Africa, same word for storm and god in, 316.
AG, Sk. root, 122.
Agents in nature, 132.
— all objects named as, 132.
— behind other phenomena of nature, 305.
Ager, field, 126 *n*.
Agni, Vedic hymns addressed to, 61.
— birth of, 101.
— Fire, one of the Devas, 120.
— etymological meaning of, 122, 126.
— names of, 123.
— the mover, 126.
— as a human or animal agent, 127.
— the tongues of, 127.
— agent of fire, 130.
— a god, 134, 135.
— the Supreme God, 143.
— biography of, 143, 144.
— facts against theories, 144.
— Weber on, 145.
— with Indra the chief Deva of the Veda, 145.
Agni in his physical character, 145.
— whence he came, 146.
— as the sun, 146.
— the sun or the fire on the hearth, 148.
— as lightning, 151.
— as Deva, bright; Amartya, undying, 156, 188, 189.
— the immortal among mortals, 156.
— the friend, helper, father, 157.
— helper in battle, 158.
— destroying forests, 163.
— the horses of, 165.
— as sacrificial fire, 165.
— the flesh-eater, 166.
— the messenger between gods and men, 168.
— as priest, 168.
— his good qualities, 169.
— hymns to, 170 et seq.
— Angiras, name of, 172.
— later development of, 177.
— identical with other gods, 178.
— supremacy of, 187.
— the quick, 188.
— as creator, ruler, judge, 194.
— sublime conception of, 196.
— later and poorer conception of, 197, 202, 203.
— one of the eight Vasus, 198.
— his love-affairs, 198.
— in the Mahâbhârata, 199.
— purifying character of, 199.
— fire, in other religions, 204.
— in our bodies, 230.
— in plants, 230.

Agni and Âtar, 232.
— the parents of, 242 *n*.
— and Hephaestos, 241 et seq., 276.
— tales about, 252, 253.
— disappearance of, 264, 268, 270.
— and Varuna, dialogue between, 265.
— later accounts of the hiding of, 267.
— in search of Indra, 271.
— three brothers of, 267.
— contamination of, 269.
— cursed by Bhrigu, 269.
— theogonic development of, 293.
— mythological development of, 293.
— ceremonial development of, 294.
— the Supreme Being, 305.
Agnihotra, or fire-sacrifice, 111-112.
Agnîshomau, 186.
Ago, agmen, 126 *n*.
ἄγος, 107 *n*.
ἄγω, to drive, 126 *n*.
Agricultural Âryas, 161.
— called krishtis, 161.
— their wealth, 162.
Â-hâva, a jug, 107.
Akbar, the emperor, 35.
— and the Vedas, 35, 38.
Al-Birûnî, 1000 A.D., 32, 33, 34.
— in India, 33.
— his knowledge of Sk., 33.
— and of the Veda, 33, 38.
Alexander's expedition to India, 27.
All-father, the, 321.
All-gods, Visve Devâs, 187.
Alphabet, the word, 273.
Alphabetic writing, invention of, 215.
— first used for books, 215-216.
— and the sixth century B.C., 218, 219.
America, sun and fire in, 149.
— storm-wind in, 311.
American languages, same word for storm and god in, 316.
AN, Sk. root, to breathe, 122.
Anala, to breathe, 122.
Ancestors, worship of, 3, 6.
Ancient life, discoveries of, 16.
— gods, mixed character of, 325.
Ancients, who are the, 277.
Angiras, name of Agni, 172.
Anima, how was the concept elaborated, 307.
Animal gods of Egypt, 128.
— deification of an, 278.
Animism, Personification and Anthropomorphism, 128, 129.
— Herbert Spencer against, 128.
— traced to language, 130, 306, 308.
Anquetil Duperron's translation of the Upanishads, 36.
Anthropological religion, 3.
Anthropomorphism, 201, 306, 308.
Anukramanîs, the, 65.
— superseded by Kâtyâyana's index, 66.
Anuvâkas, or chapters of the Rig-veda, 61.
Apollo, 11.
Aranyakas or forest books, 80.
Aristotle and language, 133.
— his mention of Skylax, 371.
ἄρουρα = Zend urvarâ, 161.
Aryan immigration into India, 86.
— religions, parallelism between, 274.
— and Semitic religions, no common source for, 274.
Aryans of the Vedic hymns, 384.
Âryas, their life, 161, 162.
Asiatic Society of Bengal, 46.
Asita, the old sage, 391.
Asoka, date of, 91.
Aspiration, inspiration, respiration, and perspiration, 194.
Âtar, fire, 227.
— no etymology, 227, 227 *n*.
— son of water, 228.
— his fight with Azi Dahâka, 228.
— plurality of, 229.
— son of Ormazd, 231.
— and Agni, difference between, 232.
Atharva-veda, translated for Akbar, 35.
— account of, 81-82.
Âtman, or self, 4.

Attâ, life, 383.
Avestic religion, is it dualistic? 233, 234.
Aztec prayer, 313.
— legends, the four beings of, 315.

BAAL, or Bilu, a solar deity, 249.
— a counterpart of Agni, 250.
Babylon and Assyria, religion in, 210.
— principal deity of, 210 *n.*
Bactria and Balhika, 370.
Balhika and Bactria, 370.
Baptism by fire and water, 283.
Barthélemy, Abbé, 46.
Bel Merodach, the principal Babylonian deity, 210 *n.*
Bha*g*, to worship, 107 *n.*
BHAR, to bear, 123.
Bh*ri*gus, the, 154.
—and Φλέγυες, 154.
Bhura*n*yu, name for Agni, 123.
Biblical criticism, 332.
Bidpai, fables of, 33.
Birth of Buddha, 351.
— of Mahâvira, 353.
— of Mohammed, 354.
— of Nânak, 355.
— of *K*aitanya, 356.
— of Christ, 356.
Bohemian saying about fire, 281.
Books of Moses, their thoughts, 213-214.
— alphabets first used for, 215-216.
Brahman, 247.
Brâhma*n*a of the Vedas, 59.
— prose, 69, 70, 71.
— period, 81, 96.
Brâhma*n*as of the Ya*g*ur-veda, 70, 71.
— of the Sâma-veda, 72, 381.
— of the Rig-veda, 73.
— the authors of, had lost the true meaning of the Veda, 74.
— of the Brâhmans, 74.
— meaning of, 75.
— large number quoted, 75.
— schools, 75.
— glimpses of life in the, 79, 80.
— cosmogonic theories in the, 247.
Brâhmans and Buddhists, difference between, 92.
— believers in miracles, 339.
Brahmodya or priestly discussions, 260.
Bread, treated with reverence, 300.
Breath of the priests, among the Slaves, 232 *n.*
Bright Ya*g*ur-veda, 71.
Bright ones, 135.
Brinton on sun and fire in America, 149.
— his Myths of the New World, 312.
Brugsch on Egyptian religion, 206.
— on letters, 215.
Buddha, date of, 86.
— birth of, 351.
— incarnation of, 353.
— wonders at the birth of, 392.
— bearing the sins of the world, 394.
Buddhism in China, 30.
— rise of, 92-96.
— a reaction against Vedic religion, 92, 94, 96.
Buddhist pilgrims, 30, 31.
— canon, 219.
— pilgrims and the Veda, 373.
Buddhists, technical terms borrowed by the, 382.
Bunsen and India, 49.
Burnouf, Eugène, and his Vedic studies, 51, 52.
— his Buddhistic work, 51.
— his discovery about Jemshîd and Zohâk, 229, 229 *n.*

CALF-KILLING to cure murrain, 289.
Castes, the four, 32 *n.*
Castrén, on sun and fire among the Fins, 151.
Category of causality, 8.
Categories of the understanding, 133.
— of language, 133.
Childhood of the world, shown in the Veda, 102-104.

Children, influence of, on religion, 202.
China, contact with, 28.
— three religions of, 29.
— Buddhism in, 30.
— writing in, 219.
Christ, birth of, in the Korân, 352 *n.*
— apocryphal account of, 356.
— purity of the religion of, 364.
Christianity, true, 332.
— and Buddhism, similarities between, 347–350, 390.
Clamor concomitans, 125.
Coincidences and dissimilarities between Buddhism and Christianity, 273.
Colebrooke, H. T., and the Vedas, 48.
Commentary of the Veda, 53, 54.
Comparative mythology, lessons of, 272.
Conceive and perceive, from capio, 194.
Concept of deity, the highest, 192.
— the result of evolution, 193–197.
Constructive chronology, 96.
Conway, Moncure, on protection of animals, 191.
Cosmogonic theories in the Brâhma*n*as, 247.
Cotton not mentioned in the Veda, 88.
Creator, idea of, in India, 195.
Creeks, belief in the sacred fire, 152 *n.*
Cult, a manifestation of religion, 299.
Cuneiform inscriptions, 17.
Customs, purpose of, often forgotten, 290.

DAHANA, the burner, 122.
Daimonion of Sokrates, 4.
Dârâ, prince, his translation of the Upanishads, 35.
Dark Ya*g*ur-veda, 71.
Darsa-pûr*n*amâsa, new and full-moon sacrifice, 112.
Darwin's Views on Language, 192.
Dasa*s*ila, ten commandments of the Buddhists, 342, 343.
Dâ*s*atayî, name for the Rig-veda hymns, 63, 64 *n.*
Dâtâ̆ras vásuâm and δοτῆρες ἐάων, 109.
David's letter to Joab, 380.
Dayânanda Sarasvatî, the modern reformer, 95.
De Brosses, and Comte, on fetishes, 115.
Deification, 118, 308, 309.
— found everywhere, 118.
— specially shown in the Veda, 118, 121.
Deity, general name of, 188.
— Deva, 189.
— highest concept of, 192.
De Rougé on letters, 215.
Deva, deus, bright, 120.
— then God, 120.
— meaning of, 134, 136.
— evolution of the word, 138.
— becomes the highest concept of deity, 139.
Deva-hood, how conceived, 135.
— not yet Godhood, 136.
Devas were recognised early, 99, 108.
— or bright ones, 336.
Devil, never supreme, 234.
Diable as iroucan, 311 *n.*
Dialogue between Agni and Varu*n*a, 265.
Dîdivi, found once in the Veda, 173.
Dies from div, 134.
Dînkard, the, 32 *n.*
DIV, Sk. root, 134.
— dies, 134.
Divine, the idea of, evolved in many ways, 139.
— the, or Infinite, 298.
— character ascribed to the founders of religion, 350.
Drift of an argument, 126 *n.*
Dual deities, 186.
Dyaus, 11.
— religion of, 327.

EARLY scepticism, 182, 183.
Ego, the, 4.
Egypt, animal gods of, 128.
— religion in, 206.
— Le Page Renouf on the gods of, 207.
— physical phenomena worshipped in, 208.
— the concept of the divine rose from natural objects in, 209.
Egyptian religion, modern character of the, 236.
— gods all meant the same thing, 238.
— zoolatry, 387.
Elijah, 222.
Epochs marked by discoveries, 216, 218.
Eskimo prayer to the winds, 313.
Ether and Agni, 126.
Euhemeristic explanations of mythology, 253.
European missionaries in India, 38.
— scholars acquainted with the Vedas, 46.
Evolution of the word Deva, 138.
— of concepts, 190.
— doctrine of, upheld by the students of language, 191.
— one powerful prejudice against, 193.
Exchange of gods, 184.
Ezour-veda, 39.
— and Voltaire, 40.
Ezra, collected books of the Old Testament, 219, 220.

FATHER CŒURDOUX, 46.
Fetish, name of, 117 *n.*
Fetishes, De Brosses and Comte on, 115.
Fig-tree, sitting under the, 348, 349.
Filial piety in China, 344.
Finland, henotheism in, 182.
Fins, sun and fire among the, 150.
Fire, lighting and keeping of the, 111.
— early conceptions of, 121, 124.
— names of, 122.
— named as active, 123.
Fire, as a Deva, 134.
— from flint, 153.
— from wood, 153.
— mythological ideas connected with, 154.
— and wood, one word for, 154 *n.*
— on the hearth, 100.
— sacredness of, 167, 167 *n.*
— flesh thrown on the, 167.
— worship of, 211.
— widely worshipped, 225.
— in the Avesta, 226.
— Âtar, 227.
— must not be blown, 232, 232 *n.*
— in Egypt, 235.
— in Greece, Hephaestos, 241.
— in Italy, Vulcanus, 244.
— philosophical aspects of, in Greece, 244.
— of Herakleitos, 245.
— and Zoroaster, 246.
— and water in the Brâhma*n*as, 246.
— as worshipped in Babylon, 249.
— from the paternal hearth, 279.
— lighting and keeping of, 279.
— Mongolian feeling for, 281.
— kindling of, in India, in a new home, 280.
— Ojibway feeling for, 281.
— baptism of, 284.
— in Mexico, 283, 284.
— purification by, 284.
— and sick child, 290.
— in the Isle of Lemnos, 291.
— of St. Brigida, 292.
— guarded by maidens, 292.
— and water, reverence shown to, 301.
— development of, 303.
— in Egypt, 304 *n.*
Fireless races, 158.
Fires in the Veda, three, 229.
— in the Avesta, five, 229.
— in the body, 230.
— sacrificial, three, 231.
— 'love the village,' 280, 281.
— lighted in Marburg from sticks, 291.
— extinguished after Plataeae, 291.

Fish, sacrifice of, 269 *n*.
Forest life, 80.
Founders of religion, divine character ascribed to the, 350.
Freyja, 324 *n*.
Fundo, 108 *n*.
Futilis, futile, 107 *n*.
Futis, a water-jug, 107 *n*.

GAMBLER, poem of the, 77.
Garcilasso's story of the Inca, 183, 184.
*G*âtavedas, name for Agni, 123, 200 *n*.
Germany, interest in the Vedas, 48.
Giuta, Gothic, to pour out, 108 *n*.
Goat, words for, 126 *n*.
God, the Father, 2.
— the negroes have a name for, 116.
— and the plural gods, 117.
— as a predicate, 115, 117, 119.
— different meanings assigned to the word, 116.
— and gods, among the Greeks, 116.
— whence comes the idea, 139.
— an innate idea, 139.
— a hallucination, 140.
— from the idea of light, 140.
— natural evolution of the idea, 140.
— natural revelation of, 140.
— of fire in the Old Testament, 223.
— concept of, a necessity to the human mind, 341.
Gods, Greek and Roman, 136.
— considered by the Christians as evil spirits, 136.
Gold, known to the united Aryans, 385.
Graven images, 201, 202.
Greece and Italy, no religious literature in, 205.
Greek accounts of India, 26.
— and Roman gods, 136.
— — — their anthropomorphic character, 136.
Greek and Roman gods, family ties among, 136.
Greek riddle, 260.
Greeks, concept of God and gods among, 116.
Grigri, or juju, 117.
Grohmann on Wuotan, 324.
Gruppe on the idea of God, 140.
Guizot, Sk. MSS. bought by, 376.

HAFIZ quoted, 362.
Hakleburg, Mount Hecla, 323.
Hapta Hen*d*u, 26.
Havis, sacrifice, 107.
Heathenish customs in Scotland and Ireland, 288.
Hekataeos and Herodotus knew of India, 27.
Helios, 11.
Henotheism, 180, 181.
— used in various senses, 181 *n*.
— in Finland, 182.
— as a phase, 328.
Henotheistic character of the Vedic gods, 179.
Hephaestos, 241.
— birth of, 242.
— and Agni, 241–242.
— etymology of, 243, 243 *n*.
Hera, 241.
Heraclitus on the finite and infinite, 157.
Herakleitos, religion of, 245.
— fire of, 245, 249.
— and gambling, 256.
Herder and the Veda, 48.
Herodotus' mention of Skylax, 371.
Hieroglyphics, known to Moses, 216.
Highest Commandments, 358.
Hiouen-thsang, 373.
— on the Veda, 374, 374 *n*, 375.
Historical method, 7.
— continuity, 7.
— growth of religious ideas, 211.
— studies, value of, 329.
Hitopadesa quoted, 362.
Holy Ghost, the, 4.
Holy, hale, whole, 108.

Homa, and âhuti, libation, 107.
Hot*ri*, priest, 107.
Hot*ris*, reciting priests, 70, 72, 73.
HU, to pour out, to sacrifice, 107, 107 *n.*
Human mind ascended from nature to nature's gods, and to the God of nature, 144.
Hurakan, heart of heaven, 314.
— lord of the winds, 325.
Hurricane, 311.

'IEPOΣ, holy, 108.
Immoral influence of some religions, 295.
Inca, story of the, 183, 184.
Independent speculation, 79.
India, Egypt, Babylon, and Persia, early contact between, 23.
— never mentioned in Egyptian or Babylonian inscriptions, 24, 25.
— Semiramis in, 25.
— Greek accounts of, 26.
— the word, 27.
— known to Hekataeos and Herodotus, 27.
— Alexander's expedition to, 27.
— Megasthenes' account of, 28.
— European missionaries in, 38.
— Xavier in, 39.
— Aryan immigration into, 86.
— art of writing in, 89.
— aborigines of, 160.
— — black skinned, 160.
Indian division of the heavens, thought to be Babylonian, 25.
— antiquity, peculiar character of, 55.
— mind, workings of the, 56.
'Ινδοί, 372.
Indra, Vedic hymns addressed to, 61.
— his strength, 187.
Indrâgnî, 186.
Infinite, the, 2.
— seen in the finite, 143.
— meaning of, 296.
Infinite, as a name, 297.
— first attempt to grasp, 335.
Inscriptions in Arabia, 215 *n.*
Irregular perfect of Veda and *οἶδα*, 57.
— — agrees with Locke's view, 57.
I-tsing on the Vedas, 375.

JEHOVAH, name and concept of, 224.
Jewish idolatry, 213.
— belief in one God, 220.
John Hacklebirnie's house, 323.
Jones, Sir William, and Sanskrit, 46.
— and the Vedas, 480.
Juju, or grigri, 117.

KAFU, koph, ape, 24.
*K*aitanya, birth of, 356.
Kalpa-sûtras, 90.
Kapi, Sk., ape, 25.
Karma, or sacrifice, 106, 110.
Kaspatyros, 372.
— for Kaspapyros, 372.
*K*âturmâsya, 112.
Kâtyâyana's index of the Rig-veda, 66.
*Kh*andas, or Mantra period, 68, 69.
Korân, account of the birth of Christ in the, 352 *n.*
Krama-text of the Rig-veda, 380.
Kratu, Sk., counsel, German Rath, 172.

LANGUAGE, categories of, 133.
— Aristotle and, 133.
Lee, Dr. Robert, on faith in miracles, 358.
Lenormant on letters, 215.
Locke's view of human knowledge, 57.
Logographi, the, of the sixth century, 218.
Logos, language, 133.
'Love your enemies,' 359-363.
Lucina, 11.
Ludwig and Bergaigne's view of the Vedic hymns, 104.

Ludwig's list of sacrificial terms in the Veda, 105 *n*.
Lustration of animals, 285.

MAHÂTMAS, 347.
Mahâvîra, birth of, 353.
Mahâyag*ñ*as, or commandments, 345, 346.
Ma*nd*ala, Delbrück, Grassmann, &c., on the seventh, 62 *n*.
Ma*nd*alas, the ten, 59, 60.
— the six family, 60.
— method in the collection of the, 60.
— names of the poets or deities of the, 62.
Manu, Laws of, translated by Sir W. Jones, 47.
— by Bühler, 47.
— age of, 48.
Manu's laws for the four castes, 345.
Manuscripts of the Veda, 42, 43.
Marco della Tomba and the Veda, 43.
Marriage in the Veda, 386.
Marus of the Buddhists, 320.
Marut, Pâli maru, 384.
Maruts, the, 317–320.
— Rudra, father of the, 320.
Mâtari*s*van, 152.
— etymology of, 152 *n*.
Max Müller's edition of the Rig-veda, 53, 54.
Megasthenes in India, 28.
Mênê, 11.
Mercury and Wuotan, 323 *n*.
Mesha, king, his inscription, 215.
Messiah, the Jewish, 394.
Metrical language, early, 108.
Mexican riddle, 258.
Mexico, storm-wind in, 312.
Michabo, the Great Light, 320.
Miracles not needed in early days, 142.
— condemned by Mohammed, 338, 338 *n*.
— condemned by Buddha, 339.
— believed in by the Brâhmans, 339.
Miracles, condemned by Christ, 339.
— Amiel on, 340.
— Newman on, 340.
— stumbling-blocks to faith, 357.
— Dr. R. Lee on faith in, 358.
Mitra, the deity, 27.
Modern superstitions, 13.
Mohammed's birth, 354.
Mongolian feeling for fire, 281.
Monotheism or Monism in the Veda, 44.
— how it arises, 328.
Monotheistic instinct of the Semitic race, 220.
Moon, new and full, 112.
Moral elements, 100.
Morning and evening meal or sacrifice, 110.
Moses, time of, writing unknown, 216.
— hieroglyphics known to, 216.
— no books existed at his time, 219.
— and his mother, 360 *n*.
Mount Sinai, 222.
Müller, J. G., on sun and fire in America, 149.
Mythology, euhemeristic explanations of, 253.
— not religion, 257.
— meaning or hyponoia of, 271.
Myths and legends, the parasites of religion, 299.

NAMING and conceiving, 124.
Nânak, birth of, 355.
Nârada, the Sage, 201.
Natural religion, three divisions of, 1.
— phenomena as viewed by nomad and agricultural people, 12.
— and supernatural, 119.
— revelation of God, 140.
— religion can lead to the highest idea of deity, 197.
— — use of the study of, 330.
— — lessons of, 331.
— — attacks on, 333.
Nature, order of, early perceived, 99.

Nature, a terror and marvel, 119.
— agents in, 132, 335.
— one agent in, 336.
Nature's gods not God, 142.
Need-fire, the, 285, 286, 389.
Negro tribes have a name for God, 116.
New Testament free from foolish stories, 203.
Nirvâna, nibbâna, 383.
Nooumena, 335.
Northern Buddhist texts, mistaken Sk. of the, 383.
Nursery-psychology, 130.

ODIN, or Wodan, or Wuotan, 321.
Οἶδα, same as Veda, 56, 57.
Ojibways, feeling for fire, 281.
Old Testament, 211.
— — an historical book, 212, 219.
— — authorship of books, 212.
— — religious ideas of, 213.
— — when written down, 214.
— — books collected by Ezra, 219.
— — writing mentioned in the, 388.
One God, belief in, among the Jews, 220.
— Abraham the originator of that belief, 220.
Ormazd, not fire, 227.
Orthodox and heterodox, 141.
Osiris, the god, 239.
Ouragan, 311.

PADA-TEXT of the Rig-veda, 380.
Pahlava, date of word, 373.
Pakthas of the Rig-veda, 372.
Paktyes, the, 372.
Paktyika, 372.
— or Afghans, 372.
Pâ*n*ini, the grammarian, 64, 76.
Paolino da S. Bartolomeo and the first Sk. grammar, 46.
Parallelism between Aryan religions, 274.
Paramâtman and Highest Self, 95.
Parishads, or schools of the Brâhmans, 66.
Par*s*u and Pârasavya, 369, 370 *n*.
— and Tirindira, 369.
Pârthavas, are they Parthians? 369.
Parthians, the, 369.
— their old name, 373.
Pâ*t*ilaputra, council of, 92.
Pâvaka, illuminating, 123.
Père Calmette and the Veda, 40, 41, 42, 43.
Persia, the bridge between India and Greece, 26, 27.
— later contact with, 32.
Persians, 369.
Persona, 307.
Personification, 306, 308.
Peru, gods of fire and water in, 150,
— worship in, 312.
Phenician letters, 215.
Phenicians, the, 23, 24.
Φλέγυες and Bh*r*igu, 154.
Physical origin of all religions, 10, 11.
— deities, Tiele on, 131.
— phenomena worshipped in Egypt, 208.
— religion, 1, 4, 7.
— — its origin, 8.
— — varieties of, 9.
— — best studied in India, 9.
— — outside India, 14.
— — definition of, 115.
— — simplicity and necessity of 336.
— — leads to moral religion, 234.
Pilippilâ, 262.
Pischel and Geldner's 'Vedische Studien,' 384.
Poem on trades and professions, 76.
— of the gambler, 76.
Poetry and mythology, 308.
Polytheism, 328.
Pons, Father, and the Veda, 45.
Pra*g*âpati, Lord of Creation, 247, 336.
Prâti*s*âkhyas, 63, 63 *n*, 64.
— date of the Rig-veda, 64, 376.
— minutiae of the, 65, 377.
Prayer better than sacrifice, 109.
Premature generalisation, 145.
Priests, various kinds of Vedic, 69, 70.
Primitive, meaning of, 14, 98, 99.

Primitive, Veda not entirely, 15.
— sacrifice, 110.
— man, 129.
— — roots express the acts of, 130.
P*ri*thu, Pârtha, and P*ri*thi, 369.
Prometheus, in the Veda, 153.
Psychological religion, 3, 5, 6.
Ptah, the god, 239.
— the artificer, 240.
Pur, the Vedic, 385.
Pythagoras and the vision of the soul of Homer, 245.

RA, the god, 238.
Rain, the first thought among men, 261.
Reformation, the, 332.
Religion, three divisions of natural, 1.
— physical, 1, 3, 5, 7.
— anthropological, 3, 5.
— psychological, 3, 5, 6.
— the three phases often contemporaneous, 5.
— ancient Vedic, 6.
— definition of physical, 115.
— influence of children on, 202.
— every, a kind of compromise, 203.
— in Egypt, 206.
— Brugsch on, 206.
— in Babylon and Assyria, 210.
— Sayce's lectures on, 210 *n*.
— none really dualistic, 234
— and mythology, difference between, 276.
— mythology and ceremonial, essential difference between, 292.
— definition of, re-examined, 294, 298.
— influence of, on the moral character, 295, 296.
— author's definition of, 296.
— Cicero on, 298, 299.
— with the Semites, 299.
— cult a manifestation of, 299.
— myths and legends the parasites of, 299.
— a knowledge of divine beings, 301, 302.
Religion, science of, founded on facts, not theories, 366.
Religions, common elements of all, 342.
— truth in all, 346.
— nature of the study of various, 363, 364.
Religious literature, none in Greece and Italy, 205.
— sanction for customs, 282.
— element, the, 300.
Renouf, Le Page, on the gods of Egypt, 207.
Revelation in nature, 141, 142.
Riddle of the five senses, 262.
Riddles, ancient, 257 et seq.
— produced mythology, 263.
*Ri*g, or *ri*k, verse, 59.
Rig-veda, M. M.'s edition of the, 53, 54.
— the only true Veda, 58.
— represents the earliest phase of Âryan thought, 58.
— Sa*m*hitâ of the, 59.
— how collected, 62, 63.
— number of hymns, 63, 63 *n*.
— early existence in its present form proved, 65.
— *S*aunaka's exegesis and indices of the, 64, 65.
— Kâtyâyana's index, 66.
— number of verses in, 66, 378.
— collection of the hymns an historical event, 68, 73.
— Brâhma*n*as of the, 70.
— nothing to do with sacrifice, 72.
— difference between it and other Vedas, 72, 73.
— age of, 96.
— *S*aunaka on the divisions of the, 379.
— various texts of the, 380.
*Ri*ta, or order, 99.
Roberto de' Nobili, 39.
Roman Catholic stories, 202.
Romanes, on human faculty, 191.
Roots, expressing actions, 124, 125, 130, 307.

Rosen's studies in the Veda, 50.
Rosetta stone, 16.
Rosmini on words, 138.
Roth's Essays on the Veda, 53.
Rudra, father of the Maruts, 320.
Rudraka and John the Baptist, 348.
Ruskin on the ancient gods, 137.

SACHAU, Dr., 33.
Sacrifice and prayer, which comes first, 105, 106.
— not an early idea, 106, 108.
— fragments left of a, 268 *n*.
Sacrifices, early, 100.
— become complicated, 113.
— must be unblemished, 171.
Sacrificial terms, 108.
St. Brigida, fire of, 292.
Sâma-veda, 67.
— Brâhma*n*as of the, 70, 381.
Sâman, a, 68 *n*.
Sa*m*hitâ of the Vedas, 59.
— of the Ya*g*ur-veda, 70, 71.
— -text of the Rig-veda, 380.
Samouscroutam, or Sanskrit, 41.
Samson's riddle, 260.
Sandrocottus, date of, 91.
Sanskrit grammar, the first, 46.
— and Sir W. Jones, 46.
— translations from the, 47 *n*.
— words in Sumerian, 381.
— of the Northern Buddhist texts, 383.
Sapta Sindhava*h*, 26.
Sâtin, Arabic covering, 87.
*S*aunaka, author of the Prâtisâkhya of the *S*âkala school, 64.
— his indices of the Rig-veda, 65.
— on the divisions of the Rig-veda, 379.
Savana, libation, 111.
Savanas, the three, 113 *n*.
Sâya*n*a's commentary, 53.
— difficulty of publishing, 53, 54.
Sayce, Professor, and the word sindhu, 87.
— on religion in Babylon and Assyria, 210 *n*.
Schopenhauer and the Upanishads, 36.
Schroeder, Professor von, on the Vedic gods, 179.
Scotland, superstition in, 289.
Seasons, and the year, invocation of, 99.
— the three, 112.
Seb, the earth, 387.
Secular ideas become religious, 278.
Self, the, 4.
Semiramis in India, 25.
Semitic nations, sacrifice among, 110.
— race, their monotheistic instinct, 220.
— really polytheistic, 221.
— their gods, gods of nature, 222.
Sick child, and fire in Scotland, 290.
Signs and sounds, 125.
— changed to miracles, 357.
Sindhu, cotton, mentioned 3000 B.C., 86, 87.
— identical with σινδών, 87.
— σινδών, 87.
— and Hebrew sâtin, 87.
Sixth century B.C., 216, 218.
— and alphabetic writing, 218, 219.
Sky, first concept of man, 261.
— as meaning rain, 261.
Skylax visited India, 26.
— and the Paktyes, the Pashtu or Afghans, 371.
— mentioned by Aristotle and Herodotus, 370.
Smârta, sm*r*iti, memory, 90.
Solar and meteoric theories, reconciliation of, 186.
— myth, the, 327.
Solemn, the meaning of, 113.
— from sollus, annus, 113.
Soma, known to the Zoroastrians and Vedic people, 101.
— giver of life, 188.
Soul, spirit, 131.
Special revelation to Abraham, 221.
Spencer, Herbert, against animism, 128.
— his agents and agencies, 132.
— a Euhemerist, 254 *n*, 255.

Sphinx, riddle of the, 260.
*S*rauta, *s*ruti, revelation, 90.
Star, auspicious, 391.
Storm and god, same word for, 316.
— -wind, 310–313, 315.
— — in America, 311.
— — in Mexico, 312.
— — in Babylon, 316.
— — in India, 317.
— — in Germany, 320.
Stabrobates, 25, 25 *n.*
Sumerian, Sk. words in, 381.
Sun and moon, invocation of, 99.
— and fire in America, 149.
— Brinton on, 149.
— J. G. Müller on, 149.
— and fire among the Fins, 150.
— Castrén on, 151.
Supernatural, the, 119.
— element, 305.
— craving for the, 337.
— as natural, 341.
Sûtra, the word, 94.
— applied to Buddha's sermons, 94.
— period, 96.
Sûtras, 81, 88, 89.
— why composed, 89, 90.
— style, 80, 90.

TABLES of the law, 216.
Tanûnapât, Vedic name for Agni, 123.
Taoism, 360.
Ten Commandments, 342.
— of the Buddhists, 342, 343.
Theogonic process, 306.
— development, 326.
Thoth, the moon, 387.
Thought and language, 307.
Three phases of religion often contemporaneous, 5.
Tiele, Prof., Le Mythe de Kronos, 187.
Tiele's theory of the gods as facteurs, 131.
— his forces or sources de vie, 132.
Tinegin in Ireland, 287.
Tirabazos, 370.
Tiridates, 370.
Tirindira and Parsu, 369.
Tiu, the god, 321.
Translations of Sk. books into Pehlevi and Arabic, 33.
Trift from treiben, 126 *n.*
Trishava*n*a, the threefold libation, 111.
Truth in all religions, 346.
'— makes revelation,' 361.
Tuesday, 321.
Tvash*t*ri, the Vedic god, 240.
— the artificer, 240.
Týr, the god, 321.

UDGÂT*RIS*, singing priests, 70.
Understanding, categories of the, 133.
Unknowable, the, 297.
Upanishad, the word, 93.
— used by Southern Buddhists, 93.
— in Pali, 93 *n.*
Upanishads, and prince Dârâ, 35.
— Anquetil Duperron's translation of the, 36.
— Schopenhauer, 36.
— the, and Âra*n*yakas, 80.
— names and number of, 80 *n.*
— after Buddha, 86.

VAHNI, fire, from same root as vehemens, 122.
Vaisvânara, useful to all, name for Agni, 123.
Varu*n*a, lord of all, 188.
Vasukra and the Veda, 34.
Vasus, the eight, 198.
Vâtes, 322 *n.*
Veda, not purely primitive, 15.
— discovery of the, 17.
— its importance, 18–20.
— unique character of the, 18.
— its age, 19–22.
— oldest monument of Aryan speech, 19.
— how it became known, 22.
— no foreign nations mentioned in the, 23.
— not mentioned by foreign nations, 23.

Veda, mentioned first by the Chinese, 28, 38.
— first committed to writing, 34.
— how it became known in the West, 38.
— and Père Calmette, 40.
— known by heart, 41, 42.
— MSS. of the, 42.
— best key to the religion of India, 45.
— Father Pons and the, 45.
— MSS. of, brought to Europe, 50.
— Rosen's studies in the, 50.
— Eugène Burnouf's studies in the, 51.
— Guizot buys MSS. of the, 52.
— Roth's Essays on the, 53.
— author's edition of the Rig-, 53.
— never published in India, 53.
— commentary of the, 53, 54.
— meaning of, 56.
— same as οἶδα, 56, 57.
— there are four, 58.
— Brahmanic view of the, 58.
— consists of Sa*m*hitâ and Brâhma*n*a, 59.
— the Sâma-, 67.
— the Ya*g*ur-, 68.
— the true, 74.
— the Atharva-, 81, 82.
— dates of the, 82.
— accurate knowledge of, necessary for studying physical religion, 84.
— from vid, to see, 84.
— a masculine, 84.
— how to fix the date of, 85, 366.
— character of the, 97.
— *Ri*ta or order in, 99.
— moral elements, 100.
— Soma of the, 101.
— childish thoughts in, 101.
— exalted thoughts in the, 102.
— sacrificial hymns are late, 105.
— Ludwig's list of sacrificial terms, 105 *n.*
— sacrifices very prominent in, 110–113.
— true antiquity of the, 250.
Veda, value of, 365.
— belief in one God, 366.
— Hiouen-thsang on the, 374, 374 *n*, 375.
— I-tsing on the, 375.
Vedângas, the six, 63 *n*.
Vedas first known, 33, 34.
— and the emperor Akbar, 35.
— and Marco della Tomba, 43.
— grains of gold in the, 44.
— monotheism or monism in, 44.
— and Herder, 48.
— and Sir W. Jones, 48.
— and H. T. Colebrooke, 48.
— interest aroused in Germany, 48.
Vedic age, true literary periods of the, 91.
— Âryas, their poetry, 155.
— gods, always human, 128.
— — though later often monstrous, 129.
— — Schroeder on the, 179.
— — their henotheistic character, 179.
— hymns, age of, 91, 96, 114.
— — simplicity of, 98.
— — sacrificial character of some, 104, 105.
— Ludwig and Bergaigne's view, 104.
— — secondary and tertiary, 114.
— — process of deification in the, 118.
— — modern date of the, 384.
— — literature, age of, 95, 96.
— period, and the original religion of India, 10, 11.
— — life during the, 76.
— religion, 6.
— — Buddhism a reaction against, 92.
— — dark side of, 197.
— texts, 219.
Verner's law, 322 *n.*
Voltaire and the Ezour-veda, 40.

WEATHER, original meaning of, 324.
Weber on Agni, 145.
Weber's idea of the Sâma-veda, 68 *n.*
Wood and fire, one word for, 154 *n.*

Words, Rosmini on, 138.
Wordsworth, 309.
Writing, art of, in India, 89.
— not known to the Vedic poets, 385.
— mentioned in the Old Testament, 388.
Wuotan, 322, 323.
— and Mercury, 323 *n*.
— Grohmann on, 324.
— from vadhas, 324.

XAVIER in India, 39.

YAG, to sacrifice, 107.
Ya*g*ur-veda, 68.
— Brâhma*n*as of the, 70.
— the bright and dark, 71.
— Sa*m*hitâ, the so-called, 71.
Ya*g*us line, 68 *n*.
Yama and Yamî, the twins, 239 *n*.
Yukatan, gods of, 314.

ZEUS, 11.
— not simply the sky, 326.
Zio, the god, 321.
Zoroaster, religion of, 226.
— and fire, 246.
Zoroastrian texts, 219.
Zulu riddle, 258, 259.

THE END.